DECISION MAKING IN PSYCHIATRY AND THE LAW

DECISION MAKING IN PSYCHIATRY AND THE LAW

EDITED BY

THOMAS G. GUTHEIL, M.D.

Codirector, Program in Psychiatry and the Law
Associate Professor of Psychiatry
Massachusetts Mental Health Center
Harvard Medical School
Boston, Massachusetts

HAROLD J. BURSZTAJN, M.D.

Codirector, Program in Psychiatry and the Law
Associate Clinical Professor of Psychiatry
Massachusetts Mental Health Center
Harvard Medical School
Boston, Massachusetts

ARCHIE BRODSKY, B.A.

Senior Research Associate
Program in Psychiatry and the Law
Massachusetts Mental Health Center
Harvard Medical School
Boston, Massachusetts

VICTORIA ALEXANDER, B.A.

Executive Editor
Program in Psychiatry and the Law
Massachusetts Mental Health Center
Harvard Medical School
Boston, Massachusetts

WILLIAMS & WILKINS
BALTIMORE · HONG KONG · LONDON · MUNICH
PHILADELPHIA · SYDNEY · TOKYO

Editor: Michael G. Fisher
Associate Editor: Carol Eckhart
Copy Editor: Janet M. Krejci
Designer: Dan Pfisterer
Illustration Planner: Ray Lowman
Production Coordinator: Adèle Boyd-Lanham

Copyright © 1991
Williams & Wilkins
428 East Preston Street
Baltimore, Maryland 21202, USA

Printed in the United States of America

Library of Congress Cataloging-in-Publication Data

Decision making in psychiatry and the law / edited by Thomas G.
  Gutheil . . . [et al.].
    p.   cm.
  Includes index.
  ISBN 0-683-03801-X
  1. Psychiatry—Decision Making.   2. Psychiatrists—Malpractice.
3. Forensic psychiatry—United States.   I. Gutheil, Thomas G.
  [DNLM   1. Decision Making.   2. Forensic Psychiatry—United States.
3. Malpractice.   W 740 D294]
RC455.2.D42D43   1991
616.89—dc20
DNLM/DLC
for Library of Congress   90-13169
                                                                        CIP

                                              91   92   93   94
                        1   2   3   4   5   6   7   8   9   10

*To our colleagues in
the mental health and
legal professions,
in hopes of continuing
the dialogue.*

FOREWORD

AN ETHICAL PRESCRIPTION FOR WHAT'S TROUBLING DOCTORS

The "big question" of ethics is "Why act ethically?" A clinical corollary to this is "Why should clinicians act ethically with their patients?" The answer to this question is not immediately apparent, in part, because acting ethically is not directly tied to the most obvious goal of medicine, namely, the good health of patients. The authors of *Decision Making in Psychiatry and the Law* did not set out to answer this question. Yet, through their careful reflections on clinical decision making, an answer to it emerges.

Of the different applications to which decision analysis has been put, some of the finest work has been done in the area of clinical decision making. This book is no exception. How clinicians, together with patients, make decisions has come under close scrutiny by practitioners from within the medical and clinical sciences because the outcome of clinical decisions can have a profound impact on the lives and well-being of patients. It is fitting that this study should be undertaken by practitioners because they are intimately aware of the consequences that their actions can have on the lives of others.

Clinical decisions can result in tragic outcomes for both the patients and the clinicians who treat them. The health of patients can deteriorate and they can die. At the same time, clinicians can be subject to malpractice suits that can destroy their careers and they must live with the emotional and psychological stress that accompanies an untoward outcome for one of their patients. But the importance of decision analysis is not restricted to the analysis of decisions that have an unhappy ending. There is also much to be learned from decisions that end felicitously. I will discuss some of the implications that decision analysis has for ethical decision making within a clinical context.

How are we to understand the domain of ethics? Although this question can be answered in more and less complicated ways, it is safe to say that one feature of decisions and actions which are within the moral domain is that they have consequences for other people. Clinical decisions are paradigmatic of decisions that affect people other than the primary decision maker, at least, if the primary decision maker is understood to be the clinician. Because of this, they fall squarely in the domain of ethics. I want to look at how analyzing clinical decisions can foster moral decision making in the clinical context. At the most general level, decision analysis asks us to reflect on our decisions in a way that we do not in our daily lives. This, combined with a good will, increases the likelihood that these decisions will be moral. But there are more specific ways that decision analysis can generate moral decision making.

Breaking a decision down into its component parts gives us access to the different reasons and considerations that have motivated it. Consider the following example. A decision to commit a mentally ill patient involuntarily, for instance, could be based on a number of considerations. Among the possibilities are preventing harm to the patient or other people and protecting the committing clinician from a legal suit should harm occur. Whether there is a treatment available that could benefit the patient should he be committed and whether commitment proceedings are a common practice in the clinician's home institution may also play a role in the decision. This rough enumeration only highlights some of the considerations which may have important moral implications.

With a list in hand of the different factors which have come to motivate the decision, the decision can be reflected on from a variety of perspectives, including medical, moral, and legal, and in terms of policy. The ethical components of the decision can be distinguished from the nonethical ones. For instance, knowing that one component of the decision to commit the patient is the availability of a beneficial treatment, we can identify a paternalistic aspect to the decision. If the *only* reason for committing the patient were to provide him with a beneficial treatment, the commitment would qualify as a paternalistic interference. That is, it would count as interfering with a person's self-regarding actions for his own sake. Looked at from the point of view of classical liberalism, such interference in a person's liberty is unethical. Of course, life rarely mirrors imaginary examples of this kind, and clinical decisions are rarely made on the basis of one consideration. Nonetheless, focusing our inquiry in this way affords us the opportunity to strengthen our understanding of the ethical aspects of decisions.

Identifying the desire to benefit the patient as a reason for committing him facilitates identifying and articulating the ethical components of the decision. Because the knowledge that a treatment is available which can help the patient is primarily medical knowledge, it might initially seem that this is a purely medical consideration. By recasting it into the language of interfering with a person's freedom of action for his own good (from medical language to moral language), the presence of paternalistic considerations is brought to light in a way that could not otherwise have been. At the same time, it should be underscored that identifying the patient's benefit through treatment, as the primary reason for treatment, was indispensable for identifying the moral component of the decision. What initially appeared to be a purely medical decision can now be viewed as the combination of an ethical and a medical decision. The information provided by recasting the "medical" into the "moral" is important because it sets the stage for other crucial inquiries. Now, the extent to which the committing physicians' values, in contrast to the patient's, should be taken into account in making the decision can be explored. Whether one is for or against medical paternalism, one is better equipped to address this issue, with the knowledge that one is acting paternalistically. Decision analysis is an important mechanism through which ethical assumptions and biases can be identified, values articulated, and ethical decisions evaluated.

Despite the moral advantages to be gleaned from the analysis of clinical decisions, it would be a mistake to view decision analysis as a panacea, capable of resolving all the moral problems that plague contemporary medicine. Decision analysis can foster moral decision making in the clinical context only in so far as the reasons and considerations that have motivated the decision are successfully identified. When the analysis of the decision is aimed at achieving moral insight, it should be undertaken by someone with a keen moral imagination. Although training in ethics is helpful in cultivating such moral insight, it is not essential. The authors of this volume, with their diverse backgrounds, are sensitive to both the ethical ramifications of clinical decision making and the clinical context in which decisions are made.

By working from within an interdisciplinary framework, these authors also succeed in transcending the blinders of their own disciplinary paradigms and, in turn, ensure that identification of the parts of the decision will not favor one discipline. The more perspectives that can be taken into account in the analysis of the decision, the less likely it is that the evaluation of the decision will merely reflect the prejudices of a single discipline. Ultimately, decision analysis can help us to know what we ought to do in particular cases; it would seem, however, that good will is necessary to inspire us.

Although good will can motivate ethical behavior, other sources of inspiration are welcome. This book suggests another important incentive. Acting ethically in a clinical context, we are told, can serve the interests of physicians by deterring patients from undertaking malpractice suits. This claim may strike some people as counterintuitive from the standpoint of ethics because, although what is morally right and what is legally required often coincide, they do not always do so. Sometimes performing the morally right action requires acting contrary to the legally mandated one. But let us look at this view more carefully.

How could, for example, providing informed consent to a patient minimize the likelihood that the patient would seek legal recourse? The obligation to provide patients with informed consent is founded on the idea that patients, as persons, have a capacity for autonomous decision making which should be respected. Respecting persons as autonomous agents requires that they be active participants in decisions that directly concern them. The process of informed consent gives patients an opportunity to be actively engaged in the decisions that will affect them.

Providing a patient with informed consent respects the patient as a person, but the ethical requirement to secure informed consent has other important implications for the patient and for the relationship between the patient and the physician. Patients who have participated in the process of informed consent have been actively involved in the decision making which will govern their health and lives. In this way, a decision is transformed from one made by a physician about a patient to one made by both patient and physician. This, in turn, has important implications for the ascription of responsibility.

It would not be surprising if, in view of their enhanced participation in the decision-making process, patients were to take more responsibility for the outcome of clinical decisions than they would have had they not given informed consent. Naturally, in the absence of empirical evidence, it is impossible to conclude that patients who have given informed consent are less likely to seek legal redress when they meet with an infelicitous outcome. But the point that needs to be highlighted here is that informed consent brings patients into the decision-making process, and it is because of this that they can be expected to bear more responsibility for decision making. Behaving ethically with patients thus carries with it substantive changes in the doctor-patient relationship which mandate different ascriptions of responsibility.

Ethical rules of thumb, such as "secure informed consent," do more than just endear the physician to the patient; they change the relationship between patient and physician in a way that needs to be reflected in how we understand individual responsibility. If a physician's acting ethically diminishes the likelihood of a lawsuit, it may well be because ethical behavior redistributes decision-making power in the doctor-patient relationship.

What strikes us as counterintuitive about the proposal that acting ethically can minimize the likelihood of legal suits is that it is difficult to conceive of 1) acting with the motive of diminishing harm to oneself with 2) acting ethically. Put differently, the self-interested desire to protect oneself from a legal suit seems to be incompatible with what we imagine motivates moral action. But it is a mistake to conflate the consequences of an action with the motive or intention with which it is performed. The consequences of an action can be intended or unintended and foreseen or unforeseen. Given this, a physician could perform the morally right action with the intention of benefitting the patient, but also foresee that an unintended consequence of the action is the minimization of the likelihood of a legal suit. In other words, the physician could both act ethically in the sense that the action is motivated by the patient's welfare and, at the same time, foresee a possible benefit to him/herself, namely, reducing the chance of being sued.

It is also possible for an individual to act ethically, yet to intend to improve his/her own lot in life. On a consequentialist understanding of morality, the intention with which an action is performed does not determine whether or not the action is to be considered moral. Actions which produce the best consequences are ethical and those which do not, are not. On this picture of morality, the failure to be able to conceive of 1) acting ethically with 2) the intention of avoiding a legal suit can be explained by the underlying conception of "morality" with which one is working, namely, deontological ethics, the view of ethics which identifies morality with intentions. Once, however, "what is ethically right" is divorced from "what is intended," as it is with an ethical theory that stresses consequences instead of intentions, the inability to conceive of "benefit to self" with "acting ethically" disappears.

The intuitions that made us question the claim that acting ethically can have risk management benefits rests on a particular conception of morality, one to which we need not be wedded. But even if we adopt an intention-based ethics, we are not forced to reject the claim that acting ethically can have risk management benefits: for the benefits to be had from ethical behavior may be foreseen, but unintended, consequences of the behavior.

We are now in a position to answer the question with which we began: "Why should physicians act ethically with their patients?" The answer to this question is twofold. Patients can benefit from being treated ethically; their autonomy is enhanced and they are treated with respect. This easily translates into the clinical benefit of raising the morale and self-esteem of a demoralized patient suffering from a chronic illness. And, if the authors of this book are right, behaving ethically can also confer benefits on the practicing clinician by diminishing the risk of being sued for medical malpractice.

PATRICIA ILLINGWORTH, PH.D.

PREFACE

This book you are holding represents, among other things, a compilation of ideas from the Program in Psychiatry and the Law at the Massachusetts Mental Health Center and Harvard Medical School—ideas that have evolved over a decade of collaborative work. The members of the Program, past and present, are listed elsewhere in this book. However, it may be valuable to place members' contributions into perspective by offering a conceptual biography, as it were, of the Program's ideas. In addition to placing this book into context, such a review may also convey some idea of the functioning of the Program itself.

The Program in Psychiatry and the Law (the Program) was founded in 1979/1980 at the Massachusetts Mental Health Center (the Center) through the efforts of Paul S. Appelbaum, M.D. Its original mandate was to serve as a training program for young forensic psychiatrists, who would learn through performing, under supervision, medicolegal and ethical consultations with the trainees and staff at the Center. To date the Program has trained eleven Chief Residents in Legal Psychiatry who form an informal nationwide group of Program associates; some still attend meetings. In the early 1980s this medicolegal training mandate was enlarged by the confluence of several conceptual streams. The first was the problem in medicine as a whole of making decisions under conditions of uncertainty, in the teeth of the possibility of tragic outcomes. Models for guiding such decision making were first outlined in a seminal text (1).

A second conceptual stream flowed from the demonstrated need of medical decision theory to transcend the limited model offered by the simplifying, certainty-driven mechanistic paradigm of medicine and to reach the probabilistic paradigm, a concept both more realistic and more suited to the inherent uncertainty of modern practice.

A third stream flowed from the unequivocal need in the medicolegal (or forensic) field for careful empirical study of medicolegal events and the decision making that informed or produced those events. We view this need for applied empiricism as so fundamental to our thinking that it has become the Program's motto: "Nobody's done the study to find out *what actually happens.*" Investigation in this area led to empirical study of drug refusal (2), involuntary commitment (3), risk perceptions of psychotropic medication (4), and suicide liability (see the discussion in Chapter 10).

The fourth stream flowed from the need for new ideas to enrich the dialogue between clinical and legal realms. In particular, although both legal and clinical realms have in common the process of decision making—indeed, that is the fundamental assumption of this book—there exists no methodology for exploration of the intuitive decision making that all practitioners employ in real life. Such reasoning had been treated by theorists as a "black box," impervious to systematic and reliable empirical analysis. The development by members of the Program of a "gray box model," which "opens up" such intuitive reasoning for scrutiny, is an important contribution by the Program to the field (5).

A fifth conceptual stream flowed from issues of the therapeutic alliance and the notion of informed consent as dialogue and ethical construct rather than legalistically mandated transfer of data. These wellsprings led to the Program's exploration of both the alliance and informed consent as forces directed toward liability prevention through their improvement of the doctor-patient relationship, the central incubator for the emotional substrate of liability (6).

A sixth conceptual stream flows from the notion that ethics represents a valuable mechanism for decision making that is older than both medicine and law and is most useful when both those disciplines have exhausted their possibilities; ethics is not merely a philosophical abstraction or a form of preaching of "right behavior." Program members apply these concepts in the regularly scheduled "Ethics Rounds" in the various departments of the Center and in their writings (7).

The newest conceptual stream to enrich the Program flows from Kohlberg's theories of the stages of moral development (8) and the manner in which these stages influence decision making. These theories have colored much of the thinking in this book and are summarized in the final chapter.

What does the Program actually look like in action? The earliest meetings of three members on a weekly basis to pool ideas and work on drafts of articles unwittingly served as the embryo for the present "think tank" component of the Program's functioning (the Program at present serving as think tank, consultation service, and clinical research unit). As interested individuals asked or were invited to attend to share ideas, discuss medicolegal points of interest, gain forensic sophistication, study decision analysis, exchange information, and nurture academic interests and concerns, the Program has grown to about twenty active participants meeting weekly; another dozen individuals, some former "actives," drop in occasionally. Attorneys, psychiatrists and forensic psychiatrists, psychologists, research methodologists, students of various disciplines, and individuals with mixed degrees (especially clinical-legal) participate; as policy the Program bars no one and invites participation without "admission requirements." The opportunity thus provided for egalitarian debate, discussion, and mutual peer enrichment around problematic cases, thorny conceptual issues, and empirical investigations has drawn practitioners experiencing the loneliness of solo practice, investigators seeking guidance on research design, undergraduates considering forensic careers, clinicans eager to sharpen awareness of medicolegal matters, and others to sit in.

One of the Program's most important structural innovations has been to include gifted medical writers as integral members to capture ephemeral ideas generated in brainstorming sessions and to edit successive drafts of those materials aimed at publication in professional journals. As a result the Program has been a prolific source for "think pieces," empirical studies (some unprecedented), and education on risk management, and a stimulus for conceptual advances in the field. The fruits of the first decade of this exhilarating process are in your hand.

REFERENCES

1. Bursztajn HJ, Feinbloom RI, Hamm RM, Brodsky A. Medical choices, medical chances: how patients, families, and physicians can cope with uncertainty. New York: Rutledge, Chapman and Hall, 1990.
2. Appelbaum PS, Gutheil TG. Drug refusal: a study of psychiatric inpatients. Am J Psychiatry 1980;137:340–346.
3. Bursztajn HJ, Gutheil TG, Mills MJ, Hamm RM, Brodsky A. Process analysis of judges' commitment decisions: a preliminary empirical study. Am J Psychiatry 1986;143:170–174.
4. Bursztajn HJ, Chanowitz B, Kaplan E, Gutheil TG, Hamm RM. Contrasting risk perceptions between medical and legal professionals regarding use of antipsychotic medication. submitted for publication.
5. Bursztajn HJ, Gutheil TG, Hamm RM, Brodsky A, Mills MJ, Levy L. Transitions in clinicians self reports of the assessment of commitability. Int J Psychiatry Law, in press.
6. Gutheil TG, Bursztajn HJ, Brodsky A. Malpractice prevention through the sharing of uncertainty: informed consent and the therapeutic alliance. N Engl J Med 1984;311:49–51.
7. Appelbaum PS, Reiser SJ. Ethics rounds: a model for teaching ethics in the psychiatric setting. Hosp Community Psychiatry 1981;32:555–560.
8. Kohlberg L. Essays on moral development. Vol. 2: The psychology of moral development: moral stages; their nature and validity. San Francisco: Harper and Row, 1984.

ACKNOWLEDGMENTS

The editors gratefully acknowledge their indebtedness to the following:

To Alan A. Stone, M.D., for opening the doors and ideas of the Harvard Law School to generations of scholars from the Program in Psychiatry and the Law and for seminal contributions to the ideas herein developed;

To Paul S. Appelbaum, M.D., for founding the Program in Psychiatry and the Law and for continuing inspiration, stimulation, guidance, and support;

To the many present and past members of the Program in Psychiatry and the Law who—although not listed as formal contributors— contributed essentially to the dialogue that shaped this book;

To Robert M. Hamm, Ph.D., for a fifteen-year course and countless innovative contributions in empirical methodology for measuring uncertainty;

To Leslie Levi, former Executive Editor, Program in Psychiatry and the Law, for her significant assistance with early chapters;

To Beth Banov, Massachusetts Mental Health Center Librarian, for great bibliographic resourcefulness and help;

To Miles F. Shore, M.D., Bullard Professor of Psychiatry, Harvard Medical School, and Superintendent, Massachusetts Mental Health Center, for striving to preserve scholarship amid the demands of adversity;

And especially to Raymond S. Meinert, Jr., Administrative Assistant, Program in Psychiatry and the Law, whose patience, effort, and ingenuity were largely responsible for the preparation of this manuscript.

ACKNOWLEDGMENTS

EDITORS

THOMAS G. GUTHEIL, M.D.
Codirector, Program in Psychiatry and
the Law
Associate Professor of Psychiatry
Massachusetts Mental Health Center
Harvard Medical School
President, Law and Psychiatry Resource
Center
Special Consultant, Risk Management
Foundation of the Harvard Medical
Institutions

HAROLD J. BURSZTAJN, M.D.
Codirector, Program in Psychiatry and
the Law
Associate Clinical Professor of
Psychiatry

Massachusetts Mental Health Center
Harvard Medical School
President, National Law, Medicine and
Psychiatry Consultants

ARCHIE BRODSKY, B.A.
Senior Research Associate, Program in
Psychiatry and the Law
Massachusetts Mental Health Center
Harvard Medical School

VICTORIA ALEXANDER, B.A.
Executive Editor, Program in Psychiatry
and the Law
Editorial Director, Massachusetts
Mental Health Center

CONTRIBUTORS

DAVID BARNARD, PH.D.
Associate Professor of Humanities
Acting Chairman Department of
  Humanities
Penn State College of Medicine

MARILYN BERNER, J.D., L.I.C.S.W.
Associate, Program in Psychiatry and
  the Law
Massachusetts Mental Health Center
Lecturer in Psychiatry
Harvard Medical School
Former Director, Adult Services
Central Middlesex Area Office
Massachusetts Department of Mental
  Health
Faculty, Law and Psychiatry Program
Massachusetts General Hospital

SUZANNE CANNING, M.D.
Forensic Psychiatrist and Associate
Program in Psychiatry and the Law

BEN ZION CHANOWITZ, PH.D.
Associate Professor of Psychology
Brooklyn College

MICHAEL L. COMMONS, PH.D
Senior Research Methodologist,
  Lecturer and Research Associate
Program in Psychiatry and the Law
Executive Director, Society for Research
  in Adult Development
Executive Director, Society for
  Quantitative Analyses of Behavior
Director, Dare Institute

ROBERT M. HAMM, PH.D.
Research Associate, Program in
  Psychiatry and the Law

Research Associate, Institute of
  Cognitive Science and the Institute
  of Behavioral Sciences
University of Colorado, Boulder,
  Colorado

MARK J. HAUSER, M.D.
Forensic Psychiatrist and Research
  Associate
Program in Psychiatry and the Law
Massachusetts Mental Health Center
Clinical Instructor in Psychiatry,
  Harvard Medical School
Consulting Psychiatrist, Massachusetts
  and Connecticut Departments of
  Mental Retardation

PATRICIA ILLINGWORTH, PH.D.
Founding Member, McGill Center for
  Medicine, Ethics and the Law
Assistant Professor, Departments of
  Philosophy and Medicine
McGill University, Montreal, Canada
Liberal Arts Fellow in Law and
  Philosophy, Harvard Law School

ERIC KAPLAN, M.D.
Former Chief Resident in Legal
  Psychiatry
Program in Psychiatry and the Law
Massachusetts Mental Health Center

LESLIE LEVI, B.A.
Former Executive Editor
Program in Psychiatry and the Law

RONALD SCHOUTEN, J.D., M.D.
Director, Law and Psychiatry Program
Massachusetts General Hospital
Instructor in Psychiatry
Harvard Medical School

EVELYNNE L. SWAGERTY, M.S.W.,
L.I.C.S.W., J.D.
Assistant Attorney General
Department of the Attorney General
Commonwealth of Massachusetts

MARK WARREN, M.D.
Forensic Psychiatrist and Associate
Program in Psychiatry and the Law
Former Medical Director, Attleboro
  Mental Health Center
Assistant Professor of Psychiatry
Case Western Reserve University

MEMBERS OF THE PROGRAM
IN PSYCHIATRY AND THE LAW

MICHELLE BELMONT, B.A.
Associate, Program in Psychiatry and
the Law

RODNEY DEATON, M.D., J.D.
Associate, Foley, Hoag and Eliot
Boston, Massachusetts

KENNETH DUCKWORTH, M.D.
Former Chief Resident in Legal
Psychiatry
Program in Psychiatry and
the Law
Fellow in Child Psychiatry
Massachusetts Mental Health Center
Harvard Medical School

MARCUS GOLDMAN, M.D.
Gaughan Fellow in Forensic and
Correctional Psychiatry, and
Clinical Fellow
Massachusetts Mental Health Center
Harvard Medical School

SUSAN G. GOODSON, M.D.
Acting Chief Resident in Law and
Psychiatry and Associate
Program in Psychiatry and
the Law
Commonwealth Fellow in Mental
Retardation
Massachusetts Mental Health Center

SUSAN HARRIS, M.D.
Forensic Psychiatrist and Associate
Program in Psychiatry and the Law
Medical Director, Nantucket Counseling
Services and ADM Services

Attleboro, Massachusetts
Director, Geriatric Outpatient
Department
Hahnemann Hospital

DAVID HOFFMAN, M.D.
Forensic Psychiatrist and Associate
Program in Psychiatry and the Law
Faculty, Massachusetts Mental Health
Center
Harvard Medical School

LYNN KENNEY, PSY. D.
Associate, Pepperdine University and the
Program in Psychiatry and the Law

RAYMOND S. MEINERT, JR., R.A.
Administrative Assistant, Program in
Psychiatry and the Law

EDWIN MIKKELSEN, M.D.
Director, Division of Child Psychiatry
Massachusetts Mental Health Center
Associate Professor of Psychiatry
Harvard Medical School

LLOYD PRICE, M.D.
Forensic Psychiatrist and Associate
Program in Psychiatry and the Law
Associate Attending Psychiatrist and
Associate Attending Child Psychiatrist
McLean Hospital
Clinical Instructor in Psychiatry
Harvard Medical School

JAMES REINHARD, M.D.
Gaughan Fellow in Forensic and
Correctional Psychiatry, and
Clinical Fellow

Massachusetts Mental Health Center
Harvard Medical School

JOSEPH A. RODRIGUEZ, ED.D.
Research Associate, Department of
  Human Development & Psychology
Harvard University and the Program in
  Psychiatry and the Law

DEBBIE ROGELL, B.A.
Associate, Program in Psychiatry and
  the Law

RONAL G. ROSSO, M.D.
Associate, Program in Psychiatry and
  the Law
Staff Psychiatrist
Taunton State Hospital

R. ANDREW SCHULTZ-ROSS, M.D.
Gaughan Fellow in Forensic and
  Correctional Psychiatry, and
  Clinical Fellow
Massachusetts Mental Health Center
Harvard Medical School

GERHARD SONNERT, PH.D.
Research Associate
Program in Psychiatry and the Law and
  the Department of Physics
Harvard University

DINA D. STRACHAN, B.A.
Medical Student,
Yale Medical School

LARRY H. STRASBURGER, M.D.
Forensic Psychiatrist and Associate
Program in Psychiatry and the Law
Assistant Clinical Professor of Psychiatry
Harvard Medical School

GERALD SWEET, PH.D.
Staff Psychologist, Framingham-Union
  Hospital
Framingham, Massachusetts
Assistant Clinical Professor
Division of Psychiatry
Boston University Medical School

CONTENTS

SECTION I. INTRODUCTION

chapter 1.

ANATOMY OF A MALPRACTICE CASE

The case example that follows has been designed as a heuristic exercise to highlight areas of decision making in psychiatry and the law. Although based on an actual psychiatric malpractice case, the details have been modified to preserve confidentiality and for didactic effect. The remainder of the book will refer back to this case example for illustration of the issues discussed.

◆

It is a busy day at the local community mental health center. Dr. Newell, the examining resident, has already seen a large number of psychiatric emergency cases. Ms. Adams shuffles into Dr. Newell's emergency room office, flops down into the chair, and stares blankly at the floor. According to the admitting clerk, she has come in because of sleep problems, depression, anxiety, crying spells, and suicidal thoughts. After some initial supportive work, Dr. Newell takes the following history.

A 28-year-old childless woman, Ms. Adams has been depressed off and on over a number of years. She and her husband have always had a stormy relationship, but the situation has become considerably worse over the last several years. Twice her husband has threatened to leave her and file for a divorce. The second time, she took a significant overdose of the antidepressant medication that her outside psychiatrist, Dr. Olsen (one of the resident's former teachers), had prescribed for the last two years. Now her husband has once more threatened to leave her. In acute distress, Ms. Adams first called Dr. Olsen, who referred her to the center for evaluation and possible admission. He is just about to leave for a one-week vacation and is concerned that his absence might be an exacerbating factor in his patient's distress. When called by Dr. Newell from the center, Dr. Olsen comments that he usually treats the patient as a moderate suicide risk, the urgency of this approach tempered somewhat by the fact that the patient herself acknowledges that she uses the threat of suicide as a means of manipulating her often inattentive and insensitive husband into making some response.

During the evaluation, Dr. Newell notes that Ms. Adams is a slight woman dressed in jeans and T-shirt, her face pale and drawn, and her washed-out-looking blonde hair in some disarray. She sits limply in her chair but also looks somewhat wary. She is manifestly depressed, tearful, and distressed that her husband might really mean what he says this time—that this last fight may, indeed, have been the last straw. Dr. Newell inquires about her recent experiences.

"How have you been eating lately?"

Ms. Adams grimaces, dabbing at her face with a crumpled tissue. "Not a whole lot. I don't have any appetite, nothing tastes good anymore; in fact, nothing has any taste at all, it seems."

"Have you lost any weight?"

Ms. Adams sighs. "I don't know. Coupla pounds, maybe. Everything still fits, anyway."

"How about sleep?" the resident asks.

"Yeah, how *about* a little sleep?" Ms. Adams gives a humorless laugh. "I barely fall asleep after a couple of hours and then I'm up again, long before the alarm. The same thing happened the last time I was depressed."

"Does anything help you get to sleep?" Dr. Newell asks. "How about the medication that Dr. Olsen gave you?"

"Yeah, that helps sometimes, not always." Ms. Adams looks at him somewhat guiltily. "I'm taking some—I have a drink or two before I go to sleep."

"How much are you drinking?"

"Maybe—a half a shot of vodka?"

"How much vodka is that, actually?"

Ms. Adams sighs in a tired manner. "About half of an iced tea glass, O.K.?"

"Every night?"

"It didn't used to be but it is now, the last two weeks."

"What does the alcohol do for you?"

"I guess it knocks me out—it turns off my mind so I can get to sleep. Doesn't work that well, I guess; I'm up at the crack of dawn."

"Do you use anything else?"

"You mean, like drugs? No, I've never messed with that."

Dr. Newell hesitates a moment, looking at her speculatively. "How bad has it gotten?"

"Do you mean if I—have I ever thought of—you know—killing myself?"

The resident nods. "I guess that's what I'm asking."

Ms. Adams draws a deep breath and holds it for a moment. "I have to tell you it sure has crossed my mind, around 4 AM some mornings. But—I wouldn't do it now."

"Why not?"

"Everything's so up in the air. I mean, it doesn't make sense."

"How would you do it if you did?"

Ms. Adams shrugs. "I don't know, I haven't given that any thought. The pills again, I guess, I don't know."

"How many do you have at home?"

Ms. Adams looks blank. "I haven't any idea."

"Why pills?"

"What do you mean?"

"What makes you think of pills to kill yourself?"

Ms. Adams frowns. "I don't know—I guess they're painless. Of course, they didn't work last time I tried them, anyway."

Dr. Newell mulls this over for a moment.

"What is your religion?"

Ms. Adams looks startled. "No psychiatrist ever asked me *that* before. It's Protestant, I guess; that's what I told the girl at the front desk. Daddy was Episcopalian and Mommy was raised Lutheran, so I guess I'm mixed. Why?"

"I was wondering if your faith was any help."

"I don't think so; not really, I guess."

"Does your religion have anything to say about suicide?"

"I don't know. You mean, like, is it a sin? I never heard about that."

The resident tries another tack. "How was your treatment going with Dr. Olsen?"

"Oh, he's very good, he's doing his best, don't blame him. It's just that I don't know if it's enough."

"How does it sit with you, his going on vacation just now?"

Ms. Adams shrugs. "He works hard, he deserves a vacation. He's gone away before, and he always leaves somebody to call."

Dr. Newell considers the clinical issues about Ms. Adams with care, writing his thoughts in the record with equal care to document reasoning. The patient is clearly facing several risk factors in relation to her depression. The first is her fear of losing her husband, the uncertainty surrounding his threat possibly making the tension even worse than it would be if his departure were certain.

In addition, during this time the therapist with the longest relationship and greatest experience with the patient—Dr. Olsen—will be unavailable. No matter who may fill in for the departed therapist, the relationship thus newly formed cannot replace the familiarity—perhaps even the comfort—of the long-term relationship. The therapeutic alliance is not as reliable as usual.

The increased use of alcohol is another risk factor, since alcohol tends to diminish inhibitions; that is, to decrease internal controls and make impulsive action more likely.

Finally, the means for suicide, in the form of the pills that she used in her previous attempt, remains readily available, and the patient has indicated that she has a supply at home. Dr. Newell is also keenly aware, however, that the real world fairly bristles with possible instruments for use by those intent on self-harm—clothes and belts, household poisons, tall buildings, fast-moving vehicles, bridges, and so on. Focusing on the pills alone could well be misleading in planning for this patient's care.

On the other side of the ledger lies the fact that the patient occasionally threatens suicide to manipulate her husband. This requires careful consideration, since even manipulators can slip in their plans and may die as a result. He recalls that more men than women commit suicide, despite the fact that more women attempt it.

He also reasons that Dr. Olsen, going on vacation while his patient is in distress, may be feeling somewhat more anxious about her than would ordinarily be the case, perhaps leading him to overread and thus overrate the seriousness of her condition. It is also possible that Dr. Olsen is withdrawing somewhat from his patient in anticipation of his departure.

Having weighed all these factors, Dr. Newell decides to suggest hospitalization to Ms. Adams. First, however, he asks her whether she can wait a little longer and promises to return shortly. She agrees to wait for him. He then steps into the clinic office and asks the nurse to keep an eye on the patient while he checks with his supervisor, Dr. Gottleib. Presenting his case over the phone, Dr. Newell outlines the decision points just noted. Dr. Gottleib asks some questions, including how confident the resident is about his data base and his assessment. She agrees with Dr. Newell's decision to offer the patient hospitalization, noting that the stress of the threatened separation appears to be fairly severe, and her supports are in some disarray. Dr. Newell returns to broach this idea to the patient.

Ms. Adams listens seriously and appears to give the matter thoughtful consideration. Then she shakes her head. She states that she does not want to be hospitalized because she has several specific plans for the immediate future, and she does not want to risk losing her new job as executive secretary in a fashion design firm by taking time off or to experience again the humiliation of being an inpatient in a mental hospital, as she did the last time she became depressed. Dr. Newell's efforts over several hours to dissuade her from her decision fail; she remains adamant.

Dr. Newell obtains Ms. Adams' permission to call her husband to come in for an interview, which might shed more light on the current situation (e.g., confirming her actual alcohol intake) and might, secondarily, aid in persuading Ms. Adams to sign in to the hospital.

Mr. Adams explains over the phone that he has been trying over many years to help his wife. She not only is angry with him most of the time but hangs up on people calling him over business matters. She also calls his office, complaining to his boss about him. He feels that she is a real threat to his survival, as well as her own. He is trying to remove himself from the situation but will continue to support her financially. Over the phone the husband expresses no interest in discussing her situation any further, in coming in for an interview, or indeed, in playing any further role in her care. "I have cut my ties with her," he says, "this time for good. She has to find her own help."

On being told of this response by her husband, the patient is crestfallen, as though she had hoped her husband might respond to this crisis. She becomes more tearful at this point and perceptibly angry.

"That's just typical of what I have to put up with," she mutters. "I should have known better than to think he'd do anything."

She draws a deep breath, then smiles wanly.

"Look, it's really been very helpful just talking to you, getting this all out. I think I'll be O.K. now."

Her refusal of voluntary hospitalization triggers the next question, the next level of assessment: does the patient qualify for involuntary commitment? The local statutory standard for involuntary commitment is "a high probability or likelihood of imminent dangerousness because of mental illness." The physician must petition the court for the patient's commitment on the basis of this standard.

In addition, the clinician must assess the negative impact of hospitalization itself: will the patient be so dismayed by the experience of being involuntarily hospitalized that she despairs, resulting in an *increased* risk of suicide? Will "taking over" for the patient intensify her feelings of helplessness? Dr. Newell recalls that hospitalization is far from a panacea. Many people commit suicide while in the hospital, even under fairly close supervision. Moreover, a fairly small number of patients sue for false imprisonment when thus hospitalized. Finally, given her statement that she has future plans and her denial of actual intent, it appears fairly likely that the court would find that she would not qualify for the standard.

Despite this view, Dr. Newell muses, there would be a particular value in petitioning for commitment anyway—a value related to Pascal's wager. Pascal suggested that it was better to believe in the existence of God and be wrong, risking nothing after death, than *not* to believe in the existence of God and be wrong, risking eternal damnation.

Comparably, it would be better—and safer—to file for commitment and be wrong than to release her and be wrong. In the face of a "tragic" choice—one where either alternative poses significant costs and potential harms—the safer course would be the one that seems more conservative in the short run: to file for commitment. The cost associated with involuntary hospitalization, although significant and likely, would still be far better borne than the less likely but much more serious cost involved in the decision not to petition for commitment—namely, suicide.

Petitioning for commitment, however, has subtle and indirect costs of its own. Over and above the trauma of putting the patient through the legal proceedings needlessly, a petition for commitment may place great strain on the treatment alliance, even so tenuous a one as the resident and patient have developed in the emergency room. Overriding the patient's stated wishes might even do harm to her relationship with Dr. Olsen. On the other hand, some patients feel more cared for when they are thus opposed; this feeling may be unconscious and not apparent in a short encounter.

Another consideration, of which Dr. Newell is more peripherally aware, is that the courts are already overcrowded, and "unnecessary" cases will only add to the congestion. Moreover, the courts make decisions about a patient's dangerousness in a variety of ways, which may be calibrated inaccurately if clinicians who don't really think their patients are dangerous keep filing for commitment. To put this another way, the clinician and even a whole institution may lose their credibility in court by petitioning too readily—a case of crying wolf that can be extremely serious for subsequent situations in which dangerousness is much clearer.

To consider whether the patient is competent to participate in planning for alternatives to hospitalization, Dr. Newell makes an informal determination, by reflecting on the quality of her interaction with him, as to whether Ms. Adams is capable of participating wholeheartedly in a dialogue about her treatment. No objective standards for this competence determination actually exist. Dr. Newell usually performs this talk intuitively by trying to decide whether the patient can engage in a dialogue centered around designing and implementing a plan for treatment. Certainly, Ms. Adams appears quite clear about who her caretakers are and what treatment consists of. This competence in part represents a dimension of the informed consent process, whereby a patient is expected to collaborate in a plan of management.

Dr. Newell phones Dr. Olsen to discuss his evaluation of the case and the decisions he has made, but Dr. Olsen has already departed on his vacation.

Although he does not believe the patient is committable, Dr. Newell once more runs past his supervisor both the new situation and his reasoning. On the basis of this information, Dr. Gottleib makes two decisions. First, she decides that the picture presented by the resident is sufficiently clear and free of ambiguity to make it unnecessary for her to interview the patient herself. This decision is based in part on Dr. Gottleib's previous experience of the resident as a solid clinician, good observer, and candid reporter, as well as on her awareness of the careful and valid decision making that he has demonstrated in previous cases.

Second, Dr. Gottleib decides, according to her own risk-benefit analysis of the situation, to accept Dr. Newell's decision not to file for commitment of the patient and to treat her on an outpatient basis for the time being. It is likely that the emergency room visit has been of some use as an emotional catharsis; further intervention can take this into account.

The resident and the patient agree, after some discussion, on the following plan. Ms. Adams will ask one of her friends, a responsible older woman, to come to the clinic and pick her up. She agrees to contact Dr. Olsen's covering physician or Dr. Newell as needed. An inpatient detoxification unit is discussed by the two parties and rejected by the patient in favor of attendance at Alcoholics Anonymous meetings, which the patient readily accepts.

Her friend arrives shortly, the plan is reviewed once more, and Ms. Adams departs, holding a card with the clinic telephone number on it.

Some days later Dr. Newell reads in the newspaper that Ms. Adams has died from a presumed overdose of her medication plus alcohol.

◆

The following morning, Dr. Newell calls up the city morgue and obtains a photocopy of the suicide note found next to Ms. Adams. It reads: "To whoever finds me: I appreciate what everyone has been trying to do for me, but it's just no use. I cannot live without my husband. Now that he has walked out on me, I cannot go on. Please do not blame the doctors, they have done the best they could. I have taken an overdose of sixty 50-milligram tablets of my medicine, with one jigger of vodka on top of it. I guess this is goodbye."

A short time later Dr. Newell and Dr. Gottleib meet for a review of the case. Such meetings are referred to by a variety of names, including quality control review, psychological autopsy, and suicide review. They serve the same educational function as the physical autopsy in medicine: learning from death. In psychiatry, however, these meetings serve an additional purpose: termination, or "saying goodbye," to the patient. For the resident (and others involved in Ms. Adams' care), death through suicide is a loss that must be mourned like other losses. This is not simply an emotional indulgence for the resident: his actual ability to work empathically with other suicidal patients will in part depend on how well he is able to work out his feelings about the loss of this one.

Dr. Newell goes over the case in detail with Dr. Gottleib, trying to recall every nuance of the patient's speech and voice, trying to recall the dialogue verbatim. Both of them pay particular attention to all the decision points along the way: admit/don't admit, medicate/don't medicate, spend more/less time talking to her, inpatient/outpatient detoxification, and so on. When this first run-through is finished, Dr. Newell sighs.

"You know, going over this, I guess the thing that really bothers me is that there isn't anything I can identify that I would do differently next time. She just wasn't that suicidal when I saw her; it seemed like a clear manipulation aimed at the husband. You should have seen how upset she got when he refused to come in for an interview. If she had really been intent on ending it all, shouldn't his reaction have been irrelevant, as far as she was feeling? Would she have gotten that upset?"

Dr. Gottleib is thoughtful. "What you say certainly fits the case with many suicides, but don't forget, the woman who overdosed may not have been the same woman you saw. Maybe after you saw her something happened—some event, an interaction with someone, a passing thought, even—that changed her whole picture in a way you couldn't foresee or control. Let's remember that some patients kill themselves as an act of hostility directed at someone else—in this case, her husband." She leans back in her chair. "But there's another angle here that I've been mulling over. Consider this: the average lay person really doesn't know how much of anything it takes to kill oneself. One patient I know seriously attempted suicide with six extra-strength aspirins—a dose so trivial that we were misled for a while as to how much he meant it. You just can't always tell."

She taps the note on the desk before her and adjusts her reading glasses to peer at the page. "That detail near the end, now, where she writes down exactly what she took—"

The resident is puzzled. "What about it?"

"You haven't seen many suicide notes, I take it?"

Dr. Newell shakes his head. "This is the only one."

The supervisor smiles grimly. "I've seen a fairly large number of them over the years, and I have never seen one in which the patient gives the exact dosage of what she took like that. Does it suggest anything to you?"

The resident frowns. "Nothing in particular, except that it seems kind of—I don't know—precise, for someone who is about to kill herself."

"I think so, too. It occurred to me that it's possible she was hoping that if the doctors who worked on her at the hospital knew exactly what she had taken, they could give her the right antidote, and she wouldn't actually die."

Dr. Newell stares at her. "But that's ridiculous! It doesn't work that way! Besides, there *is* no antidote. You have to give supportive care until she washes the stuff out of her system, assuming you get to her in time."

"Absolutely. I quite agree. But she wouldn't know that. In fact, I can't think of any other more likely way to read the situation as it stands. Picture it as it might be from her viewpoint: she takes the overdose, counting on the note to give the doctors the information they need to save her. When she pulls through, her husband—who now feels incredibly guilty for leaving and frightened about almost losing her—changes his mind and comes back to her, on his knees, so to speak. It's a pretty common scenario for suicide attempts. But I would guess she just misjudged how lethal the overdose really was."

Dr. Newell looks dismayed. "You're saying that she was trying to con her husband and she died by accident!" He pauses, letting it sink in. "My God, what a waste!"

Dr. Gottleib sighs. "I'll buy that." She pauses. "How are you holding up?"

Dr. Newell looks startled. "Me? I'm O.K., I guess. I mean, it was a real shock to see it in the paper. I couldn't sleep for two nights afterward, going over it again and again in my mind."

The supervisor nods understandingly. "I know what you mean. We've all been through such nights. You said you were shocked—were you mad, too?"

Dr. Newell looks puzzled. "What, you mean, mad at her? What for?"

The supervisor does not respond, but looks steadily at the resident.

"Oh. I see what you mean. Am I mad at her for doing this: for dying, for copping out, for putting me in this position. Well, I guess I am. Sure. I mean, if she wanted help, why didn't she just follow up on the plan we made? It was reasonable, and it would have been helpful—at least, I think so."

"I think so, too." Dr. Gottleib pauses. "Tell me, what did you feel in the room with her?"

Dr. Newell squints with the effort to recall. "Sorry for her, I guess. She seemed to be a nice lady in a lot of pain who just couldn't cope with the situation. I found myself wishing I could just—I don't know—shake her husband, grab him and shake him, make him understand, make him stay."

"What are you missing about her?"

"What?"

"What are you missing about her? You met her, you had a short but intense relationship, and now she's gone. What do you miss about her?"

"I never thought about that." He pauses, then says slowly, "I guess I liked the way she seemed so real in the office; you know, her suffering was really present, right on the scene. She had an appealing sort of no-nonsense quality that I found myself liking."

Dr. Gottleib nods. "Some of that came through as you spoke about her. Do you plan to go to the funeral?"

Dr. Newell looks aghast. "I wouldn't dare! They'd—I don't know—attack me, murder me, eat me alive!"

"You mean her family? I can see how you might feel that way, but remember: this family has been struck by lightning, by a human catastrophe. They need help now, in getting over this loss, and so do you. Give it some thought. Going to the funeral may help you say goodbye. Have you contacted any of the family?"

The resident grimaces. "I sure did, and it was not my idea of pleasant. The husband refused to come in or to have anything to do with the clinic. Ms. Adams' mother came in for a couple of sessions, though; she seemed to get some relief out of them. That whole side of the family is furious with Mr. Adams, and the mother spent a lot of time sounding off about how her daughter was too good for him, that sort of thing. At the end she thanked me for letting her get it off her chest."

The supervisor nods. "That is why our reaching out to the family is so important, no matter how uncomfortable we may feel about it. It does help, and it is unlikely anyone else really understands the welter of feelings that come up after a suicide." She pushes her chair back. "Keep me informed about how you're doing."

Dr. Newell, rising, smiles ruefully. "Thanks. See you at the funeral, I guess."

Dr. Gottleib smiles warmly. "Right."

———◆———

Some weeks after this conversation takes place, Mr. Adams is seated in his living room, staring out the bay window, which commands a view of a narrow strip of lawn and the state highway beyond. It is late evening. His face is puffy with alcohol and sleeplessness, and he swirls a drink absentmindedly in a wide, shallow glass. Again the scenes from his wife's funeral scroll across his mind like a newsreel: the closed casket; the minister's sanctimonious graveside speech and his pointed remark about a "God who never abandons us, but who abides with us through all adversity"; the hatred on the faces of his wife's family; the uneasy sympathy of his friends from work ("Tough one," "Sorry about this," "A real shame") and their averted eyes, showing no accusation at all, none at all.

Worst of all are the dreams, all on the same theme: his wife, or her mother, screaming at him, blaming him, or—even worse—*not* blaming him, telling him to forgive himself. When he snaps awake from each of these dreams, the first thing he notices is the empty space by his side in bed. No wonder he doesn't sleep much, he muses.

The phone rings. It's one of his oldest friends, calling to see how he is doing. He tells the truth, and his friend is dismayed. "Jesus, couldn't they do anything?" the friend bursts out. "Couldn't they stop her?"

Mr. Adams is about to respond that the doctors did all they could, when he suddenly freezes, mouth still open, phone in his hand, staring without focus out the window. An idea has suddenly taken shape in his mind: could it be someone else's fault?

His friend is making "Are you there" noises from the receiver, and Mr. Adams, shaking himself, brings the conversation to a close, pleading excessive grief. Then he sits down again. His position is identical to that in which he sat before, but there is a difference: the blank, defeated expression on his face is gone, and his mind seems to be working.

Later that night, as Mr. Adams sits in front of the TV, a commercial rivets his attention. Over a sustained shot of a judge's gavel, a theatrical voice is affirming that those in the audience may well have a claim for various kinds of damages that they are unaware of, and that the only way to be sure is to call the law offices of a local attorney, whose name Mr. Adams recognizes from weekly ads in his newspaper television guide. Grabbing a pencil, he jots down the number in the margin of his crossword puzzle.

Mr. Adams' first thoughts upon awakening the next morning are of the TV commercial. "What about that psychiatrist, Dr. Olsen? She spent hours with him, telling him things she never told me, coming home crying some days and happy—like she was in love—on others. That guy wouldn't even answer my questions about how she was doing when I called! Where the hell was *he*? And then the S.O.B. didn't even come to the funeral. He sent some student of his!"

The excitement of that most intoxicating of feelings—righteous wrath—makes Mr. Adams' hands tremble as he pours himself a cup of coffee. On impulse, he decides to call an old friend from high school, Jameson, now an attorney in town. Jameson's small general legal practice handles only about one malpractice case a year, but his early work with a larger firm (before branching out on his own) has given him a taste of the malpractice field. From this experience he is also well aware of the hidden costs, emotional and financial, to plaintiffs, and the consequent need to screen carefully any potential case.

They meet the next day. Mr. Jameson listens carefully as his old friend tells his story. In recounting the history, Mr. Adams is tempted to gloss over the frequent quarrels with his wife and her earlier suicide threats, but he finds himself confessing his feelings of guilt over the matter and is surprised to feel relieved. After he finishes, Mr. Adams looks at Mr. Jameson and asks: "What d'ya think, Bill? Should I sue?"

Jameson leans forward in his chair and rests his elbows on the desk. "I think you're asking me two questions."

"What do you mean?"

"Well, you're asking me first if you have a case. That's a complicated question. You may have a case, but it will take lots of research and review by experts in the field to establish if there is any evidence of malpractice. The death of a young woman is very sad, and jurors are usually touched by that. But juries also take into account the nature of the doctor-patient relationship, how much control the patient had over her own behavior, and the doctor's overall conduct: how much effort was put in, whether it met the standard of practice, and so on. There is always lots of expert testimony, but what it comes down to is whether or not the jury thinks it's fair to take money from the doctor, as punishment, and give it to the person suing."

"So you're saying that the jury may take a look at me and decide, even if the doctor made a mistake, I was also to blame and so I don't deserve any money?"

Jameson nods.

"Well, look, suppose they don't find out about the fights?"

"I'm afraid that will all come out at trial: fights, threats, your sex life. It's all fair game for the defense. And that brings me to the second part of your question: whether it will be worth it or not." Jameson leans back, his tone becoming somewhat academic. "In making your decision whether or not to sue, you have to consider the costs as well as the benefits. A lawsuit is a long, physically and emotionally draining process. Lots of personal information will come out, and it gets into the papers. You have to think about that. Let me ask you something. What are you hoping to get by suing?"

Mr. Adams has been distracted by uneasy thoughts as he contemplates the vision of his personal life spread over the front page of the local shopper's weekly. Jameson's question catches him a bit by surprise, and he draws on reserves of anger in response.

"I want those irresponsible doctors punished. They took over control of my wife's life and then, when the going got tough, they threw their hands up. They never told me this might happen. If anybody is at fault, it's them, not me! They need to be taught a lesson so that—so that—so they don't do this to some *other* poor patient."

Mr. Jameson shakes his head ruefully, sensing the futility of influencing his friend's decision. He decides to give it one more try.

"Look, you might be right. There are some bad doctors out there, and I've sued some of them. And on your case, sure, I haven't looked over the records yet or talked to an expert. If you would like, I'll send them to one of our experts, who is very objective and has helped me with a number of cases. But I feel an obligation to give you my gut reaction, as your lawyer and your friend. No matter what, this will be a tough case, personally damaging to you and extremely difficult to win. From what you have told me, the jury is not likely to be sympathetic to your position unless the doctors were reckless in their treatment. In other words, realistically, I don't think you have much chance of winning. And what are you trying to win? You're not likely to get the millions you may think: your wife hadn't worked in years before her present job and her prospects for employment were mixed under the best of circumstances. You have no children who could claim a loss. And your claim for loss of the relationship would be hard to prove, given what you've told me."

After staring at his knees for a moment, Mr. Adams looks up: "I need to show it was their fault, not mine."

Jameson is impressed by this flash of insight on the part of his old friend. "Okay, you're doing this because you're angry. Suing seems like a great release, at first. But it's not the answer. I think you need to talk to somebody about this, your minister, or a counselor of some sort. Do that, then give me a call. If you're still convinced you want to go ahead, I'll take the case for you. But I don't think a lawsuit is a good substitute for talking to someone about this awful thing that's happened to you."

Mr. Adams slowly realizes what is being said to him. His face reddens. "You're telling me that I should see a shrink to talk about how some other shrink killed my wife? *You're* the one who's nuts! I'm getting out of here. If you won't help me, I'll find someone else who will." With that, Mr. Adams grabs his coat and storms out of the office.

Upon returning home, he immediately picks up the phone to make an appointment with the law firm advertised on TV. To his surprise it turns out that he will never see the smooth young attorney from the commercial, since that individual, lending his name merely for recognition, acts as a broker and farms out all cases to a small local law firm that specializes in plaintiffs' cases. At his appointment he meets

Mr. Lyons, the young attorney assigned to his case. Mr. Lyons listens carefully to essentially the same story that Mr. Jameson heard. This time, however, Mr. Adams downplays his checkered relationship with his wife, stresses how dependent his wife was on her therapist, and voices previously unspoken concerns about her medications and her stability. He now asserts he had "no idea" of the seriousness of his wife's depression or that she might kill herself. He admits that they were having marital problems and were separated but points out that this was actually a positive step, a cooling off period to help them both think things over. He told her he was leaving, he claims, only out of frustration and to force her to "straighten up."

"If the doctor had told me how unstable she was, I never would have done that," he adds with great sincerity.

After listening carefully to this story, Lyons asks many detailed questions about the state of the marriage. He also inquires about the probable emotional impact of the litigation on Mr. Adams. Mr. Adams dismisses the implicit warning.

"I know all that. I've talked it over with a lawyer friend of mine. I know it will be tough, but I'm willing to do it if it will help save someone else's life."

Mr. Adams has succeeded in convincing himself of his altruistic motives, and his conviction carries through. Mr. Lyons is impressed. It strikes him that this may be one of those cases in which justice can actually be done, and the deterrent force of malpractice litigation put to good use.

After gathering some more information on Ms. Adams' education and work history—that is, her potential for future employment and earnings that could represent a loss caused by her death—Mr. Lyons explains the contingency fee arrangement. He informs Mr. Adams that litigation is expensive, that the case will be reviewed by at least one expert psychiatrist to decide if there is evidence of malpractice, and that the firm will make an estimate of the economic damages resulting from her death. Once that is done, they will meet again and decide whether or not to file a suit.

Mr. Lyons reminds Mr. Adams that he doesn't have to put up any money for the research or the trial costs. Mr. Adams is relieved; he and his wife had minimal savings and very high medical bills. "Instead of charging you for all this and getting an hourly fee, we receive nothing if we lose and one-third of the award if we win. If we decide to take your case, we will take the risk, based on our belief that it is a winnable case."

Mr. Adams' expression turns speculative. "How much do you think we can, you know, get?"

"Well, with the death, pain and suffering and lost income, we always ask for at least $5 million. That's almost routine."

Doing some quick mental arithmetic, Mr. Adams feels the gambler inside him stir to life, and feels a peculiar mixture of excitement and guilt. The two then shake hands and agree to talk when the research has been completed.

———◆———

A few months later Mr. Lyons is poring over the six-inch-thick file of case materials, when a senior partner in the firm stops by the office.

"That the Adams file?"

Lyons pushes his hair back out of his eyes. "Right. Medical records, outpatient and inpatient charts, doctors' office notes—the works. I'm just going over it for the third time."

"Something or nothing?"

Lyons looks thoughtful. "Something, I think, but it has the usual problems. The quote, loving and bereaved husband, unquote, seems to have been fed up with the deceased and was pretty much out the door: hardly a sympathetic plaintiff. The decedent was suicidal for most of her life, according to this, and just managed to hang on for all these years. At one point one of her doctors wrote that the choices were between locking her up for the rest of her life or getting her to take responsibility for herself." Lyons ticks off points on his finger. "They did offer her a hospital bed, but she refused after reassuring the doctor that she would come for help if she got worse. They did not think she was committable. The documentation seems pretty good, and there's not a lot of evidence so far that people ignored her complaints. On top of that, our economist confirms what I suspected: low lost income, little earning potential or education, and high costs. She gave me one set of numbers that suggested that Ms. Adams cost less dead than alive! That's the bad news."

Lyons changes hands for the other side. "The good news is that her regular psychiatrist took off on vacation even though she was in bad shape, and he prescribed the medication she actually used to kill herself. A resident made the decision not to hospitalize with supervision only over the phone. The husband tells a convincing story and might come across as sympathetic if we coach him. No one ever told him the risks of suicide, and it's pretty obvious that the doctor took her threats too lightly."

"So, what are you saying?"

"I'm saying that if you want my gut reaction, the doctors made a mistake, but it wasn't obvious malpractice. She lied to the guy in the emergency room, and the husband wasn't willing to help, no matter what he says. That woman was a disaster waiting to happen, and so was their marriage. Thank God they didn't have any kids."

The senior partner nods approvingly: "Very interesting. Luckily, you don't sit on the jury. You make some good points, and we'll have to deal with each of them at trial. But the most important thing you said was that there was no 'obvious malpractice.' That's irrelevant. The jury will look at a lot of things."

The senior partner begins to pace the office, his voice taking on a pontificating tone. "They might see this suicide as just the patient's problem. They could be tipped by many things: who looks better on the stand, who sounds better, what seems fair. But if we can present this right, they might see it as the doctor's problem. If you're telling me that there *may* have been some malpractice, even if it's not obvious, we should go ahead. Tell you what: you want to run it by Dr. White? He's usually pretty reliable."

"That's the problem, Ed. He is so damn reliable we won't know if there's really a case there, even if he gives the green light. Anyway, I thought I'd look at the case law first."

The partner nods as he turns away. "Run it by White anyway, and also send it to Flaherty. Flaherty has a few more opinions in his book than 'Yes, it's the worst case of malpractice I've ever seen.' "

After reviewing the case, Dr. Flaherty drafts a report to Mr. Lyons. He points out the strengths and weaknesses of the case, with special emphasis on the quality of documentation by Dr. Newell, the efforts to get supervision on the case, and the patient's participation in the treatment decision. He also highlights the importance of the marital relationship and the long-term nature of the patient's illness. He concludes by saying that he finds no evidence of malpractice in the case.

Shortly after receiving the same materials from Mr. Lyons, Dr. White seats himself at his desk and arranges the documents in the Adams case in a neat stack before him. Pulling a yellow legal pad from a desk drawer, he jots down numerous brief notes in a careful hand as he flips rapidly through the materials.

Several hours later, Dr. White assembles his notes before him, props them up on the pile of documents, and begins to write the draft of an opinion letter to the plaintiff's law firm. The final letter, which is a succinct two pages, outlines several negligent acts by the physicians involved and draws a direct causal connection between them and the patient's death. Dr. White's letter closes with the statement that malpractice, in his professional opinion, has clearly occurred. To no one's surprise, Dr. White finds gross negligence at almost all the decision points in the case.

Mr. Lyons and the senior partner read and re-read both reports, then meet to make a decision.

"Well, what do you think now?" the senior partner asks.

"I'm exactly where I was before, Ed. And Flaherty's report only supports it more: there is little evidence of malpractice."

"But what about White? He's a psychiatrist, too, isn't he? He makes a good case for malpractice."

Lyons is annoyed. "Come on, Ed. He *always* does. I'm not impressed."

"You don't have to be impressed, the jury does. Look, we don't decide the cases, they do that. We advocate, they decide. That's how the job is divided up." The partner puts his feet up on Mr. Lyon's desk. "Now, we have three questions to answer here: First, do we have a good-faith belief that there was malpractice in this case? I say, yes: White's review and the husband's story give us that. It's not frivolous, it's not a nuisance suit.

"Now, the second question is a business decision: Are we likely to win or likely to lose? Given the whole situation, I say we're more likely to win: we've got the emotions on our side.

"Finally, are we likely to win enough to make it worthwhile to the firm? Now, as I read it, the damages won't set any records, but they will be all right. And remember, costs come off the top before we take our third."

Sensing his colleague's unease, the senior partner turns reassuring. "I know you have some questions about the case, but that's the nature of the business. That's why we have an adversarial system. That's what we're here for, to represent one side. Now, if you want off the case, I'll understand. It's up to you. Let me know tomorrow."

Mr. Lyons ponders the arguments. He believes in the importance of people getting their day in court, and he believes in the need to represent every client zealously. How else could the system work? But he has often felt the tension between these legal missions and the merits of the case. On the other hand, he has not forgotten his upcoming annual evaluation and the potential promotion. He sighs. "Perhaps I should have gone to medical school after all."

Suddenly resolved, he phones his senior partner and tells him he has decided to stay on the case.

The suit is filed against Drs. Newell and Gottleib. Dr. Flaherty receives a check with a letter thanking him for his work and telling him that his services will no longer be needed on this case. Dr. White is retained as the plaintiff's expert.

———————◆———————

At another law firm in town, Mr. Shields, an associate assigned to the defense team for the doctors in the Adams case, is going over the clinic notes from Ms. Adams' last visit, underlining certain sections and making cryptic notations (such as "stat?" and "check exp") in the margins. This task completed, he stacks together a massive bundle of papers, some of them stapled into inch-thick sections, others clasped into large three-ring binders. Juggling the unwieldy pile on out-stretched arms and steadying it with his chin, he backs carefully out of his office, turns around, and sidesteps painstakingly down the hall to the partner's office.

Fortunately, the door is open. Mr. Shields hurries over to the desk and plunks the pile of papers down on an unoccupied corner, letting his breath out in a "Whew!"

"A little light reading for those long afternoons," he says dryly, taking a chair.

The senior partner smiles. "How are you coming with it?"

"O.K. It seems to be a pretty solid case. The documentation is better than average, the right questions were asked, and so forth. The strongest point—this is just my initial opinion, you understand—is the fact that Newell got two consultations during the process. That's a big help in determining the standard of practice issue."

The partner nods. "I agree. What next?"

Mr. Shields unfolds a handkerchief and wipes his brow. "I've just finished flagging the various parts for our expert. Who will that be, by the way?"

"Probably Joe Gordon, if he's free."

"I don't recognize the name."

The partner registers mild surprise. "Funny you shouldn't. I guess you just missed being on a case with him. We use him a fair amount. High-level professor at the university, resume like a phone book, extremely convincing in court. Also, a straight-shooter."

Mr. Shields looks puzzled. "What do you mean? He's honest?"

"That too. But what I meant was, he's objective. If he says there's a case to defend, there is. He's not just drumming up business."

"Sounds good. Should I call him up?"

"Yeah. His number's in the file. Make sure he has the time to review this case. If he does, send him a formal letter asking him to render an expert opinion and enclose in that letter a statement of the standard. Remember it?"

Mr. Shields narrows his eyes in concentration and quotes slowly. "Whether, in the treatment of Ms. Adams, the standard of care displayed by Drs. Newell et al. fell within the standard of care of the average prudent practitioner at the same level of training and specialization at that time under the same circumstances."

The partner nods approvingly. "Close enough. Then, at the same time you send him that letter, send him a xerox of everything in this pile."

Mr. Shields looks sourly at the tower of documents. "It'll take an orange crate to send all this in."

The partner smiles. "It won't be the first one he's gotten from us."

◆

Some time later Dr. Gordon sinks into a recliner chair in his living room and places a coffee mug on an end table at his side. He glances at the mantel clock and notes the time on a corner of the manila folder, labeled "Adams v. Newell et al.," on his lap. Like many experts, he is paid by the hour, and time recording is second nature by now.

Pen in hand, he takes a bundle of papers from the stack next to the chair and begins to read. At intervals he also makes cryptic notations in the margins, such as "standard?" "NB," "good," "doc." and—on one occasion—"drivel!"

When fatigue brings the session to a close, Dr. Gordon jots down the time and stands, kneading the small of his back. Then he prepares for bed. His wife, who is sitting propped against the headboard grading some papers, looks up as he slides under the sheets.

"How's it going?"

Dr. Gordon grunts. "O.K. Good, solid case, nice records. But long! Papers probably weigh more than the patient."

Ms. Gordon looks sympathetic. "What is it, honey, another suicide?"

" 'Fraid so. A lot of the last bunch have been suicides. Stands to reason, I guess; that's where the bad feelings are."

His wife looks puzzled. "You mean the doctors feel badly about their mistakes?"

It is Dr. Gordon's turn to look puzzled. "What mistakes?"

"I mean, the malpractice. Isn't that when a doctor makes a mistake?"

Dr. Gordon punches his pillow into a more agreeable shape. "That's the theory, honey, but it's not how it really works. Malpractice is supposed to be when a doctor falls below a certain standard of practice. That's how it's described in the law itself. In the real world, malpractice suits come from a bad outcome plus bad feelings: anger, guilt, entitlement—you name it." He sighs. "Seems like suicide is the bad outcome that leaves the worst feelings; I guess that's why there are so many of these cases."

"But, Joe, what I don't see is, how is the jury supposed to figure all that out?"

Dr. Gordon considers. "I guess that's where the expert comes in. I teach them about it."

◆

Sometime later at his monthly poker game with two other psychiatrists, a CPA, an internist, two surgeons, and a trial lawyer, Dr. Gordon has just collected a modest pot. While the chips are being swept from the table and some of the players depart in search of new beers, one of the psychiatrists asks Dr. Gordon, "How's the forensic world these days? Any hot cases?"

"A few," Dr. Gordon acknowledges. "I'm in the middle of a suicide case now."

"In-hospital?"

"No, emergency room visit. You know I can't give you the details, but it involves a patient in outpatient treatment who made a clinic visit, then suicided. All the involved docs are being sued."

The other psychiatrist shakes his head, the mournful expression on his face seeming to convey, "What else can you expect these days?" The trial lawyer, returning from the refrigerator, overhears the last part of this conversation and asks, "Wait a moment. The woman suicided while under treatment? Isn't that malpractice?"

Dr. Gordon looks at him with surprise and annoyance. "Jesus, Steve, didn't you learn anything in law school?"

"I know, I know, there has to be a doctor-patient duty and there has to be negligence directly causing the damages. But I mean, just off the record, isn't it negligent—don't you think it's negligence when someone kills himself while he's treating with a psychiatrist?"

Dr. Gordon turns in mock dismay to his psychiatric colleagues who are staring at the lawyer with nervous expressions. "You see what we're up against? Even the lawyers jump to that conclusion! No wonder juries are hard to convince." He turns to face the lawyer directly, "No, Steve, a suicide in treatment is not malpractice unless someone has been negligent, and in this case, I personally think no one was."

The lawyer shrugs and begins to arrange his chips in neater piles. "Well, good luck with it anyway, Joe. I don't do any malpractice work myself, but I know about juries. Hope your jury sees it your way."

Dr. Gordon shrugs in turn. "Not my problem. I just testify."

◆

The task of winnowing through the Adams file consumes large segments of several weekends. Finally, Dr. Gordon uncovers his dictating machine and records his preliminary report, flipping through the documents to cite the precise entries that support his opinion. The report covers twenty-four single-spaced pages but can be summed up in one sentence: Dr. Gordon's opinion, to a reasonable degree of medical certainty, is that the defendant physicians met the standard of care in their treatment of Ms. Adams. Dr. Gordon buttresses this view with a careful analysis of the risks versus the benefits at all the decision points along the way and describes the tensions among the patient's needs, rights, autonomy, and protection.

On the basis of this opinion, the defense officially names Dr. Gordon as its expert. Had Dr. Gordon's opinion been "unfavorable"—that is, had he felt that the care was, indeed, negligent—the law firm might have settled the case immediately or, following standard legal practice, sought another expert in the hope that a different opinion would emerge. Instead—based on the strength of the expert's reasoning in his report, the attorneys' feeling for the case, and a series of cost-benefit calculations—the doctors' defense team advises their clients not to settle but to defend (i.e., fight) the case in court.

Now the two experts, as well as other individuals who may have information relevant to the case, are deposed (examined under oath) by both sets of attorneys. The original parties to the case were deposed earlier, and transcripts of their depositions make up a large segment of the pile of records representing the data in the case. This "discovery" phase ensures that both sides have access to more or less the same data base for the trial.

As the time for the trial draws closer, the defense attorneys meet with Dr. Gordon to explore his reasoning and ask questions that have not been addressed in his report. Dr. Gordon indicates the precise places in the record that support his reasoning and explains how he drew his conclusions from them. From these record entries the attorneys develop questions that they might ask Dr. Gordon at the trial, with the goal of illuminating these points for the jury. Finally, the defense team sits back.

"I guess that's it," Mr. Shields says. "Just bring an up-to-date resume in case they want to see it. Also, don't bring your notes to the witness stand. I don't want them to have anything extra to go fishing through."

Dr. Gordon nods. "No problem; I think I have the case pretty well in mind. And, as I recall, if they want me to pay attention to a particular line or word, they'll show it to me anyway."

"Right. We'll be calling you so you'll know exactly when to show up at the courthouse. Anything else?"

"Just to remind you: there's nothing I love better than lots and lots of advance notice."

Shields smiles. "Don't we all. We'll do our best, but you know how courts are."

Dr. Gordon nods. "I'm beginning to get an inkling."

———————◆———————

After numerous postponements, the case of Adams v. Newell et al. is scheduled for an approximately four-day period in March, six years after the suicide of Ms. Adams. The plaintiff's side is presented first. The plaintiff's witnesses, interviewed on direct examination and then cross-examination, include Mr. Adams, one of his friends, Dr. Olsen, Dr. Newell, Dr. Gottlieb, and Dr. White. The direct examination of Mr Adams downplays the marital discord and emphasizes his bereavement and loss. The friend testifies concerning his observations of Mr. Adams' distress and grief. Cross-examination by the defense attempts to bring out the evidence of martial strife and threatened abandonment elucidated in the evaluation itself and revealed in the clinic note.

Dr. White is the final plaintiff's witness. A short, elderly man with white hair, he wears a pinstriped blue suit and gold-framed half-glasses. When he takes the stand, he beams and nods at the jury, many of whom beam back. Other jurors hide smiles at his manner, somewhere between that of a classics professor and an elf.

Dr. White's direct examination establishes that he had been affiliated with several hospitals decades ago and was in part-time private practice until his retirement five years earlier. He now teaches a little and consults on legal cases. He has reviewed with care the materials in the case, and his direct testimony concludes with his opinion that the doctors demonstrated negligence in their care of Ms. Adams.

In direct examination of his witness Mr. Lyons brings out the reasoning behind this opinion in terms of what should have been done, drawing on Dr. White's own experience with patients. Stress is laid upon the use of medications.

"Dr. White, do you have an opinion concerning the advisability of allowing Ms. Adams to have all those drugs around, feeling the way she did?" Mr. Lyons inquires.

"I certainly do."

"Could you give that opinion to us, Doctor?"

"Certainly. To allow a woman in as deep despair as poor Ms. Adams to have access to enough drugs to poison herself is, in my opinion, the very height of negligence. It is tantamount, I might say, to handing a loaded gun to a child."

On hearing this, the jurors look uneasy. Expressed in these terms, it does sound like a reckless act.

In his cross-examination of Dr. White, Mr. Shields is guided by several details from Dr. Gordon's expert witness report. He first obtains some information about Dr. White's consultative practice with law firms. It appears that Dr. White consults only to plaintiff's law firms and receives a flat fee rather than an hourly rate.

"Now then, Doctor," Mr. Shields begins, "you have testified that you have read the records of the doctors who were actually there, on the scene, examining Ms. Adams. You have read those, have you not?"

"Certainly."

"In those records did you see *anything*"—Shields pauses for effect—"that would lead you to believe that Ms. Adams was psychotic or committable or incompetent, in contradiction to the opinions of the doctors who were actually there, on the scene, at the time, directly talking to and working with Ms. Adams?"

"I most certainly did," Dr. White asserts confidently.

Mr. Shields, who has turned away, as if the answer were so self-evident as to make the question rhetorical, spins around in feigned surprise. "You did?"

"Certainly."

Simulating bewildered disbelief, Mr. Shields asks, "What evidence was there that she was psychotic?"

"The depth of this woman's despair was clearly great enough to be considered psychotic," Dr. White explains, also adopting the tone of someone explaining the obvious.

"Was she hallucinating? Delusional? Paranoid?" Mr. Shields barks.

Dr. White's quiet voice is in sharp contrast. "She was not."

Mr. Shields nods. "She was not. What evidence was there that she was committable?"

Dr. White spreads his hands. "Her clear suicidal intent, of course. I would never let such a person leave my office without ensuring that she would be placed in a hospital immediately, with precautions against suicide instituted."

"Doctor, do you call her explicitly stated intention not to kill herself but to follow a program of treatment, as we have heard—do you call that a clear sign of suicidal intent?" Mr. Shield's tone is sarcastic, dismissing.

Dr. White shrugs. "The woman was too ill to be relied on to decide things for herself. That is why hospitalization was mandatory, in my view."

"Which brings me to the next point," Mr. Shields says without dropping a beat. "What evidence was there that she was not competent to set up a plan with the doctor and follow through on it, just as she told the doctor, who was there on the scene at the time, that she intended to do?"

"Clearly, her despair was so deep that it was foolish to believe her plans, her schemes for this and that." Dr. White pats the top of the witness stand for emphasis. "The woman needed care, and she was too sick to do anything for herself. It is as simple as that."

Mr. Shields snorts, eyeing the jury as if to say, "Can you believe this?"

"You maintain she was incompetent despite the fact that the doctor—who was actually there, on the scene, at the time—carefully tested her ability to understand him, at not one but several points during the interview, and as he has testified, she *never* tested out as incompetent?"

"Certainly," says Dr. White.

Mr. Shields turns away with a look of disgust on his face that the jury can plainly read. The effect of an exchange like this last one would ordinarily be fairly destructive to Dr. White's credibility to the jury but—as an "old court hand"—Dr. White has remained throughout the cross-examination apparently unshaken in his aplomb when confronted with the internal contradictions in his own testimony. Moreover, when agreeing with attorney Shields about such a contradiction, and hence seeming to concede a weakness in his argument, Dr. White responds with an emphatic "Yes! That is exactly correct!," smiling all the while—a tactic that confuses some of the jury members, who receive the impression that White and the lawyer on the opposing side are somehow in agreement. Thus, these jurors are unsure whether Shields or White has scored a solid point.

Whenever this tactic is employed, Shields responds with an effective counter-move. By means of body and facial language as well as tone of voice, he treats all of Dr. White's disagreements as though they were agreements, points scored by Shields. Thus, for example, after White has resolutely refused to buy a hypothetical example and has forcefully disagreed, Shields swings to face the jury, hand outstretched toward Dr. White, and smiles confidently at them as if to say, "There! You see? He has to admit it!" As a result of this maneuver, several other members of the jury are left with the perception that the "doctors' lawyer" has just scored a significant triumph of logic over the opposing witness. Interestingly, such a maneuver, being nonverbal, does not appear in the court reporter's transcript of the case, despite its powerful influence.

Shields winds up by turning toward the judge and saying flatly, "I have no further questions for this witness," in a tone that seems to convey, "What could you expect from a witness such as this?" Dr. White is excused. Leaving the stand, he nods cheerfully to the jury. One of the younger jurors reflexively nods back, then looks embarrassed.

In opening its own side of the case, the defense brings Drs. Newell and Gottleib back to the stand to refresh the jurors' memories with their appearance, demeanor, and testimony. Both physicians respond well on the stand—nervous but genuine and likeable. The defense has advised them to have their spouses sit with them in the back of the courtroom before they go on the stand, with the specific aim of rounding out their reality as people to the jury. Although the present case is theoretically decided by the jury's verdict about the presence or absence of malpractice, the defense knows that the heart of such a case is often the question of whether the jury unconsciously (or even consciously) identifies with the dead patient—"This horrible thing could have happened to me, and they must pay for their failure, lest it happen to me next time"—or with Dr. Newell—"That is the kind of doctor I would want to take care of me; he probably did the right thing then, as he would again later, if I were his patient."

Mr. Shields guides each doctor in sequence through the events and decision points along the course of the interaction with Ms. Adams, taking pains to bring out the decision making that went into each step.

"Did you consider hospitalization for Ms. Adams?" Mr. Shields asks Dr. Newell.

"Yes, I did."

"Did you offer it to her?"

"Yes."

"And what happened?"

"She chose not tᴏ accept it."

"She chose not to. Did you consider that to be a competent choice on her part?"

Dr. Newell nods. "Yes, I did."

"Why?"

"She had demonstrated all along a clear understanding of the pros and cons of this plan during our discussion."

"Could you have hospitalized her anyway?"

"Well, I could have petitioned for commitment by the court."

"Did you consider that?"

"Yes."

"Did you do it?"

"No."

"And why not, Doctor?"

"Because, when I put together the advantages and disadvantages, it came out clearly on the side of agreeing to the plan we both set up."

"Both of whom, Doctor?"

"Ms. Adams and myself."

"That was your decision, Doctor, to follow your plan?"

"Well—mine and the patient's."

Mr. Shields nods approvingly. "And did you review that decision with your supervisor?"

"Yes, I did."

"And what was her opinion?"

"That our plan was the most appropriate one."

"Appropriate to Ms. Adams's needs at the time?"

"Yes, sir."

"Thank you, Doctor."

Mr. Shields frequently bolsters attempts like the foregoing to bring out the reasoning by having the doctors read aloud from the chart, since good documentation is one of the strengths of the defense's case. In addition, quotation from the record is a way of demonstrating that these assessments occurred at the actual time of the evaluation—that the physicians are not making up their reasoning by hindsight, after the fact.

Dr. Gottlieb is the next witness. Since, as Dr. Newell's supervisor, she is next in the hospital chain of command, her exposure to liability is as great as—or possibly greater than—Dr. Newell's own, according to the legal doctrine known as *respondeat superior.* This doctrine holds people in positions of authority vicariously responsible (or liable) for the actions (or nonaction) of those who work for them. Because of her greater experience and authority, Dr. Gottlieb is an important witness for both the plaintiff and the defense. For the plaintiff, she is a potential "deep pocket"—a source of settlement or judgment dollars from her own malpractice insurance policy, apart from Dr. Newell's. In fact, it would amount to legal malpractice if the plaintiff's attorneys ignored her role in this case and did not name her as a defendant. For the defense, Dr. Gottlieb represents a greater potential risk of exposure because of her position of authority and concomitantly greater insurance coverage. As a result, both the direct and cross-examination of Dr. Gottlieb are extensive and extremely detailed.

Attorney Shields encourages Dr. Gottlieb to elaborate on the reasoning underlying her clinical decisions, including her decision not to come in to the clinic to see Ms. Adams and her decision not to hospitalize the patient against her will.

Dr. Gordon is the final witness for the defense. He is a tall, thin, somber-looking individual with thinning black hair salted with gray, wearing tortoise-shell glasses and a navy blue suit. His facial expression at rest is that of someone who is obligated to give you the news that you have cancer. However, when answering questions, his manner becomes animated, and the enthusiasm of the dedicated teacher shines through.

Drawing on this quality as a strength for the witness stand, Mr. Shields has decided, in consultation with his senior partner, to "give the witness his head" whenever possible—that is, to allow Dr. Gordon to give, in answer to questions, mini-lectures to the jury. While there is some risk that the jurors will be put off by excessive pedantry, abstruse jargon, or a condescending manner in the expert's presentation, they may respond positively to the right expert, feeling that they are being let in on the "trade secrets" of what doctors really think and do behind the scenes. Ironically, the effectiveness of this approach rests in part on the fact that doctors are generally perceived—perhaps realistically—as talking far too little to their patients and keeping things hidden. Thus, the expert will be seen in marked contrast as a doctor who will talk, who will take the time to tell the jury what is really going on.

To get to this phase of the direct examination, Mr. Shields passes quickly but comprehensively over Dr. Gordon's impressive credentials, publications, and achievements and presents the standard in the form of a question to the expert.

"Do you have an opinion, Doctor, to a reasonable degree of medical certainty, whether the care of the defendant doctors in this case met the standard for the average prudent practitioner at the level of training and experience at that time and under those circumstances?"

"Yes, I have an opinion," Dr. Gordon responds.

"And what is that opinion, Doctor?"

Despite his experience on the stand and his awareness of the somewhat ritualistic nature of this part of the direct examination, Dr. Gordon notes that he always feels slightly tense at this exact point, in response to the suspense of the moment, the "punch line" of the defense case. Thus, he is aware of a slight edge in his voice as he answers, "That they met the standard."

Two jurors, who have unconsciously held their breath for this moment, begin breathing again. Mr. Shields now asks for Dr. Gordon to defend—i.e., give the basis for—his opinion. He poses a series of open-ended questions that will permit Dr. Gordon to teach freely about suicide, assessment and management, and the patient's competence to participate in treatment planning. Since the jury is showing every sign of becoming engrossed in this inside information, Mr. Lyons jumps up with an objection every so often in order to break the flow. In doing so he is aware that he must not overdo this approach, since the jury, or the judge, may become irritated and alienated by too many interruptions.

On cross-examination of Dr. Gordon, Mr. Lyons adopts an attitude of barely restrained hostility, a posture designed both to intimidate the witness and to suggest outrage at Dr. Gordon's ostensible folly or duplicity in presenting such testimony.

"Now, Doctor," Mr. Lyons asks, on a steadily rising tone of disbelief, "are you seriously suggesting that this poor sick woman, bent on self-destruction, should not have been hospitalized?"

Dr. Gordon frowns. "That she 'should not'? No, that was not my testimony. It was appropriate that she be offered hospitalization, and she was."

"And what happened, Doctor?" Mr. Lyons demands fiercely.

"She refused."

"So this suicidal woman WAS NOT HOSPITALIZED!" Mr. Shields's voice is now twenty decibels above normal volume.

"Since she was not committable, she was not." Dr. Gordon's voice is deliberately soft, so that Lyons's still echoing tones sound excessively—even foolishly—loud in contrast.

"Her not being committable: that is merely your opinion, isn't it, Doctor?" In Mr. Lyons's inflections, the word "opinion" has the tone of "lunatic, hallucinatory fantasy."

"It is my opinion, yes."

"It's your OPINION, is that right, Doctor?"

"Yes."

Throughout the rapid and sarcastic inquiries that Mr. Lyons fires at him, Dr. Gordon responds with the same politeness and pedagogic enthusiasm that he showed on direct examination. One result of this style is that even those jurors who are not immediately convinced by the testimony perceive him as even-handed.

Finding relatively little to attack and wanting to end on a note of emotional strength, Mr. Lyons glowers at the witness and intones, "Regardless of what the doctors were *trying* to do, poor Ms. Adams is dead! Would you agree with me on that, Doctor?"

Fleetingly, Dr. Gordon feels the impulse to assert in response that the patient's being dead is beside the point, that the fact that she would suicide is now known only by hindsight, that the relevant question is the standard of care for a prospective judgment. Instinctively, he senses that any attempt to cram these points into his response cannot help sounding defensive. Besides, these points can be made by the defendant's attorney on summation. He contents himself with a simple "Yes."

"She's dead, isn't she doctor?"

"Yes," Dr. Gordon repeats.

With a contemptuous backhand gesture Mr. Lyons flings his yellow legal pad of trial notes onto his courtroom table and says, in a voice heavy with mingled scorn and disgust, "NO further questions!" His manner is that of someone who might well have further questions, lots of further questions, but whose stomach has been so turned by what he has heard that he has lost all will to ask them. The emotional intensity of this moment makes several jurors feel quite anxious.

After Dr. Gordon has been excused, each attorney presents his summation to the jury, and then the judge gives the jurors their instructions. As she explains their task in this case, the judge's face is set in lines of intense concentration. The jurors take this to signify that the case is a very serious and important one, and they feel inspired to do their job with care. In reality, the judge's concentration is a reflection of the complex and delicate decisions that go into choosing and delivering the instructions. Most judges have a number of standard instructions, either mandated or approved by law, about which there is little or no controversy in a given case. In every case, however, attorneys for the plaintiff and the defense present the judge with instructions that are favorable to their own theory of the case and argue the merits of these instructions. The judge then has to select those that she feels give the fairest statement of the law—or use other instructions that she has selected—to ensure that nothing in the instructions will serve as the basis for an appeal of the case.

While judges are the least accountable individuals in modern society—they cannot be sued, fired, or otherwise held responsible for their decisions—they are exquisitely sensitive to having their decisions reversed (i.e., overruled) on appeal to a higher court. When a jury trial is appealed, it is the judge's instructions to the jury that often come under close scrutiny. Such reversals are public information, reported, together with often lengthy textual explications of the issues and grounds for reversal, in various legal newsletters, journals, and—eventually, in some cases—even legal textbooks; judges thus rule under the scrutiny of the future. Judges closely follow the patterns of appeals and reversals of their own and fellow judges' opinions; issues of peer competitiveness and self-esteem are closely interwoven in these results.

---◆---

The jurors listen attentively to the judge's instructions and some take notes. Others, perceiving the somewhat ritualistic nature of this courtroom event, allow their minds to wander, already considering the central question in any trial involving a battle of experts: which side do you believe?

The jury adjourns to the room set aside for their deliberations. The four days of trial have not allowed much time for them to size each other up or to form any but the most superficial relationships. They all sense a shared seriousness of purpose, however, and there is relatively little shuffling around and fiddling with papers. Mr. Prentice, the chosen foreman, somewhat self-consciously lapses into his professorial manner—he teaches political science at a local college—and asks for discussion. There is no moment of uneasy silence, since the group contains a number of enthusiastic talkers, most of whom immediately begin to share their views, vociferously and simultaneously. Prentice waves a hand for silence and the din subsides.

"I hate to do it, people, but I think we're going to have to go with raising hands. Let me call on you before you speak or we'll be here forever, okay?"

There are nods of grudging agreement all around, and four hands shoot up immediately. Mr. Prentice points. "Yes, Mr., uh, Riley, is it?"

"Yeah," Mr. Riley acknowledges. "The way I see it—the old lady doctor—the teacher, you know?" Several jurors nod. "She didn't even bother to come in herself to see the lady—the sick lady, I mean. Now that bothers me. I just don't think that's right."

Mr. Prentice recognizes a woman juror, who is looking askance at Mr. Riley with some hostility, since she is in the same age group as the doctor that Riley has termed the "old lady."

"Her age has not a jot to do with it," Ms. Winthrop states firmly in cultured accents. "Her failure to be present on the scene simply does not seem to me to be proper medical conduct, even in these excessively casual times."

Ms. Bunting, called on next, has just rolled her eyes while Ms. Winthrop has been intoning her opinion. "That's so irrelevant! Honestly, it's like—you're missing the whole point! That doctor, the young one—"

"Dr. Newell," Mr. Prentice inserts, helpfully.

"Yeah, him! He spoke to her on the phone the first time, so she gets her two cents in, and then, if that's not enough, like, he calls again to get even more advice! Now isn't that being real careful, like that tall doctor was saying?"

Mr. Nicholson, a college student in government who considers himself pre-law, breaks in without waiting for Mr. Prentice's call. "Exactly! That's exactly the point! You see, he was taking the patient very seriously. Now in my book, that just isn't negligence."

Almost all the jurors are drawn into the discussion. One juror believes that the short psychiatrist who smiled a lot was probably right because he seemed sincere like her grandfather, whom he strongly resembled; in contrast, another juror is scornful of the way the short expert kept "smirking at all of us."

Mr. Prentice, taking his responsibilities as foreman seriously, continues to remind his fellow jurors of the judge's instructions on the law and guides them in their attempts to apply it to the facts of this case. Mr. Mitchell jabs the table for emphasis.

"The woman *told* them she was going to do it, and she went right out and did it. They knew it was gonna happen, and they didn't do anything, not a thing! If that ain't malpractice, I don't know what is."

About half the jury sees it that way: the suicide was completely foreseeable. The other half is swayed by the slow, deliberate, somewhat pontificating manner of Ms. Grady, a local Latin teacher. "In a limited sense, yes, Mr. Mitchell, what you say may well have some merit—some merit, indeed—but let us not forget that she also indicated, with equal force, that she would *not* commit suicide in her conversation with the doctor, and it appears—at least, the evidence suggests"—her eyes sweep the other jurors' faces, gathering support—"that she was fully 'compos mentis' at the time." She catches Mr. Riley's uncomprehending look. "That means she was in full possession of her faculties, Mr. Riley," she explains graciously.

"If her faculties were in such great shape, why is she a stiff now?" Mr. Riley mutters, too low for anyone else to hear the words; however, Ms. Grady, with a teacher's trained sense of even covert rebellion in the class ranks, snaps him a sharp glance.

The jury remains about evenly divided on whether the suicide was foreseeable or not, and whether, as a result, the patient should or should not have been hospitalized. A majority is very concerned that the "doctor's medicine is what did her in," but all of them have grasped the paradoxes of pharmacologic treatment of depression.

The majority of the jurors feel that, if two psychiatrists disagree as did the experts in the trial, this says more about the murkiness of psychiatry than about the issue of malpractice in this particular case. Mr. Prentice attempts some clarification of the role of the American adversarial system of justice. He is less successful at making this point than one of the younger jurors, who reports having seen on television how even fingerprint experts disagreed in one particular case. This report somehow carries conviction, and the issue fades somewhat from the forefront of discussion.

As the hours pass, a consensus gradually forms on the side of "no malpractice." The explicit core of this view is the fact that the patient could have made the choices not to die and to call the available doctors and, for unknowable reasons, elected not to do so. However, this consensus has several unconscious determinants as well, most of which would be denied if the jurors were asked directly about them (as most decision-makers reject nonrational explanations for their decisions).

One such unconscious factor is a shared impression of Mr. Adams as something of a sleazy character. The jurors universally believe—his testimony to the contrary—that he was going to run out on his wife, a move rendering him, in their instinctive view, "undeserving" of gain from the process in which they are engaged.

In addition, the jurors liked the doctors they saw on the stand. The "good feeling" thus generated went a long way toward creating the sense that they "probably did the right thing." Complementing this view is a sense that Ms. Adams was the agent, rather than the victim, of her suicide. While the suicidal person is, by definition, both agent and victim of suicidal action, one or the other of these aspects may dominate the jury's perceptions with determinative effect.

Finally, in the jury's awareness, the experts did not make impacts as distinct as might be imagined. Both seemed articulate and sincere; both made points, the significance of some of which was obscure; both seemed to know what they were doing; and the difference in their credentials really did not register as substantive. Thus, in the jury's unconscious the experts tended to cancel each other out.

———◆———

The jury finds for the defendant doctors. The case is not appealed. The malpractice insurance premium rates increase somewhat for Drs. Newell and Gottleib, since they have been sued, but not as much as would have been the case if they had lost. Mr. Adams becomes more depressed but eventually spontaneously recovers. Dr. White shrugs. Dr. Gordon chooses to believe that his testimony was the decisive feature in the case. Mr. Lyons is annoyed but moves rapidly on to new cases. Mr. Shields is praised by the senior partner and, on the strength of this, proposes marriage to the woman he has been dating for a long time.

SECTION II. APPROACHES TO DECISION MAKING

chapter 2.
PROBABILITY, DECISION ANALYSIS, AND
CONSCIOUS GAMBLING

Why is it useful for clinicians to think about how they make decisions? As the case of Ms. Adams amply illustrates, there are many junctures at which the choices made by the clinician, together with the patient's choices and chance, can have serious, even life-or-death consequences. In making these choices we know that we stand to be judged in two tribunals—that of the law and that of conscience. Clearly, the emergence of potential legal liability as a prominent fact of professional life accounts in part for the increased motivation to understand, and modify, how and why we decide to do what we do. Our hope is that by examining the process of decision making, we will learn to make better choices and, if necessary, to demonstrate to a judge or jury that even a decision resulting in a tragic outcome was based on sound general principles. Even in this litigious era, however, probably the most unforgiving judge we face is our own conscience. Here, too, we seek to be judged fairly.

Decision making itself has come under scientific scrutiny, and specialized techniques have been developed to analyze the process of making a decision. In an age that places great reliance on science and technology, the study of decision making has evolved its own science and its own technology. Clinicians can benefit from mastering the critical use of these disciplines. As with other technologies in medicine (diagnostic tests, medications, therapeutic procedures), we must learn that the application of decision-making technology can never fully replace the wisdom gained by experience and intuitive understanding.

As preparation for examining the specific clinical issues addressed in later sections of this book, we will consider in this section some general perspectives on decision making and their application to clinical practice in psychiatry. They represent two approaches to the pursuit and use of knowledge that differ from one another in their assumptions about certainty and uncertainty.

MECHANISTIC AND PROBABILISTIC PARADIGMS

To begin to look at the different perspectives on decision making, we need to understand the contexts from which they arise; in other words, we must consider how we see the world. Do we believe that every problem has a specific, objective solution and that all questions have answers (whether or not we know them) that are certain and consistent? Or do we believe that uncertainty and subjectivity inevitably enter into any given situation—both question and answer, problem and solution? Our expectations and beliefs in these areas influence the manner in which we make decisions, the facets of a situation we take into account and those we disregard.

We can characterize these views as representing two models, or paradigms: the mechanistic and the probabilistic. The mechanistic paradigm seeks certainty and assumes that it can be attained. Conversely, the probabilistic paradigm holds that nothing can be known with absolute certainty and that the pursuit of knowledge must be tempered by this recognition (1).

The mechanistic paradigm is defined by three principles. The first is deterministic causation, the idea that one or more specific causes can be isolated to explain a given effect. According to the second principle, the cause (or causes) of a given effect can be proved to exist by means of a "crucial experiment," which will always produce the same results when repeated. The third principle holds that all scientific knowledge (that is, knowledge gained from crucial experiments) is objective.

The mechanistic paradigm has been the accepted method of searching for answers and "truth" since Sir Isaac Newton established the three principles enumerated above. But why do we place importance on this paradigm in particular? One reason is that, in our society, physics has traditionally been used as a model for scientific thought, which in turn has been made a model for rational thought in general.

Claude Bernard, one of the founders of modern medicine, proposed that Newton's mechanistic principles be used as the guidelines for "modern medical science." In his Principles of Experimental Medicine, published in 1865, Bernard states:

> As a science, medicine necessarily has definite and precise laws which, like those of all the sciences, are derived from the criterion of experiment . . . the principles of experimental determinism must be applied to medicine if it is to become an exact science founded on experimental determinism instead of remaining a conjectural science based on statistics. A conjectural science may indeed rest on the indeterminate; but an experimental science accepts only determinate, or determinable phenomena (2).

Can the world be understood as absolutely certain? Are events really predictable? In terms of our introductory case, was there any way to determine absolutely whether or not Ms. Adams would commit suicide? In Newton's time it was thought that the world was certain but that human beings were limited in their knowledge of the world by imperfect instruments of measurement. Uncertainty was a condition of human perception, not a condition of reality. Einstein's theory of relativity marked a dramatic departure from Newton's ideas of time and space but was still grounded in the mechanistic paradigm.

The shift to the probabilistic paradigm was sparked by quantum mechanics and the realization that chance and cause are related. If A is said to cause B, some degree of chance, or probability, characterizes the relationship between A and B. Uncertainty is not simply in the eye of the beholder, as the mechanistic paradigm would have us believe, but is at the very center of reality. To understand the relationship between cause and effect, one must understand the probabilities involved. This realization in turn led to Heisenberg's principle of uncertainty, which holds that the act of observation influences the object being observed.

Thus, in shifting from a mechanistic to a probabilistic approach, we can no longer remain detached spectators observing an isolated and independent system. Instead, we become active participants in a process—as much a part of the system of causes and effects as the observed subject.

The probabilistic paradigm also rests on three principles, which parallel those of the mechanistic paradigm. First, causes are not static but dynamic, acting—and interacting—differently at different times; the same effects may sometimes have different causes and vice versa. Second, since the observer influences that which is observed, there can be no crucial experiment. Third, no cause or effect can be entirely objective (or entirely subjective).

In a world where causes and effects are multiple, dynamic, and influenced by the act of observation, experimentation becomes an opportunity to note and interpret the interplay of change and chance, observer and observed. Experiments, by their very nature, are interactive. They mirror rather than distill the multitude of interactions that occur among people and objects.

As a probabilistic experiment, the interaction between doctor and patient can be seen as a dynamic, reciprocal relationship in which each influences and is influenced by the other. In this context diagnosis becomes a form of treatment, treatment a form of diagnosis, and both a form of education for the two players.

When Dr. Newell weighs the many factors in Ms. Adams' case, as part of the process of deciding on a course of treatment, he is engaging in a style of probabilistic experimentation that we call gambling. If we set aside its pejorative connotations, a gamble is simply an experiment in which the consequences of choosing one course of action over another are interpreted as a matter of relative costs and benefits. When we gamble, we keep in mind our estimate of the probability that something will happen and the value it will have for us if it does happen.

In the medical setting both doctor and patient participate in the gamble. The knowledge, values, and feelings of each influence the gamble and are therefore essential to the diagnosis and treatment. For example, Ms. Adams' aversion to hospitalization is an important factor in Dr. Newell's subsequent decisions concerning treatment. We consider conscious gambling at more length in a later section of this chapter.

Thus, experimentation under the probabilistic paradigm becomes an opportunity for the discussion and interpretation of values and beliefs. In this way the subjective dimensions of objective knowledge are revealed. Moreover, as one articulates one's values and beliefs and examines them rationally in the company of others engaged in the scientific enterprise, they become a form of knowledge. Whereas the mechanistic paradigm draws a sharp division between the objective and the subjective, excluding the latter from scientific thought, the probabilistic paradigm places them on a continuum, where knowledge, including scientific knowledge, may be more or less subjective and more or less objective, but not exclusively one or the other.

To summarize the different scientific perspectives exemplified by the mechanistic and probabilistic paradigms, the former seeks to purify knowledge of values and beliefs in the search for certainty; the latter embraces values and beliefs as one of many forms of knowledge that can help us come to terms with uncertainty.

DECISION ANALYSIS

Now that we have some idea about what the probabilistic paradigm is, how it acknowledges uncertainty and incorporates it into decision making, we need to find a method of interpreting uncertainty constructively and applying it to our advantage. Decision analysis is one such method.

While it is usually considered a decision-making tool, decision analysis has the equally important function of helping people justify their decisions to themselves and others. Decision analysis is not an all-purpose technological "fix." It does not take all the guesswork or all the emotion out of decision making, nor is it foolproof armor against bad outcomes or against regret. When appropriately applied, however, it can reduce these inherent pitfalls of decision making.

Decision analysis is a step-by-step procedure enabling us to break down a decision into its components, to lay them out in an orderly fashion, and to trace the sequence of events that might follow from choosing one course of action or another. This procedure offers several benefits. It can help us make the best possible decision in a given situation. Moreover, it can help us to clarify our values, that is, the preferences among possible outcomes by which we judge what the best decision might be. Decision analysis can also be used to build logic and rationality into our intuitive decision making—to educate our intuition about probabilities and about the paths of contingency by which our actions, in combination with chance or "outside" events, lead to outcomes.

A less apparent but nonetheless critical function of decision analysis is to help us make and carry out decisions that are emotionally charged. Decisions that involve potentially tragic consequences, such as Dr. Newell's decision not to hospitalize Ms. Adams against her will, may lead to self-blame or fear that one's esteem will fall in the eyes of others. In such situations, moreover, the possibility of reprisals (economic, political, or legal) raises the ante even further, as it did when Mr. Adams decided to sue Drs. Newell and Gottlieb. The more fraught with anxiety the decision, in sum, the more helpful decision analysis can be.

Decision analysis provides a framework for thinking consciously and critically about the choices we must make. We can conceive of it as a method of solving problems that evolves naturally, by a series of relatively simple steps, from our usual ways of thinking. Kenneth Hammond has theorized that people use different modes of thinking, or cognition, in different kinds of situations and that these modes represent a continuum from the most intuitive to the most analytic (3, 3a). The particular mode (or combination of modes) that one uses depends on the situation and the decision task. Both the cognitive mode and the decision task have distinctive features. For example, intuition is more rapid than analysis and tends to give equal weight to all associations that come to mind, while analysis tends to use more complicated weighting schemes.

Hammond has also suggested that scientific reasoning varies along a similar continuum. He describes the most analytic reasoning as that best suited to the physics laboratory, and the most intuitive as the reasoning of a scientist making public policy outside his or her area of expertise (4). These cognitive modes vary on a number of features, such as the covertness of the reasoning and whether attention is focused on individual situations or on variables and relations among variables. In the case of Ms. Adams, decision making by the examining physician partook of cognitive modes that were both intuitive (e.g., speculating about the impact of Dr. Olsen's vacation and his threshold of concern) and analytic (e.g., noting that more women attempt suicide but that more men succeed—a conclusion drawn empirically from statistical analysis of large data bases).

Cognitive continuum theory suggests that decision-making aids can be tailored to the kind of cognition prevailing in a particular situation. Certainly, formal decision analysis is not appropriate for all situations. If we are to approach our decisions consciously, then, a preliminary step is to select the most appropriate method of decision making.

Like Hammond's cognitive modes, conscious approaches to decision making occupy a continuum from the most intuitive to the most analytic. These approaches, which are described below, include acknowledging the decision, listing its pros and cons, structuring the decision, estimating the probabilities and values involved, and calculating the expected values. Some decisions can benefit from the simple, largely intuitive recognition that one has a choice to make. Others might call for the analytic panoply of a formal decision analysis.

Acknowledging the Decision

Human beings often make decisions impulsively and unconsciously, taking action before careful consideration. The first step beyond such unconscious decision making is to recognize that there is a decision to be made. It is generally useful to set off the consideration of a decision from the flow of action and feeling in which we live. Simply by stopping to think, we can break the often untrustworthy connection between impulse and action.

Listing the Pros and Cons

Listing the possible outcomes, advantages, and disadvantages of a decision in an orderly way can help the decision maker keep in mind factors that otherwise might be overlooked. As Benjamin Franklin wrote to the British scientist Joseph Priestley in 1772:

> When these difficult cases occur, they are difficult, chiefly because while we have them under consideration, all the reasons pro and con are not present to the mind at the same time; but sometimes one set present themselves, and at other times another, the first being out of sight. Hence the various purposes or inclinations that alternatively prevail, and the uncertainty that perplexes us. To get over this, my way is to divide half a sheet of paper by a line into two columns; writing over the one Pro, and over the other Con. Then, during three or four days consideration, I put down under the different heads

short hints of the different motives, that at different times occur to me, for or against the measure. When I have thus got them all together in one view, I endeavor to estimate their respective weights; and where I find two, one on each side, that seem equal, I strike them both out. If I find a reason pro equal to some two reasons con, I strike out the three . . . and thus proceeding I find at length where the balance lies; and if, after a day or two of further consideration, nothing new that is of importance occurs on either side, I come to a determination accordingly. And, though the weight of reasons cannot be taken with the precision of algebraic qualities, yet when each is thus considered, separately and comparatively, and the whole lies before me, I think I can judge better, and am less liable to make a rash step, and in fact I have found great advantage from this kind of equation, in what may be called moral or prudential algebra (5).

By looking at a list of pros and cons critically, whether from the perspective of time or with the help of others, we can discover which questions give us the most difficulty, that is, which ones we tend to exclude from consideration.

Structuring the Decision

Making lists in columns is a stopgap measure that oversimplifies the structure of most real-life decisions. First, it assumes that there are just two possible actions, the advantages of one being the disadvantages of the other. Second, it assumes that there is only one choice point, with all the outcomes in question flowing from the action chosen. In reality, a decision sets in motion a chain of controllable and uncontrollable, predictable and unpredictable, events. Its outcomes are connected with one another and with subsequent choices made by the decision maker and others.

A decision tree can be drawn to capture this sequence of chosen actions and chance events. It embodies the basic vocabulary of decision analysis: actions taken by the decision maker, events beyond the decision maker's control, and outcomes (intended and unintended) that result from actions in combination with events. The decision tree is a visual representation of a decision structured in terms of contingencies—that is, relationships among actions, events, and outcomes. A decision tree (Fig. 2.1) is one way in which Dr. Newell might have structured his options for treating Ms. Adams.

An early application of the principles of decision analysis to a legal decision grew out of an 1871 case in which the Long Island Railroad was sued for damages by the family of a man who had been killed while

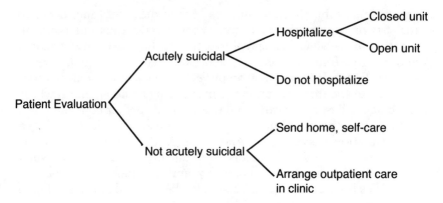

Figure 2.1. The decision tree.

saving a small child from being hit by a train. The railroad argued that since the man had voluntarily placed himself in danger, the railroad bore no responsibility for his death. However, the jury's verdict, affirmed on appeal, was that the man's death was attributable not to his own negligence but to that of the railroad engineer (6).

A commentary published in 1915 in the Harvard Law Review made it clear that the verdict turned on the question of the reasonableness of the man's decision (of necessity made in haste) to act to save the child. The commentary broke down this question into the following components:

1. The magnitude of the risk was the probability that [the man] would be killed or hurt. That was very great.
2. The principal object was his own life, which was very valuable.
3. The collateral object was the child's life, which was also very valuable.
4. The utility of the risk was the probability that he could save the child. That must have been fairly great, since he in fact succeeded. Had there been no fair chance of saving the child the conduct would have been unreasonable and negligent.
5. The necessity of the risk was the probability that the child would not have saved himself by getting off the track in time. (7)

"Here," the commentary concluded, "although the magnitude of the risk was very great and the principal object very valuable, yet the value of the collateral object and the great utility and necessity of the risk counterbalanced those considerations, and made the risk reasonable." Although the language used here is not that of the modern decision analyst, the reasoning it conveys amounts to a decision analysis in a nutshell. The decision tree might contain just one choice node, where the decision maker chooses to act in one way or another, and two chance nodes, where the world—chance, reality, nature—responds in one way or another. The man had two options, and the world had two to four ways to respond.

In reality, of course, there is more to it than this. First, this tree is narrow. It leaves out other possible actions, such as trying to alert the engineer to the situation, and other events, such as a third party removing the child from the tracks. (Even though these other events fall into the class "child gets out of way" and so would be implicitly included in the tree, if they are named explicitly it is easier to think about them.) The decision tree also leaves out other consequences besides life and death—for example, varying degrees of injury and lasting disability that the man or child might suffer.

Second, this tree is shallow; it stops after one event. It might have been extended to include further actions taken by the individuals or families involved (such as the decision to sue) and subsequent events reflecting the losses they would suffer, and gains they would realize, from the death of a loved one and their responses to it.

A decision tree is a more powerful tool than Franklin's list of pros and cons, but it too has its pitfalls. The terms in which the decision is framed—what is included, what is left out—may influence the decision in unintended, unrecognized ways. Moreover, the danger of illusory completeness, of premature closure, is probably greater with the tree than with the list. A list is open-ended; more items can always be added. A tree, with its interrelated parts, requires greater effort to change. Adding detail in one place may mean adding equivalent detail in several other places. The additional time and effort required for revision, together with the appearance of completeness, may tempt the decision maker to stop thinking too soon or to leave out things that would be uncomfortable to consider. On the other hand, as the philosopher John Dewey (8) pointed out, one can extend the tree indefinitely into the future, so that a final outcome is never reached. One can also adorn the tree with so much detail that one loses the tree for the forest. A decision tree is necessarily an abstraction of reality. In using it one must balance accuracy of representation against ease, convenience, practicality, and relevance. (9)

Estimating Probabilities and Values

Another advantage of the decision tree over the list of pros and cons is that it offers the ability to weigh the items being considered (the branches of the tree) in terms of either their likelihood of occurrence or their importance. The structure provided by a decision tree does not by itself do this, but once we have the tree, we can incorporate estimates of probability and value into a decision. It seems, in fact, that the structuring of a decision makes some such estimation almost irresistible. Although mathematical calculations did not figure in the case of the man who saved the child from the train, the commentary included informal, broadly quantitative estimates of the probability that the man could save the child ("fairly great") and that he himself would be killed or hurt ("very great"). It also noted that the man's life and the child's were both "very valuable."

There are various ways of estimating the probability that an event will occur. One way is to calculate the relative frequency with which the event in question occurs over a large number of trials in similar circumstances, as when one determines the probability of the effect of an antidepressant on depression by performing large numbers of clinical trials with depressed patients.

This presumably objective method is of no use, however, in dealing with unique events. For example, Ms. Adams' condition at the time that Dr. Newell evaluated her may have differed from her state of mind after she left the clinic. Perhaps her initial feelings of despair and helplessness, tempered by her visit to the clinic and Dr. Newell's empathic response to her pain, once again flooded her when she was alone. With a change of mood and state of being came a change of perceived choices. When Ms. Adams was with Dr. Newell she apparently wanted to live; later, alone, she chose suicide. Thus, values and perceived options can shift with changes in relationships and circumstances.

Moreover, the very act of deciding what category of events is relevant to predicting the probability of an individual event requires a subjective judgment of similarity—that is, a judgment as to what events are comparable enough to form a group from which a probability could be calculated. Subjective judgment also comes into play in adjusting the estimate because of changing conditions or because the event in question is somehow atypical of its category. Such decision-making dilemmas often arise in psychiatric settings.

Another way to estimate probabilities is by using subjective judgment intentionally from the start. As noted earlier, a subjective estimate is based on the degree of belief a person has that something will happen. For example, in the Long Island Railroad case, the man had to make a subjective judgment about the possibility of saving the child on the track, since no statistics were available, and even if they had been, he would have had no time to consult them (9, 10).

Psychologists have found that subjective probability estimates can be reasonably accurate when the people making them are knowledge-able about what they are estimating as well as experienced in probability estimation. On the other hand, people tend to overestimate low probabilities and underestimate high ones. One way to check the soundness of subjective estimates is to see whether they are consistent. For example, if you think the probability of being offered a job promotion is 0.7, then you should also think that there is a 0.3 probability that you will not be offered the promotion. It is always a useful exercise to ask yourself both questions.

The estimation of values, like that of probabilities, has both its simple and complex sides. If the event probabilities are the same for each possible action, all one needs to know about the values of alternative outcomes is which is higher or highest. If two bets give the same odds, but one offers a higher payoff for the same investment, one does not need to calculate mathematically which bet is more advantageous. In most cases, however, values must be combined with probabilities in a way that requires us to respect their numerical properties.

Some outcomes are easily measured—for example, monetary units gained or lost. Others are hard to express numerically, especially those that are intangible. When we are faced with outcomes of very different kinds, their values may appear to be incommensurable. We can compare the dollar costs of two medical treatments, but how do we measure monetary cost against pain, disability, or years of life? The man who saw a train bearing down on a small child had to choose between two lives that were valuable along different dimensions: one life, his own, had a longer past, while the other, not his own, had a longer future.

Calculating Expected Values

The purpose of quantifying the probabilities and values of all anticipated outcomes is to combine them, so that we can know the "expected value" of our actions. The expected value of an action is the sum of the values of the possible outcomes, each multiplied by the probability that it will occur. In common sense terms, it is the average result (good or bad) that could be expected from an action if the same choice could be repeated many times. Thus, an action that leads, with a probability of 0.3, to an outcome with a value of 10, and otherwise leads to an outcome of 0 value, has an expected value of 3. Knowing the expected values of possible actions may help us decide among them when we could otherwise have no idea which is best (11).

Clinical Contribution of Decision Analysis

Psychiatrists facing difficult clinical decisions may well find that a formal decision analysis is neither useful nor appropriate. In the psychiatric setting it is often not possible to obtain precise measurements of probabilities and values. Even so, the perspective of decision analysis—the way in which it makes decision making conscious, methodical, and critical—can in itself be beneficial. Simply breaking down a decision into its components (actions, events, and outcomes) and observing the relationships among them may help the decision maker focus on the dimensions and qualities of the choice to be made. The principles of decision analysis offer a systematic approach to decision making that fosters consistency among the decisions one makes; that can be justified to others, if a decision is questioned; that can be taught to others, so that decisions can be more or less consistent among decision makers; and that can be evaluated and improved, if necessary. One of the most valuable features of this approach in the clinical setting is that it can be shared, providing an opportunity for treatment decisions to evolve from a genuine collaboration between physician and patient (12, 13).

DECISION MAKING AS GAMBLING

Another way to approach decision making—one that is less formal and systematic than decision analysis—is to think about the process as a type of gambling. In an uncertain world every choice is a gamble in that one can never be entirely sure of the outcome. Both decision maker and gambler consider the possible gains and losses associated with a choice of actions and try to weigh the gains against the losses by estimating their probability and value. Of course, gambling in this broader sense is not simply a game. The consequences of our gambles in life are both more far-reaching and less clear-cut than they are in a game (1).

Although we can never be sure just how much we stand to win or lose by a decision, in approaching it as a gamble we can gain some understanding of the stakes involved. With time and experience, we can learn how we gamble and whether we are gambling reasonably. This kind of conscious gambling is not easy. It forces us to acknowledge the uncertainty in our lives, as well as the limits of our ability to control the consequences of our decisions. The paradox is that by recognizing the limits of our ability to know and to control, we gain greater knowledge and, through that knowledge, exercise greater control.

Failure to recognize or accept the role of uncertainty in decision making results in unconscious gambling. The more anxiety one feels in the face of uncertainty, the more likely one is to gamble unconsciously. This type of decision making is mechanistic in style, framing a decision as an all-or-nothing proposition that results in a total gain or a total loss. The unconscious gambler tends to consider only one cause and one outcome at a time, with no recognition of the roles played by chance, change, and the very act of making a decision. This deterministic, polarized view of causation results in unconscious gambling, guided by the assumption either that one has total control over the outcome of a decision (all that is needed to win is skill or information) or that one has no control (all one can do is try to minimize the loss).

Conscious gambling, in contrast, is probabilistic in style and philosophy. In fact, it is an informal application of the probabilistic paradigm, reflecting the three principles of that approach. The person who makes a decision by gambling consciously allows for the interplay of chance and change in the outcome (first principle), recognizes human judgment and choice as inescapable components of the decision (second principle), and draws on varieties of knowledge—statistical data, experience, values, beliefs—in making the decision (third principle).

In the clinical setting and elsewhere, conscious gambling is most fruitful when it is a cooperative rather than competitive or solitary venture. Decisions about treatment involve at least two players (patient and physician) and often more (the patient's family, the physician's colleagues). It makes sense that those who have a direct stake in a decision play a part in the process of reaching that decision. To gamble cooperatively, they must agree on the goal of the gamble and the possible gains and losses—they must agree that the goal is worth the gamble. Two (or more) people who gamble cooperatively thus share responsibility for both the process and the outcome of their joint decision making.

Dr. Newell and his supervisor gamble cooperatively when they review the question of Ms. Adams' suicidality and weigh the risks and benefits of hospitalizing or releasing her. They hope to choose a course of action that will allow all parties involved to win. In a somewhat different light, Dr. Newell gauges Ms. Adams' ability to gamble cooperatively with him when he assesses her competence to participate in treatment planning.

One of the most important skills in gambling is the ability to know when to gamble. Some situations are governed largely by nature; others are more susceptible to human intervention. They differ in terms of the degree of control that one may be able to exercise by applying one's skill (14). To gamble appropriately and reasonably, the decision maker must be able to "read" the situation as one that invites careful gambling.

Like decision analysis, conscious gambling looks at the components of a decision in terms of probabilities and values. In addition, skilled gamblers are sensitive to the influence of time and context on their gambles, to changes within and outside themselves. They know that over time probabilities, values, information, and beliefs change, as well as circumstances. One gamble affects the next, and the value of each lies not so much in the particular outcome as in how one interprets it.

Conscious gambling does not come easily. It must be exercised and developed over time. It requires both trust and skepticism, vigilance and flexibility. Knowledge gained from previous gambles can help guide those that will be made in the future. By gambling consciously, we have the opportunity to correct our errors and to hone our decision-making skills. Perhaps most important, we gain knowledge about ourselves, about how we feel, believe, and act in a world of possibility and uncertainty.

REFERENCES

1. Bursztajn HJ, Feinbloom RI, Hamm RM, Brodsky A. Medical choices, medical chances: how patients' families and physicians can cope with uncertainty. New York: Routledge, 1990.
2. Bernard C. Principles of experimental medicine. New York: Dover, 1957:139–140.
3. Hammond KR. The integration of research in judgment and decision theory. Report No. 226, Center for Research on Judgment and Policy, Univ. of Colorado, Boulder, 1980.
3a. Hammond KR. Principles of organization in intuitive and analytical cognition. Report No. 231, Center for Research and Judgment and Policy, Univ. of Colorado, Boulder, 1981.
4. Hammond KR. Toward increasing competence of thought in public policy formation. In: Hammond KR, ed. Judgment and decision in public policy formation. Boulder: Westview Press, 1978:11–32.
5. Bigelow J, ed. The complete works of Benjamin Franklin, vol. 4. New York: Putnam, 1887:552. Cited in Hogarth RM. Judgment and choice: the psychology of decision. Chichester, UK: Wiley, 1980:142.
6. *Eckert v. Long Island R.R.* 43 NY 502 (1871).
7. Terry HT. Negligence. 29 Harv Law Rev 40, 42:44 (1915).
8. Dewey J. On certainty. In: Ratner J., ed. Intelligence in the modern world: John Dewey's philosophy. New York: Random House, 1939:275–291.
9. Bursztajn HJ, Hamm RM, Gutheil TG, Brodsky A. The decision-analytic approach to medical malpractice law: formal proposals and informal syntheses. Med Decision Making 1984;4:401–414.
10. Hamm RM, Clark JA, Bursztajn HJ. Psychiatrists thorny judgments: describing and improving decision making process. Med Decision Making 1984;4:461–414.
11. Bursztajn HJ, Hamm RM. The clinical uses of utility assessment. Med Decision Making 1982;2:162–165.
12. Bursztajn HJ, Gutheil TG, Cummins B. Legal issues in inpatient psychiatry. In: Sederer LI, ed. Inpatient psychiatry: diagnosis and treatment. 3rd ed. Baltimore: Williams & Wilkins, 1986:338–356. 1991, in press.

13. Bursztajn HJ, Hamm RM, Gutheil TG. The technological target: involving the patient in clinical choices. In: Reiser SJ, Anbar M, eds. The machine at the bedside: strategies for using technology in patient care. Cambridge, UK: Cambridge University Press, 1984:177–191.

14. Langer E. The illusion of control. Personality Social Psychol 1975;35:311–328.

chapter 3.
SUBJECTIVE ASSESSMENT IN CLINICAL DECISION MAKING AND MALPRACTICE LIABILITY

The probabilistic paradigm, as discussed in Chapter 2, rests on the principle that causes, effects, and the act of observing them are all part of a dynamic (rather than static) process of reciprocal influence. In the scientific realm this means, among other things, that no variable can be truly independent, since it is subject to the perception and interpretation of the observer, who by identifying and naming it a variable in some sense gives it existence. Thus, in a probabilistic (as opposed to mechanistic) world, no knowledge is absolutely objective, existing independently of the observer (or knower) of that knowledge. And just as the object of observation is affected by the observer, so the observer is influenced by that which is observed—the experimenter is part of the experiment. The therapeutic process, from this perspective, is truly a two-way interaction: therapist and patient influence and are influenced by one another. In fact, the psychodynamic therapist is trained to attend not only to the patient's behavior and responses to the therapist but also to the feelings and responses that the patient evokes within the therapist.

In physics, instruments are constructed to observe phenomena that might otherwise be unobservable; in psychiatry those instruments are human. In both cases, however, the act and the object of observation are filtered through the perception of the observer, who must be alert to the distortions that the filtering process entails. Indeed, in psychiatry these very distortions help point the way to observation and interpretation. The probabilistic principle that no information or act of observation is completely objective is thus vividly enacted in each therapeutic encounter, as the clinician uses both inward and outward perception to evaluate or treat the patient.

Psychiatry, perhaps more than any other scientific discipline or medical specialty, exemplifies the intimate connection between observer and observed, and the critical use of subjective experience as a source of knowledge. Although subjective knowledge plays a part in all instances of scientific observation and interpretation, the therapeutic relationship is perhaps unique in capitalizing on that role.

In the current atmosphere of malpractice phobia, many psychiatrists feel pressured to deemphasize subjective data and reasoning, which they fear will not hold up under legal scrutiny in the wake of a tragic outcome. Psychiatrists who look to subjective data—their perceptions of their own and/or the patient's feelings—when making crucial clinical decisions often ask themselves, "Is this really evidence that will withstand adversarial questioning in court? Do I have enough 'hard' evidence to commit (or discharge) this patient?"

Psychiatrists' mistrust of subjective data and subjective judgment stems in part from the technological revolution in medicine (1–3) and its glorification of mythical "exact" science grounded in objective verification (4). This historical trend is reflected in the movement to have psychiatry return to a medical model (5–7), with findings reported in precise numerical form (8). Particularly in such a high-risk procedure (legally and emotionally) as suicide assessment, fantasies about both science and the law may join to produce a damaging form of defensive medicine (9). For example, a preoccupation with judicial acceptability can mask the denial of clinically valuable subjective responses (e.g., hate) that the clinician finds unbearable. That is, the wish for legally defensible procedures may lead to clinically inferior forms of practice. This problem is discussed at length in a later chapter.

The practicing clinician who feels the pressure to conform to an unrealistic standard of objectivity is faced with a bewildering dilemma. The psychodynamically trained therapist is taught by theory as well as experience that both a patient's report of a feeling and the clinician's reaction have an irreducibly subjective component. No one has seriously proposed that the risk of a patient's committing suicide can be assessed without resorting to such data. "How could the law require," the clinician might reason, "that I not avail myself of what has been shown in practice to be indispensable to good patient care?" Yet the fear persists that the courts demand exactly that.

A side benefit of the otherwise troubling proliferation of malpractice claims in recent years is that there is now enough case law on record to permit some generalizations about how the courts decide such cases. These generalizations are largely reassuring. The courts have shown a realistic recognition of the uncertainties inherent in clinical practice. Recent case law sanctions careful consideration of subjective as well as objective data in the assessment of both the risks of suicide and the therapeutic costs and benefits of different treatment options.

Liability for malpractice has four components: duty of care, negligence, harm, and causation of the harm by the negligence (see Chapter 4). It is in terms of the second and fourth components that the legal status of subjective assessment must be considered. We will look first, therefore, at how the courts view the use of subjective data in the light of the standards of negligence applied in medical malpractice law. We will then consider how the subjective assessment of a patient's competence to give informed consent may affect the subsequent legal determination of the cause(s) of the patient's suicide. In both cases the thorough consideration of subjective data, framed by consultation, documentation, and critical use of heuristics, will be shown to conform both to sound clinical practice and to legal standards of due care.

THREE STANDARDS OF CARE

A court may appeal to any or all of three standards of care in deciding whether a physician sued for malpractice has been negligent. The court may measure the physician's handling of the case against the standard of care maintained by other physicians in the same specialty. The court may compare the expected costs and benefits of the tests or treatments chosen with those of alternative courses of action. Or the court may simply attempt to establish what a "reasonable and prudent practitioner" would have done under similar circumstances. Recent malpractice case law confirms that a psychiatrist who takes subjective data into account in the assessment of suicide risk may be considered, under all three of these interpretations, to be exercising due care. ·

What Would Other Psychiatrists Do?

The oldest tradition of negligence law holds that one has exercised due care if one has done what other psychiatrists in the community would do in similar circumstances (10). For the purpose of establishing a standard of care, the relevant professional "community" has been defined increasingly in national rather than local terms (11, 12), but the principle remains the same. This standard is very supportive of the use of subjective data, since the psychiatric community does in fact regularly consider subjective data in suicide assessment (9).

Professional custom, then, is the clinician's first bulwark against hindsight, by which a bad outcome is itself assumed to be conclusive evidence of negligence. Grieving families have naively assumed that the fact that a loved one committed suicide while under a psychiatrist's care proves that the psychiatric care was at fault. The clinician need not fear, however, that the courts will accept this facile reasoning. Against the charge that one "should have" adopted a more restrictive treatment plan, the demonstration that one has followed procedures recognized as acceptable by one's profession is a strong defense. For example, in the case of a patient who jumped out of a hospital window after she had been transferred to a less secure ward, the court cited the community standard in rejecting her suit, which was based on hindsight, against the psychiatrist who had transferred her (13). In availing oneself of this defense, however, it is essential to introduce expert testimony as to the soundness of one's assessment of the risk of suicide and/or the adequacy of the precautions taken to avert a recognized risk (14). Furthermore, the expert witness is expected to testify to the existence of a generally accepted medical standard rather than simply professing a personal opinion. In a case that involved the suicide of a previously homicidal patient, the court ruled that the plaintiff's expert witness had not established a clear medical standard that a homicidal patient should also be considered potentially suicidal (15). Where there is no one clear professional standard, a psychiatrist may (by analogy with other medical specialties) be able to demonstrate that due care was exercised through the use of methods approved by a "respectable minority" of the profession (16, 17).

Documentation of one's clinical reasoning, whether in adherence to or deviation from standard practice, is the first commandment of due care (9, 18). The second is consultation with colleagues (itself, when documented, evidence of attention to community standards). Consultation provides an opportunity to ask questions about one's use of subjectivity, such as "Would other clinicians feel as I do toward the patient?" "Would my colleagues take into account these same subjective factors? What would they do in such a case?" "Would a supervisor remind me of other considerations that I might be overlooking?" By considering these questions before making a crucial clinical decision, the psychiatrist is both providing good care and conforming to the community standard of due care.

What Are the Risks and Benefits?

The Learned Hand rule, which establishes a quasi-mathematical standard for judging what is best for the patient, came into being in negligence law (19) and later in medical malpractice law (20) as a corrective to the exclusive reliance on professional custom. Briefly stated, the rule holds that "negligent behavior is the failure to invest resources up to a level that [is commensurate with] the anticipated saving in damages" (21). This cost-benefit approach to the determination of due care remains controversial as an alternative to the notion of an accepted professional standard (10, 21).

For our purposes, however, what matters is that this seemingly objective standard, which would appear to favor numerical data, is actually quite hospitable to subjective data and intuitive clinical judgment. In psychiatry as in other areas of medicine, the insistent search for objective data through indiscriminate diagnostic testing does not stand up under cost-benefit analysis. For example, objective data that might serve as suicide indicators, such as blood or cerebrospinal fluid neurotransmitter levels (22, 23), must be interpreted in the context of a subjective understanding of the patient if they are to have diagnostic value, given the low frequency of suicide attempts in a general psychiatric population (24). Moreover, by ensuring judicial consideration of therapeutic benefits as well as risks, the cost-benefit criterion protects the clinician against the excesses of "judgment by hindsight."

Psychiatrists have been found liable for failing to recognize the risk of suicide (25) and for underestimating the seriousness of the risk and thereby failing to take adequate precautions to counter it (26, 27). However, a psychiatrist will not be found liable for failing to prevent suicide at any price. In the first place, the courts recognize that no amount of precautions can give absolute protection against the possibility of suicide (28). The courts further recognize that the decision to hospitalize a patient (by suggesting voluntary admission or by petitioning for commitment), to place a hospitalized patient under closer observation and restraint, or to discharge a patient cannot be made solely with a view toward minimizing the risks attendant upon allowing the patient greater freedom (9).

A leading authority on medical malpractice law asserts that "freedom for a psychiatric patient is a matter of medical judgment on the part of the treating psychiatrist. As long as he is informed about and alert to the patient's condition, it is usually quite difficult to prove lack of due care in what is often considered a calculated risk inherent in modern psychiatry" (18). The therapist who reduces restraints on a patient is accepting an increased risk of suicide attempts in the short term in return for long-term therapeutic benefits aimed at fostering the patient's recovery and rehabilitation. On the other side of the same coin, the possible benefits of more intensive monitoring and protective control must be weighed against the risks of regressive loss of ego strength, stigma, reduced capacity to function autonomously, and recurrent suicidality. In the words of one court decision that disallowed a malpractice claim on these grounds, "Modern psychiatry has recognized the importance of making every effort to return a patient to an active and productive life. Thus the patient is encouraged to develop his self-confidence by adjusting to the demands of everyday existence. Particularly because the prediction of danger is difficult, undue reliance on hospitalization might lead to prolonged incarceration of potentially useful members of society" (29). To impede the recovery of large numbers of patients in order to attempt to protect a few from harming themselves at a particular time would not only be bad social policy (30), it would profoundly decrease many individuals' constitutionally based freedoms, including the right to the "least restrictive alternative" among medically adequate treatments (31, 32).

The courts have given considerable deference to the judgment of psychiatrists in the delicate balancing of these risks and benefits (33–35). They have ruled that a psychiatrist may properly weigh the risk of suicide against such factors as the patient's emotional reaction to restrictive management, the anticipated effects of such management on the patient's physical condition, the therapeutic advantages of greater autonomy and a more open milieu, and the greater probability of obtaining informed consent to treatment in an atmosphere agreeable to the patient (36). In 1981 a psychiatrist in a New York state hospital was judged to have made a nonnegligent error of judgment in failing to order suicide precautions for a patient diagnosed as suicidally depressed. The error became a negligent one, the court ruled, only when the patient became psychotic. That is, the benefits of the less restrictive approach taken by this psychiatrist no longer outweighed the costs once the diagnosis changed (37). Thus, while a psychiatrist may be held liable for deficiencies in clinical reasoning, the courts do recognize the need for clinical reasoning as well as the principle of cost-benefit analysis as a framework for decision making.

To establish in court that one could reasonably have concluded that the expected benefits of a given course of treatment outweighed the expected costs, one must document the factors (subjective as well as objective) that one took into account in reaching this conclusion. Without such documentation one may be left defenseless against judicial hindsight about what one did or did not consider (38). One should enter into the record that one asked (either of oneself or in consultation with colleagues) questions about one's use of subjective reasoning, such as the following: "What stands to be gained, or lost, from one course of action versus another?" "What are the probabilities involved?" "What is the likely impact on the patient's immediate safety? On the patient's ultimate well-being? On the therapeutic alliance?" "Am I sure enough of a high probability of small gains to risk a very low probability of a large loss?" "Are there any objective data (e.g., statistics concerning suicide) that I might look at to confirm the conclusions I have drawn from subjective factors?"

Finally, the informed consent procedure provides an opportunity for an explicit review of costs and benefits with both the patient and one's colleagues (39). Through this procedure the patient can be involved to the greatest possible extent in deciding which costs and benefits are most salient to the choices at hand. Questions framed in the language of costs and benefits also facilitate consultation with colleagues, which is the cornerstone of community standards.

What Would a Reasonable and Prudent Practitioner Do?

The third way of establishing due care is by some variation of the following formula: "A physician who undertakes a mode or form of treatment which a reasonable and prudent member of the medical profession would undertake under the same or similar circumstances shall not be subject to liability for harm caused thereby to the patient" (40). This standard can be viewed as a synthesis of the other two. A reasonable and prudent practitioner would practice in a manner consistent with the accepted standards of the profession, and a reasonable and prudent practitioner would also be cognizant of the expected risks and benefits of interventions under consideration.

The reasonable and prudent practitioner formulation appears frequently in judicial decisions rendered in malpractice cases involving suicide. The courts ask two related questions: Could the psychiatrist reasonably have been expected for foresee the likelihood of a suicide attempt or to take greater precautions to prevent it? Or could the psychiatrist reasonably have concluded that the risk of suicide was outweighed by the benefits of less restrictive therapy (14, 15, 29, 30, 33, 41, 42)? This conceptualization clearly contains no threat that a psychiatrist's use of subjective data will be held to be ipso facto negligent. Nor does it imply that subjective clinical assessment is anything but a clinically and legally sound procedure.

According to another interpretation of this criterion (43), a reasonable and prudent practitioner is, among other things, one who practices "in the light of the present state of scientific knowledge" (44). In this view, the uncertainty with which the courts recognize the prediction of suicide to be fraught (15, 33) reflects a larger uncertainty inherent in the universe described by modern science (4, 45). One recent court decision stated that "accurate predictions of dangerous behavior, and particularly of suicide and homicide, are almost never possible" (29). Another noted that "physicians and other professionals practice the arts and must be allowed a wide area of discretion" (13). But there is no need to appeal to the "art" of medicine when 20th century science has itself been engaged in the exploration of uncertainty.

Thus, Havens' description of suicide as "the final common pathway of diverse circumstances, of an interdependent network rather than an isolated cause, a knot of circumstances tightening around a single time and place" (46) is consistent with contemporary scientific practice, which views causation in probabilistic rather than mechanistic terms, as discussed earlier. Attention to the impact of the therapeutic alliance on the risk of suicide and to the impact of suicide assessment on the alliance (47) exemplifies the modern scientist's sensitivity to the effects of observation on that which is observed. The careful observation and interpretation of subjective data that emerge from the therapeutic alliance are thus seen to be essential to the scientific procedure of data gathering, especially since 20th century scientists have questioned whether any data can be completely objective or completely subjective (4). There is room for both the uncertainties of subjective data and the probabilistic assumptions of modern science within the framework of the law, which acknowledges degrees of uncertainty in its three common standards of legal proof: "preponderance of evidence" (understood as roughly 51% certain), "clear and convincing evidence" (roughly 75% certain), and "beyond a reasonable doubt" (roughly 90 or 95% certain) (48).

To demonstrate reasonableness and prudence, the clinician should document (in addition to the considerations listed under the first two standards of negligence) an awareness of clinical uncertainty and an effort to cope with it through the estimation of probabilities.

Relevant questions about one's use of subjective reasoning include: "Am I focusing on how the multiple causes of the patient's illness operate in combination with one another and with chance?" "Am I looking at the patient in the context of the therapeutic alliance and the therapeutic milieu?" "Am I taking into account the effects that my own feelings (e.g., countertransference hate) may have on the patient as well as on my evaluation?" (49). This type of reasoning gives strong if not conclusive evidence that due care has been exercised in the treatment of a suicidal patient. Of course, the documented attempt to act reasonably and prudently does not prove that one actually acted that way. The fact of having proceeded with deliberation does not excuse acts that are in substance indefensible.

PROXIMATE CAUSE AND THE COMPETENT ASSUMPTION OF RISK

For a psychiatrist to be held liable for malpractice, not only must the psychiatrist be negligent and the patient suffer physical or emotional harm, but the negligence and harm must be connected. That is, the injury or death must follow directly from the therapist's negligence, so that the latter can be said to constitute a "proximate cause" (9). To be ruled a proximate cause, the physician's negligence need not be the sole cause of the patient's injury (50), but a direct causal link between the two must be found. On this principle a psychiatrist was held not liable for a suicide that took place several weeks after the psychiatrist had let the patient leave the hospital. In the court's view this interval allowed for too many intervening causes to assign a clear causal role to the decision to discharge the patient (41).

Can the patient's own actions be said to constitute an independent intervening cause? A review of case law on the analogous issue of contributory negligence indicates that much depends on whether the mentally ill patient can be expected to have a normal person's capacity for rational self-protection (51, 52)—that is, competence. The patient, mentioned earlier, who sued her psychiatrist for allowing her the freedom to attempt suicide by transferring her to a less secure hospital ward was held to be contributorily negligent because she did not give the psychiatrist sufficient information to make a better judgment (13).

Another negligence case with important implications concerning the patient's responsibility for harm to self occurred in New York in 1981. Here the state was held not liable for the self-inflicted injuries suffered by a voluntary patient who had escaped from a mental hospital. The court noted that an involuntary patient would have required greater safeguards and therefore would have been entitled to damages under the same circumstances (53). The court's reasoning implies that the burden is on the clinician to foresee more dangers in the case of involuntary (and, by implication, incompetent) patients, because their capacity to participate in a meaningful informed consent process is questionable.

Conversely, if a patient who has been found competent to give informed consent subsequently suffers damage resulting from a suicide attempt and the patient's therapist is sued, two lines of defense (other than contributory negligence) may be available. First, the patient may be said to have assumed the risks that were explained in the informed consent discussion. Thus, the notion of a patient assuming some personal risk (or responsibility) is appropriately invoked by those courts that uphold treatment choices agreed to by the physician and patient, provided that they were reasonable ones. However, a patient is not considered able to assume the risks of treatment that the courts find to be patently negligent (18).

Furthermore, even a psychiatrist who is found negligent may be relieved of liability if the causal connection fails, as when a competent patient's suicide is regarded as a voluntary act and therefore as an intervening cause of the outcome. This reasoning formed the basis of a 1981 Texas decision (54), which has been summarized as follows:

In the case of a patient who committed suicide unexpectedly, without forewarning, by overdose of the antipsychotic drug Etrafon, the court held that a Veterans Administration psychiatrist was not negligent in his treatment of the patient (which included prescription of this drug), while the hospital pharmacy was negligent in dispensing excessive quantities of the drug. In neither instance, however, was liability exacted. The court held that since the patient's intentional (but unforewarned of) overdose was not a foreseeable consequence of the pharmacy's negligence (or of the psychiatrist's, even had he been negligent), the act itself and not the prior negligence was the proximate cause of the harm suffered (43).

It is too soon to tell whether or not this decision represents an emerging legal trend. In the same year, a Pennsylvania court came down on the opposite side of the question (55). The potential implications of this development for psychiatric malpractice law are enormous and strike directly at the unique position of psychiatrists as being responsible for the behavior of others (namely, their patients) (56).

Whether the salient legal issue in a particular case is contributory negligence, assumption of risk, or proximate cause, there is room under the law for attributing intentionality to the suicidal act of a competent patient. The psychiatrist's evaluation of a patient's competence to make treatment choices becomes, then, a major intuitive clinical assessment that the courts, recognizing the uncertainty inherent in the prediction of suicide, are prepared to take seriously. The stronger the therapist's documented grounds for finding the patient competent, and thus able to act truly voluntarily, the more remote the prospect of malpractice liability is likely to be (39, 57). The assessment takes place largely in the context of the attempt to obtain informed consent. Informed consent is thus not only itself a legal requirement (58) but also another facet of the judicially sanctioned use of subjective data in clinical assessment (59).

HEURISTICS AND SUBJECTIVE REASONING

A key ingredient in the interpretation of subjective data is the use of heuristics, the strategies that one employs, unconsciously or consciously, to arrive at a simplified understanding of a complex situation. The more ambiguous that situation, the greater the tendency to depend on simplifying strategies in making sense of it. Heuristics can be quite useful, but if they are not employed consciously and critically, they may lead to errors in reasoning and judgment. Thus, awareness of how one uses heuristics is essential for careful interpretation of subjective data. Several heuristics that play an important part in the intuitive assessments that clinicians make are discussed below.

Availability refers to the tendency to equate the importance of a decision factor with the ease of its recall. Memory, of course, is selective and is often influenced by environmental clues. For example, one's mood may trigger recall of an event experienced in a similar mood (60). Used uncritically, availability supports repression. Used critically, however, it can be an important means of tracking countertransference in the clinical setting. The memories available to the therapist are clues to the feelings that the patient evokes in the therapist, and in turn to the patient's memories (61).

Another common heuristic is *recency*, the tendency to give greater weight to more recent information. As a check against this bias, recall that in the introductory case Dr. Newell obtained information from Dr. Olsen about his previous treatment of Ms. Adams. The resident also reasoned that Dr. Olsen's imminent departure at a time when his patient was in distress might have led him to overestimate the dangerousness of the situation. Thus, Dr. Newell attempted to compensate for any bias toward recency in his own reasoning and also in Dr. Olsen's reading of the situation.

Dr. Newell's consideration of statistical data on suicide (more women attempt it but more men succeed in the act) in light of his observations of Ms. Adams is an example of *anchoring* and *adjustment*. Using this heuristic, Dr. Newell was able to account for both objective and subjective information, anchoring on the statistical data and adjusting for the particular features of the case. If Dr. Newell had overlooked the applicable statistical information and simply considered his own observations, he would have been ignoring the base rate, that is, allowing the vivid personal experience of his encounter with Ms. Adams to overrule the abstract, generalized information provided by statistical rates.

Another heuristic that plays a part in the interpretation of subjective data is the *confirmation bias*, a form of selective perception in which one seeks data that support one's hypothesis and rejects data that do not. Closely related to this bias is the *single-cause heuristic*—the tendency to focus on one cause and underestimate or discount others. As a check against both of these biases, Dr. Newell examined and weighed a host of factors in assessing the risk that Ms. Adams might commit suicide. Consultation with his supervisor also provided a safeguard against the various forms of selective perception.

In weighing the risk factors involved in the case at hand, Dr. Newell considered both internal causation (for example, aspects of Ms. Adams' personality and her mood and bearing during the clinic visit) and external causation (possible loss of her husband, her increased use of alcohol, and so forth). Again, by considering the multiplicity of factors, external and internal, and discussing them with his supervisor, Dr. Newell objectified his use of this internal/external heuristic and attempted to check any bias toward one or the other dimension of causation.

A related heuristic is *locus of control,* the tendency to discount one's own influence on the behavior of another person. Used unconsciously in the clinical context, this heuristic encourages the assumption that a patient's behavior and state of mind are subject solely to influences outside the therapist. Used consciously and critically, locus of control accounts for the causal role of the therapist as a presence in the patient's life—a direct reflection of the probabilistic principle that the observer affects that which is observed. In examining the risk factors for Ms. Adams, Dr. Newell considered the effect of Dr. Olsen's absence at a time of crisis in his patient's life, thereby acknowledging the influence of this therapeutic relationship on the patient's state of mind. Dr. Newell reasoned that any substitute (short-term therapy that he or the covering physician might provide) would probably not be as influential.

Finally, in reviewing the case after Ms. Adams' suicide, Drs. Newell and Gottlieb demonstrated a critical use of hindsight. They reexamined the decision not to commit Ms. Adams and the outcome of that decision in light of the uncertainty of the situation at the time. If used uncritically, hindsight encourages the assumption that an outcome could have been predicted, thus offering false hope of an escape from uncertainty. Clinical hindsight is often used uncritically in a suicide review, as Light has pointed out in his description of the typical review, where "much evidence points to the inevitability of suicide, much more so than presentations made by the same therapist about the same patient at conferences while he was living" (62). In fact, uncritical hindsight can act as a false standard for evaluating the use of other heuristics. Thus, if one falls prey to the retrospective assumption that Ms. Adams' suicide was certain to occur, one may conclude, for example, that Dr. Newell should have given greater weight to the immediate information at hand (recency) rather than compensating for this heuristic by considering the patient's previous treatment and Dr. Olsen's possible overestimation of the latest crisis.

All these heuristics represent both an opportunity and a danger in the context of subjective reasoning in suicide assessment. If the clinician is not aware of using them, they can lead to biased observation and interpretation. Used critically, however, they help guide the clinician's intuitive reasoning. In this respect, the heuristics conform to the legal standards of due care enumerated earlier. In fact, the clinical guidelines suggested by those standards act as correctives to the unconscious use of heuristics. For example, when Dr. Newell consulted with his supervisor, thereby conforming to the community standard of due care, he was correcting for possible biases introduced by the heuristics of availability and confirmation bias. His telephone conversation with Dr. Olsen, another reflection of the community standard, acted as a corrective for the recency bias. By considering statistical information as part of his risk-benefit analysis (Learned Hand rule), the resident was consciously applying the anchoring and adjustment heuristic (anchoring in objective data and adjusting for the particular clinical case), itself a corrective for the tendency to ignore the base rate. The reasonable and prudent practitioner standard is reflected in Dr. Newell's consideration of multiple causes, acting as a corrective for several heuristics (single cause, confirmation bias, internal attribution of casuality, external locus of control, and hindsight).

CONCLUSION

A psychiatrist is held legally responsible for: 1) practicing in accordance with the established standards of the profession; 2) considering, in the course of diagnosis and treatment, which among the available options offers the highest expected ratio of benefits to costs; and 3) doing what a reasonable and prudent practitioner of psychiatry would do under similar circumstances. On the evidence of recent trends in malpractice case law, the courts recognize that a psychiatrist who gives careful, documented attention to subjective as well as objective data in assessing the risk of suicide is acting in fulfillment of all three of these requirements. In addition, a psychiatrist is required by law to obtain informed consent to treatment. The assessment of a patient's competence to give informed consent is another form of partly subjective assessment with considerable implications for malpractice liability, since liability for a patient's suicide may be substantially restricted in the case of a competent, informed, consenting patient (39). Most important, all of these legal requirements conform to sound clinical practice and can be used to guide the interpretation of subjective data in suicide assessment.

To turn away from the complexities of such data out of a fear of vulnerability to malpractice claims is a misguided form of defensive medicine, one that can be detrimental to patients. Indeed, subjectivity is of the essence in psychiatry, but it must be disciplined not only by reflection on experience, such as that obtained through clinical supervision (63), but also by consultation, documentation, and the use of sound interpretive frameworks for clinical judgment. These measures have strong clinical as well as legal rationales (64).

Unlike defensive medicine, this approach to subjective assessment is consistent with good psychiatric practice. One does not directly document one's adherence to the judicial criteria for due care. Rather, using the language or risks and benefits, one documents the clinically indicated considerations and precautions, which satisfy the judicial criteria because they constitute good practice. Legal principles thus reinforce clinical wisdom, and the psychiatrist can use these principles to guide the process of intuitive judgment that is the cornerstone of suicide assessment.

REFERENCES

1. Foucault M. The order of things. New York: Random House, 1970.
2. Reiser SJ. Medicine and the reign of technology. New York: Cambridge University Press, 1978.
3. Hacking I. The emergency of probability. London: Cambridge University Press, 1975.
4. Bursztajn HJ, Feinbloom RI, Hamm RM, Brodsky A. Medical choices, medical chances: how patients, families, and physicians can cope with uncertainty. New York: Delacorte/Seymour Lawrence, 1981.
5. Hackett TP. The psychiatrist: in the mainstream or on the banks of medicine? Am J Psychiatry 1977;134:432–434.
6. Ludwig A, Othmer E. The medical basis of psychiatry. Am J Psychiatry 1977;134:1087–1092.
7. Bursten B. Psychiatry and the rhetoric of models. Am J Psychiatry 1979;136:661–666.
8. Nussbaum K, Puig JG, Arizaga JR. Relevance of objective assessment to medicolegal psychiatry. Am J Forensic Psychiatry 1981–82;3(3):17–20.
9. Gutheil TG, Appelbaum PS. Clinical handbook of psychiatry and the law. New York: McGraw-Hill, 1982.
10. Esptein RA. The limits of medical malpractice. N Engl J Med 1978;298:1311–1312.
11. *Tallbull v Whitney*, 564 P2d 162 (Mont 1977).
12. *Robbins v Footer*, F2d 123 (DC Cir 1977).
13. *Dillman v Hellman*, 283 So2d 388 (Fla App 1973).
14. *Meier v Ross General Hospital*, 69 Cal2d 420, 71 Cal Rptr 903, 445 P2d 519 (1968).
15. *Fernandez v Baruch*, 52 NJ127, 244 A2d 109 (1968).
16. *Bruce v United States*, 167 F Supp 579 (DC Cal 1958).
17. *Kortus v Jensen*, 237 NW2d 845 (Neb 1976).
18. Holder AR. Medical malpractice law, 2nd ed. New York: Wiley, 1978.
19. *United States v Carroll Towing Co.*, 159 F2d 169 (2d Cir 1947).
20. *Helling v Carey*, 83 Wash2d 514, 519 P2d 981 (1974).
21. Schwartz WB, Komesar NK. Doctors, damages and deterrence: an economic view of medical malpractice. N Engl J Med 1978;298:1282–1289.
22. Ostroff R, Giller E, Bonese K, Ebersole E, Harkness L, Mason J. Neuroendocrine risk factors of suicidal behavior. Am J Psychiatry 1982;139:1323–1325.
23. Brown GL, Ebert MH, Goyer PF, Jimerson DG, Klein WJ, Bunney WE, Goodwin FK. Aggression, suicide, and serotonin: relationships to CSF amine metabolites. Am J Psychiatry 1982;139:741–746.
24. Baldessarini RJ, Finklestein S, Arana GW. The predictive power of diagnostic tests and the effect of prevalence of illness. Arch Gen Psychiatry 1983;40:569–573.

25. *Farrow v Health Service Corporation*, 604 P2d 474 (Utah 1979).

26. *Wright v State of New York*, 31 AD421, 300 NYS 2d 153 (1969).

27. *Vistica v Presbyterian Hospital Center*, 67 Cal2d 405, 62 Cal Rptr 577, 432 P2d 193 (1967).

28. *Skar v City of Lincoln, NE* 599 F2d 253 (8th Cir 1975).

29. *Johnson v United States*, 409 FSupp. 1283 (D Fla 1981).

30. *Fiederlein v City of New York Health and Hospitals Corporation*, 80 (App Div) 2d 821, 437 NY2d 321 (1981).

31. *In re Jones*, 338 F Supp 428 (DC 1972).

32. *J. L. v Parham*, 412 F Supp 112, (DC Ga 1976).

33. *Baker v United States*, 226 F Supp 129 (SD Iowa 1964).

34. *Schwartz v United States*, 226 F Supp 84 (DDC 1964).

35. *Zilka v State*, 52 Misc 2d 891, 277 NYS 2d 312 (Ct Cl 1967).

36. *Topel v Long Island Jewish Medical Center*, 431 NE2d 293, 55 NY2d 682 (1981).

37. *Weatherly v New York*, 441 NSC 2d 319 (NY Ct q Cl 1981).

38. *Abille v United States*, 482 F Supp 703 (ND Cal 1980).

39. Gutheil TG, Bursztajn H, Brodsky A. Malpractice prevention through the sharing of uncertainty: informed consent and the therapeutic alliance. N Engl J Med 1984;311:49–51.

40. *Hood v Phillips*, 554 SW2d 160 (S Ct Tex 1977).

41. *Paradies v Benedictine Hospital*, 77 App Div 2d 757, 431 NYS 2d 175 (1980).

42. *Runyon v Reid*, 510 P2d 943 (Okl 1973).

43. Gutheil TG, Bursztajn H, Hamm RM, Brodsky A. Subjective data and suicide assessment in the light of recent legal developments: I. Malpractice prevention and the use of subjective data. Int J Law Psychiatry 1983;6:317–329.

44. Berman AL, Cohen-Sandler R. Suicide and malpractice: a test case of "standard of care," in Proceedings, Fourteenth Annual Meeting, American Association of Suicidology, Albuquerque, NM: 1981:15–16.

45. Havens L. The risks of knowing and not knowing. J Social Biol Struct 1982;5:213–222.

46. Havens LL: The anatomy of a suicide. N Engl J Med 1965;272:401–406.

47. Eisenberg GC, Barnes BM, Gutheil TG. Involuntary commitment and the treatment process: a clinical perspective. Bull Am Acad Psychiatry Law 1980;8:44–55.

48. Stone AA. Mental health and law: a system in transition. New York: Jason Aronson, 1976.

49. Perr IN, Sindell DI. Subjective complaints, psychiatric testimony, and attorneys' tactics in handling an adverse witness. Psychiatr Q 1965;39:328–346.

50. *Bender v Dingwerth*, 425 F2d 378 (US Ct App 5th Cir 1970).

51. *Bennett v New York*, 299 NYS 2d 288 (NY 1969).

52. *Mochen v State of New York*, 352 NYS 2d 290 (NY 1974).

53. *Koenigsmark v New York*, 437 NYS 2d 745 (NY App Div 1981).

54. *Speer v United States*, 512 F Supp 670 (ND Tex 1981).

55. *Vattimo v Lower Bucks Hospital, Inc.*, 428 A2d 765 (Pa Commw Ct 1981).

56. *Tarasoff v Regents of the University of California*, 131 Cal Rptr 14 (Cal 1976).

57. Gutheil TG, Bursztajn H, Brodsky A. The multidimensional assessment of dangerousness: competence assessment in patient care and liability prevention. Bull Am Acad Psychiatry Law 1986;14:123–129.

58. *Harnish v Children's Hospital Medical Center*, 387 Mass 152 (1982).
59. Mazur DJ. Translating court decisions into ethical-legal guidelines for patient-physician communication about medical risk. Presented at the Fifth Annual Meeting of the Society for Medical Decision Making, Toronto, 1983.
60. Bower GH. Mood and memory. Am Psychologist 1981;36:129–148.
61. Day M. Counter-transference in everyday practice. In: Issues in psychotherapy, vol. I: counter-transference. Boston: Boston Institute for Psychotherapies, 1981.
62. Light D. Becoming psychiatrists: the professional transformation of self. New York: Norton, 1980.
63. Bruch H. Learning psychotherapy: rationale and ground rules. Cambridge, MA: Harvard University Press, 1974:101–117.
64. Bursztajn H, Gutheil TG, Hamm RM, Brodsky A. Subjective data and suicide assessment in the light of recent legal developments. II: Clinical uses of legal standards in the interpretation of subjective data. Int J Law Psychiatry 1983;6:331–350.

chapter 4.

MANAGING UNCERTAINTY: THE THERAPEUTIC ALLIANCE, INFORMED CONSENT, AND LIABILITY

A woman went to her gynecologist for a check-up because of certain symptoms she was experiencing. After an examination, the gynecologist said that she would require a certain procedure, which he recommended that she undergo. Then he said, "Now, the law requires me to give you the following information," and he began a singsong chant that seemed to be about possible side effects, risks and benefits, outcomes, and the like. The woman stared, slack-jawed, at the gynecologist, trying to make sense of his recitation, and finally gave up. "This is clearly something he has to do for himself," she thought. "It has nothing to do with me. Why should I listen?"

―――――――♦―――――――

The case of Ms. Adams, described in the opening chapter of this book, illustrates the role of decision making in medicolegal contexts from the many viewpoints: patients, family members, doctors, lawyers, judges, and juries. Subsequent chapters will examine the decision-making mechanisms that these actors employ as they face various medicolegal dilemmas.

Each of these dilemmas evolves, however directly or indirectly, from the interaction between two parties: the patient and the physician. In this chapter we will examine the interpersonal dimensions of decision making that shape and are shaped by that interaction. In other words, we will be examining decision making as a bipersonal field.

From this vantage point, we will address four related topics: first, the therapeutic alliance; second, the informed consent process; third, the determination of competence; and fourth, the role of these dyadic elements both in managing uncertainty and in preventing liability.

THE THERAPEUTIC ALLIANCE

We might begin by attempting a definition, since the therapeutic alliance has been described in various, occasionally conflicting terms (1). The concept of an alliance appears to have its wellspring in Sigmund Freud's "analytic pact" (1) and was given its first explicit voice in Freud's 1920 paper (2) as follows: "The physician then works hand in hand with one portion of the pathologically divided personality, against the other party in the conflict."

The conceptual underpinning of this formulation is that each patient is an internally divided system, with the elements in conflict with one another. In the particular form of alliance under consideration here—which we have elsewhere termed the "rational alliance" (1)—the therapist attempts to make a connection with the part of the patient that is considered to be adult, able to shift between inner and outer reality, and comfortable with both ordinary feelings and unconscious drives. "Opposing" this aspect of the personality are the infantile, unrealistic, immature, and pathologic dimensions of a person's psychological makeup. Since, in the process of psychotherapy, the patient's difficulties can be resolved only by means of action from within, as it were, the therapist attempts to form a link with the reasonable, or healthy, dimensions of the person against the unreasonable, or unhealthy, dimensions of the same person.

Putting aside for the moment the simplicity of its depiction here, this form of collaboration represents the usual interaction between psychotherapist and patient. The patient, in effect, says to the therapist, "Help me deal with these self-defeating and repeating patterns in my life that seem to lead me to act against my own best interests." Responding to this request, the therapist works with the patient's capacity for self-observation, recognition of difficulty, and ability to change. In the introductory case, for example, Dr. Newell essentially attempts to invoke, recruit, and then collaborate with Ms. Adam's healthy self—the part of her that does not wish to die and is willing to work toward the resolution of her difficulties—against the self that feels depressed, abandoned, hopeless, and perhaps suicidal.

The problem with this plausible formulation is that in practice it is not so simple. Therapists often work with individuals whose rational side has been functionally submerged under illness, be it depression, psychosis, various forms of intoxication, or similar disruptive influences. How is the therapist to be reassured that the collaboration is a genuine one, that an alliance is established with the best (healthiest) side of the patient? There are several answers to this important question. One, to be addressed later in this chapter, concerns the process by which the therapist determines whether or not the patient is competent to participate in the various elements of the treatment plan.

Another answer concerns the fundamental wish for certainty and perfection that pervades all interactions between doctor and patient. The experience of being ill evokes feelings of helplessness, and wishful thinking may be used as a defense against such feelings. With illness undermining any sense of control that one may have felt over one's body—and one's life—the temptation is to find some other source of control. The wish for certainty and perfection may thus become lodged in the encounter between patient and physician, the latter seen as the keeper of the magical power that will cure the patient (2).

The patient's wish for certainty may have a significant effect on the physician as well. Aware that the patient expects a perfect outcome, the physician may fear that failure to provide it will be litigated as if it were negligence. (As we will shortly see, this view is not entirely fantasy.)

For example, a severely ill schizophrenic boy, denying the severity of his illness, expresses total confidence in the power of the physician to cure him. The physician is uncomfortable with this presumption of certainty. Feeling—perhaps correctly—that hopes this high must inevitably be disappointed, the physician emphatically counters all expressions of optimism, ostensibly to eliminate unrealistic expectations of perfect results. The patient, however, begins to feel that the physician's repeated deprecation of his hopes represents defeatism, opposition to him, or a covert wish to bail out of the case. To save his hopes he struggles with the physician, attempting to get him to change his mind. As a result of both the physician's self-protective stance and the patient's resistance, each becomes alienated from the other.

Thus, the physician may experience the patient's natural longing for certainty as a threat. The intrusion of this threat tends to drive a wedge of mutual distrust between physician and patient.

Note that the alliance depicted here is not rational, since it is not a collaboration between the physician and the patient's realistic, healthy self. Rather, it is an "irrational" or "narcissistic" alliance (1), in which the patient approaches the physician as the child approaches the parent, with magical expectations of the physician's (parent's) omnipotence.

Wishes for certainty and perfection are not necessarily limited to the patient's side of a medical interaction. The physician may well be subject to similar wishes, nurtured not only by the patient's magical expectations (which in turn are triggered by the experience of being ill) but also by medical training and socialization in the profession. Hilfiker (3) has pointed out the pitfalls of medical perfectionism:

. . . we physicians are even less prepared to deal with our mistakes than the average layperson is. The climate of medical school and residency training, for instance, makes it nearly impossible to confront the emotional consequences of mistakes; it is an environment in which precision seems to predominate . . . the medical profession simply seems to have no place for its mistakes. There is no permission to talk about errors, no way of venting emotional responses.

Thus, the physician, as well as the patient, may turn to fantasies of perfection as a hedge against uncertainty and the anxiety it provokes. Clinicians have been known to resort to extensive testing in the quest for certainty, relying on the illusory precision provided by technology, and sometimes overusing it (4, 5). This approach serves to drive physician and patient apart instead of bringing them together before their common problem, the uncertainty of medical practice.

Several other types of alliance may occur between physician and patient. Although the list is too long to discuss all of them here, one additional form is important for us to consider. Termed the "situational alliance" (1), it plays a part in many clinical arenas, as well as in liability prevention, as we will see later in this chapter.

Perhaps the easiest way to grasp the meaning of a situational alliance is to imagine two shy strangers fortuitously standing side by side on the street to observe a huge fire that has just broken out in a building across from them. Under the spell of a shared event—witnessing a catastrophe—they might fall easily into conversation, without being introduced and without their usual shyness serving as a barrier. They have been brought into an unself-conscious relationship (alliance) by virtue of a common situation.

In a comparable manner, doctor and patient can develop a comfortable relationship through their joint acknowledgment of the uncertainty of clinical practice. The experience of uncertainty links them together instead of driving them apart. Like other difficult experiences, this one, when shared, is more easily borne and may become more manageable. Thus, the situational alliance provides a useful model for sharing uncertainty.

Over time, the alliance—which may take a situational, irrational, or narcissistic form at the beginning of treatment—tends to evolve toward the rational form (appeal to reason) as the patient progresses through treatment, experiences personal growth, or gradually accepts the illness and develops skills to cope with it.

INFORMED CONSENT

The second element of medical decision making as a joint undertaking of patient and doctor is the notion of informed consent. As we use the term here, informed consent is the process by which the patient decides whether or not to undergo a particular medical procedure. The patient participates in this process willingly and with the benefit of sufficient information to be able to make a rational and personal decision about the procedure. Thus, informed consent is really informed decision making, although historically the term refers to an agreement rather than a decision.

The topic of informed consent is too extensive to address here in its entirety; however, suitable reviews have been undertaken elsewhere (6). Informed consent has been a doctrine of particular interest to medicolegal scholars, since it embraces issues of autonomy and paternalism, rationality and irrationality in decision making, competence, and liability.

Informed consent has three components. The first is competence, which might be defined as a capacity to take in, process, assimilate, and employ information in guiding a decision. Note that competence is not a state or condition so much as a potential. It can be impaired by various medical and psychiatric illnesses, by age (too old or too young), and by other factors as well.

What may be obscured by the notion of competence as a capacity or potential residing within the patient is the fact that its assessment—ostensibly a measure of the patient's status, like the measurement of blood pressure—is itself a bipersonal process.

Consider this hypothetical situation. A mentally ill man suffers from the delusion that other men hate him and wish to kill him. (This is, in fact, not uncommon in some cases of paranoid schizophrenia.) If a male psychiatrist attempts to assess his competence, the patient may become so anxious or upset that the assessment itself impairs his competence. If a female physician performs the assessment, however, it may proceed comfortably for both parties, and the patient may be deemed competent to give informed consent.

Factors on the physician's side may also affect, even contaminate, the assessment process. For example, when Dr. Newell considers Ms. Adams' capacity to participate in treatment planning, he employs his own informal and pragmatic standard of measurement. There is no formal or widely employed standard for determining a person's competence to engage in an outpatient care plan, as there is for, say, competence to stand trial. As a result, the relative rigor of Dr. Newell's own standard, the degree of intuitive empathy that be brings to the measurement, his own idiosyncratic sense of what faculties in the patient are required for competence—all play a role in his determination.

The assessor's clinical skills and sensitivity in eliciting information also influence the results of a competence assessment. The evaluator who is brusque, intimidating, unsympathetic, or uncompromising may impair the patient's performance. On the other hand, a sympathetic assessor, attuned to the patient's suffering and the stress of the examination itself, may be sufficiently supportive to bring out the patient's best endeavors and, consequently, to arrive at an evaluation that suggests greater competence than might otherwise be the case.

Thus, the patient's competence may be influenced or even impaired by the person performing the assessment. That person's style and personality may also impinge in various ways on the task of assessment. Clearly, then, competence assessment is a form of decision making that is interactive, partaking of various levels of communication (verbal and nonverbal) between patient and physician.

The second component of informed consent is voluntarity. In fact, the patient's willingness to participate in a particular treatment plan is the essence of consent. Involuntary interventions made in an emergency (such as interrupting a seizure or performing cardiopulmonary resuscitation or secluding an out-of-control psychiatric patient) do not meet this criterion. Such interventions, necessarily made without heed given to the patient's consent, are legally justified as responses to emergency conditions.

Certain kinds of coercion would also interfere with the notion of voluntarity that rests at the heart of the consent process. For example, to say to a patient in a psychiatric hospital, "Unless you agree to take this medication, you can't go to dinner," represents a violation of the principle of voluntarity. The means of coercion in this case is a none-too-subtle form of blackmail.

The third element of informed consent is provision of information. In this area an important philosophical evolution has occurred over the decades since the 1960s. Before that time, the physician obtaining informed consent for a particular procedure was expected to provide information about it that was similar to the information customarily provided by other physicians at that time and in that particular area of specialization and training. The standard was thus based on a physician-centered criterion. Gradually, the standard has shifted to a criterion centered on the patient; that is, the physician is expected to provide information that the patient would wish to know or would need to know.

An example of a patient-centered criterion is the decision in *Harnish v Children's Hospital Medical Center* (7), a landmark informed consent ruling in Massachusetts. The case involved a malpractice suit brought by a woman who had undergone surgery for removal of a tumor in her neck. In the course of the operation, her hypoglossal nerve had been cut, resulting in allegedly permanent loss of tongue function.

The patient sued for malpractice on the grounds that the hospital and physicians involved were negligent in failing to inform her that loss of tongue function was one of the risks of the surgery. She claimed that "the purpose of the operation was cosmetic, that the loss of tongue function was a material and foreseeable risk of the operation, and that, had [she] been informed of this risk, she would never have consented to the operation." She did not, however, claim that the physicians were negligent in performing the surgery.

Although a medical malpractice tribunal dismissed the claim, on appeal the state Supreme Court upheld it in part. The decision established a precedent for informed consent law in Massachusetts.

In its ruling the court acknowledged that failure to obtain informed consent (in this case, the alleged failure to provide adequate information for the patient to give informed consent) may represent a deviation from the standard of care that is sufficient to confirm a malpractice claim. The court also recognized the difficulties that physicians face in obtaining informed consent, including the problem of communicating complex scientific information to laypersons and the problem of selecting the information to communicate, since any procedure carries an almost infinite number of "remotely possible risks."

In considering the patient's rights, the physician's obligations, and the inherent complexity of informed consent, the court offered the following opinion on the kind and extent of information that the physician must provide to obtain informed consent:

The patient's right to know must be harmonized with the recognition that an undue burden should not be placed on the physician. These interests are accommodated by the rule that we adopt today, that a physician owes to his patient the duty to disclose in a reasonable manner all significant medical information that the physician possesses or reasonably should possess that is material to an intelligent decision by the patient whether to undergo a proposed procedure. The information a physician reasonably should possess is that information possessed by the average qualified physician or, in the case of a specialty, by the average qualified physician practicing that specialty.

Thus, the court used a physician-centered criterion ("average qualified physician") to determine the information that the physician should possess. To address the problem of selection, however, the court ruled that the physician should provide all information that is material to the patient's decision whether to undergo the procedure in question. The court defined materiality as follows

Materiality may be said to be the significance a reasonable person, in what the physician knows or should know is his patient's position, would attach to the disclosed risk or risks in deciding whether to submit or not to submit to surgery or treatment. . . . The materiality determination is one that lay persons are qualified to make without the aid of an expert.

Harnish suggests that the physician must adopt a layperson's perspective to gauge the importance that a patient would ascribe to a particular risk in deciding whether or not to consent to the procedure in question. In this manner, the clinician is advised by the court, in essence, to indulge in a form of guided empathy, an identification with the patient's point of view, in providing information. Thus, under *Harnish* the informed consent procedure is divided into two components, with a different criterion applied to each. The first component is the information that the physician possesses, which is subject to a physician-centered criterion. The second component is the physician's selection of information to convey to the patient, which is subject to a patient-centered criterion. In selecting information to provide the patient, the physician should be guided by what the patient (in some interpretations the "average" patient) would wish to known about the procedure.

While the notion of a patient-centered standard may aid the clinician in deciding what information to provide, other models have also been proposed. A simple working model that would probably encompass the requisite information in most jurisdictions is the following. The information that a patient would want to know and that a physician would do well to proffer includes the risks and the benefits of the proposed treatment, the risks and benefits of alternative forms of treatment, and the risks and benefits of no treatment (i.e., the consequences for good or ill if the proposed procedure is rejected by the patient).

Whatever model is used, the informed consent process may have unanticipated side effects that counter the desired result. On the one hand, frank acknowledgment of serious risks may engender feelings of helplessness in the patient, in part because the uncertainty of the intervention has been made so explicit. The potentially destructive impact of this revelation, in our experience, is often heightened when the information is presented simply by handing the patient a list of possible outcomes as part of a "consent form." Even in the best of doctor-patient relationships, the explicit acknowledgment of how many things can actually go wrong in this most uncertain of all possible worlds can evoke feelings of dismay and fear.

On the other hand, a lengthy listing of risks and benefits may be interpreted as the last word on the procedure or treatment under consideration, thus giving the patient an illusory sense of certainty and control. In other words, the volume of the information provided speaks to the patient's wish for certainty, giving the impression that "all bases have been covered." The physician may well collude in this misinterpretation, both by hiding behind the illusion of an all-knowing science and by assuming that a long recitation of risks will provide protection against liability. The irony is that this unwitting collusion may well make the physician more rather than less vulnerable to a malpractice suit, should the patient's expectations be disappointed (8).

Putting it in more succinct terms, then, the Scylla and Charybdis between which the informed consent process must steer are the potential exaggeration of how little and the potential exaggeration of how much the physician knows about the possible outcomes of the procedure.

Regrettably, the growing use of the consent document itself may sabotage the principles of informed consent as a dyadic process militating in favor of liability prevention. Clarification of this point requires some examination of the informed consent form, but first a caveat is in order. Clinicians who work for facilities that require an informed consent form as the preferred vehicle for the transaction should use the form forthrightly. It would be the height of folly to go against the policy of the institution for which one works. However, such forms are best used cautiously, with an understanding of the many difficulties that they pose. More importantly, such documents should never replace the dialogue between patient and physician that we are describing here.

The first problem with the consent form is the context in which it is signed. It is not unheard of for patients who have received preoperative medication to be given the form to read while they are already in a partially clouded state of mind and to be told that they must sign it in order for the operation to occur. This ritualistic adherence to the notion of a patient "giving consent" is far removed from the exchange of information, dialogue, and reasoned decision making that the entire informed consent process is designed to accomplish. No information changes hands, no discussion occurs, and no rational decision is made. We have referred to this as "pro forma informed consent" (9). In fact, it might facetiously be termed "formed consent" rather than "informed consent."

The second major difficulty with consent forms is an inherent tension in the use of written materials to accomplish the negotiations of the procedure. A form that covers all possible complications and outcomes of a given medication, for example, will be incomprehensible to anyone except a research pharmacologist. On the other hand, a form that is too concise may well omit details that are important to the patient. Thus, the form long enough to be complete may be incomprehensible, and the form short enough to be comprehensible may be incomplete.

Third, an institutional consent form is generally written by the attorneys retained by the hospital as "house counsel." Thus, the document tends to be designed not so much to inform the patient as to protect the hospital (i.e., against all allegations of failure to obtain informed consent).

To add to this problem, consent forms are often written in legal "boilerplate," that is, language borrowed from local precedent-setting case law to speak to certain legal principles that have already been "court-tested"—a very desirable quality in legal documents. Unfortunately, legal boilerplate resembles no human speech and meets only the ritualistic needs of the occasion, not the communicative and educational ones.

In part because of the legalistic language in which the typical consent form is written, the reading level required to comprehend it is similar to that required to read *Scientific American*, a level that only a fraction of the average physician's patients—and, for that matter, not all physicians—might reach. These comprehension difficulties are, of course, intensified if the patient suffers from intellectual deficits, has an illness with symptoms that strike directly at the intellectual and cognitive processes (such as dementia in the elderly), or is not a native English speaker.

In view of these problems with language and technicality, the hope that a signature on the consent form will provide protection against all allegations of failure to obtain informed consent might well be dashed in the courtroom. For example, one clinician uses a consent form for each medication he prescribes, with the list of risks taken from the drug package insert. The first paragraph of the document begins: "I, _____ am a patient of _____, M.D. Dr. _____ has informed me that he recommends that I receive the medication _____ for the treatment of my illness. He has informed me of the nature of the treatment and has explained to me the risks and possible side effects, including muscular dystonia, motor restlessness, akathisia, hyperreflexia, opisthotonos, . . . [etc.]." If a patient signed this document and subsequently sued for failure to obtain informed consent, the plaintiff's attorney could simply ask the physician to read the form to the jury. By the third technical term, those members of the jury who were not utterly bewildered would probably be asleep. Such a jury might readily identify with the patient's bewilderment and question the credibility of the physician's claim that the patient understood what the transaction was all about.

The most serious problem with the consent form, however, is not its language, the response it elicits in the patient, or the circumstances in which it is proffered and signed. The overriding danger of the form is that it tempts the clinician to treat the transaction as a discrete task that is accomplished, and thus terminated, once the patient has signed the form. This unfortunate misuse of the form defeats the very purpose of informed consent, which is to foster and sustain an ongoing dialogue between patient and physician, as part of the process of joint decision making. Ideally, informed consent is never over. At any point along the way, the patient should feel free to ask questions about the impact of the treatment, the impact of the medication, the effects of the procedure, and so on. The physician who genuinely believes that informed consent is over and done with when the form is signed may well respond brusquely or impatiently to subsequent questions, concerns, or fears that the patient voices about the evolution of the illness or treatment, whether or not the outcome is an unfortunate one. Thus, even when the patient receives a precise answer to a question, the physician's tone or manner may discourage rather than encourage the open discourse that we envision here.

All judicial models of informed consent rest on one of the most tenaciously held assumptions of the legal and judicial community: that decisions are made rationally on the basis of the information that has been provided and by careful weighing of the risks and benefits (10). Most clinicians, on the other hand, are keenly aware that the overwhelming majority of decisions are made on the basis of unconscious processes, subjective impulses, "visceral" reactions, transferences of various kinds, etc. The wishes for perfection and certainty earlier alluded to also enter into decision making, although on an obviously nonrational basis.

If decisions are influenced by so many factors not encompassed by rationality and logic, is the physician's provision of factual information simply a charade in the name of informed consent? This is indeed one possible view of the procedure. However, the process of obtaining informed consent offers the clinician a valuable opportunity to promote a true collaboration with the patient.

The key is to acknowledge and empathize with the patient's wish for certainty. The clinician should establish contact with this wish by using such language as, "I wish I could give you a medication that was sure to have only positive effects," or "There's just no guarantee you'll live through this operation—I wish there were" (8). Note that these formulations approach the question of uncertainty in real-life medical practice "from the patient's point of view." That is, the clinician acknowledges the patient's wishes, identifies with them, and expresses regret that they cannot be realized. Thus, doctor and patient are united—ruefully, as it were—in a shared wish that human affairs could be certain and a shared realization that they are not. This delicate elimination of magical wishes is fostered and supported by the physician's position "next to" (rather than "across from") the patient, in what we can now recognize as a situational alliance. The appeal to reasonableness in facing reality—in this case, the uncertainty of medical practice—also promotes a rational alliance between physician and patient as two adults acknowledging that things can and do go wrong.

This approach to the informed consent process has been described as weaning the patient from the fantasy of certainty (8). By saying to the patient, "I wish it were possible to have a side-effect-free medication," for example, the clinician pays respect to the human longing for a sure thing. Validating the patient's wishes and at the same time implying that they cannot be met, such expressions pave the way for a more explicit statement of the uncertainties inherent in medical treatment. Thus, the clinician can promote an alliance with the patient that is grounded not in secret (or even explicit) expectations of certainty but rather in the joint recognition that medicine offers the hope of a powerful yet imperfect human science.

INFORMED CONSENT AND THE THERAPEUTIC ALLIANCE IN LIABILITY PREVENTION

With this as background, we are now ready to consider how informed consent and the therapeutic alliance can be used in the service of liability prevention. Liability is technically defined in the law as consisting of four elements, which the plaintiff (patient or survivors) in a malpractice suit must prove to exist by a preponderance of the evidence (i.e., more likely than not).

The first element is the duty of care that the physician owes the patient. In a liability action the plaintiff must establish that the person on whose behalf medical liability is claimed was actually a patient of the doctor and was thus owed a duty of care. This duty has been interpreted broadly in case law. Even an offer of care (e.g., in the course of an emergency room intervention) or a consultation by telephone may establish the duty of care (see Chapter 12 for a closer look at the clinical and legal implications of medical communications by telephone).

The second element of liability is a breach of the duty of care in the form of negligence. The allegation here is that the doctor failed to practice in accord with the standard of care represented by a capable physician (or, depending on the wording of the applicable local statutes, that level of diligence or expertise expected, at the time and under comparable circumstances, from the average practitioner or average reasonable practitioner with a comparable degree of training or specialization). Thus, the professional peer group is the reference standard used to determine whether a certain action or failure to act is negligent. In the eyes of the law, negligent care is that which falls below or deviates from the care provided by the average practitioner in the field in which the defendant practices.

Furthermore, such a breach or deviation must result in explicitly claimed harms or damages that the patient has suffered, in the form of injury, death, or the like. In the introductory case, Mr. Adams claimed that his wife's death was the result of Dr. Newell's alleged negligence. Harm is thus the third element of medical liability.

The final element is causation. The plaintiff must show that the claimed harms are the direct result of the claimed negligence. The law refers to this notion as "proximate cause": the negligence must have been the proximate cause (immediate and determinative precipitant) of the actual harms. In legal teaching the proximate cause is often identified by means of a "but for" test, as follows: *"But for* the particular negligence, the resulting harms would not have occurred."

Note that treatment without *informed* consent may represent malpractice, assuming that all the other elements are present, since obtaining informed consent before performing a medical procedure is widely recognized as part of the standard of care. Treatment without *any* consent is considered a battery ("unconsented touching"), which is both a crime and a civil wrong.

Before the 1982 *Harnish v Children's Hospital* case, claims of malpractice were usually made on grounds other than failure to obtain informed consent. *Harnish* brought informed consent issues to the forefront of malpractice law in Massachusetts. Its influence is potentially quite broad, since such high court decisions are often cited in other jurisdictions. *Harnish* has probably contributed to the impression that the procedure for obtaining informed consent is easily assailed in the courtroom. Nevertheless, attorneys for plaintiffs, like clinicians, frequently assume that a signature on a consent form presupposes valid informed consent. (According to a survey conducted by the Risk Management Foundation of Massachusetts (11), 159 of 1200 liability claims filed between 1976 and 1986 involved an informed consent issue. We expect that proportion to increase considerably over the next few years, in the wake of *Harnish*.)

Although the four elements of liability—dereliction of a duty that is the proximate cause of harm—represent the formal technical definition of malpractice established by the law, the Adams case suggests that in the real world other factors intervene. Liability claims evolve not from purely legal considerations but from the malignant synergy of a bad outcome in the context of bad feelings. Once one understands that these are the true wellsprings of litigation, it is clear that, theory aside, malpractice litigation does not necessarily signify actual bad practice by a physician or actual deviation from the standard of care.

A simple "thought experiment" may clarify this point. Most laypersons are aware of umambiguous instances of bad care that are not litigated and, similarly, of careful work by conscientious physicians that nevertheless results in a lawsuit. These common observations tend to support our point that although claims of malpractice may reflect the state of the patient-physician relationship, they do not necessarily reflect bad practice.

What kinds of bad outcomes trigger litigation? Most cases involve injury or death; some, discomfiture of a very severe sort, such as lasting pain or physically disturbing side effects of treatment. Sequelae of procedures, such as postoperative scarring, complications, loss of function, and side effects of treatment, are other typical examples of bad outcomes.

The bad feelings in question are more complex. Especially in cases of suicide—one of the worst outcomes and known for its capacity to leave the worst feelings in its wake—the emotion in question may be guilt on the part of a surviving family member. In the introductory case, for example, Mr. Adams experiences significant guilt after his wife's suicide, feeling that he has caused her death by walking out on her. Tort litigation becomes a vehicle for transferring this guilt to Dr. Newell. If the physician is found liable, Mr. Adams will not have to bear all the blame. This legal/emotional paradigm is characteristic of litigation in the psychiatric realm, where suicide is generally recognized as the most common ground for malpractice claims. In fact, a 1983 survey performed by the American Psychiatric Association Insurance Trust suggests that claims for suicide occur twice as often as the next most common ground for litigation in psychiatry. Attempted and completed suicides are grouped in separate categories; if they are combined, the gap between suicide and other grounds for malpractice claims is even wider. Moreover, a suicide case is occasionally brought forward as a claim of improper diagnosis, misdiagnosis, or fracture (as when a patient jumping from a window breaks a leg but does not die), so that a closer analysis of cases would probably show that the factor of 2 is an underestimate.

Another bad feeling that may serve as the emotional trigger in malpractice litigation is rage, particularly in reaction to a bad outcome coupled with arrogance, indifference, or insensitivity on the physician's part. In a crisis the patient, feeling powerless, may suppress any expression of anger at the physician's conduct. After the crisis is over, however, the rage may be vented through litigation. In this context a claim of malpractice has a clear-cut retaliatory thrust.

A third bad feeling is grief in the wake of a loss, whether loss of life or loss of a body part or function. More subtle, perhaps, is the loss of a perfect outcome, which flows from the wish for certainty. Although grief is part—perhaps a necessary part—of human experience, it is not always welcomed, and in fact may be avoided, whether consciously or unconsciously. Thus, the patient (or family), feeling bereaved, may litigate in an effort both to obtain restitution and to avoid or postpone mourning for the loss experienced.

A closely related feeling might be termed "failure of magic" or "perfectionistic disappointment." As discussed earlier, the experience of being ill sometimes fosters magical (infantile) hopes for a panacea from the physician. Disappointment in a bad outcome may then lead to a lawsuit.

Litigation is sometimes triggered by surprise, particularly in the case of unexpected complications, side effects, or treatment results. The patient's sense of betrayal—that is, betrayal of the patient's trust in the physician and the treatment—turns surprise into a "bad feeling" in the sense that we are using that term here. It is a clinical truism that when a patient feels prepared, a particular side effect or complication is likely to be taken in stride ("Ah, yes, that's the muscle stiffness the doctor warned me about"). In an unprepared patient, the identical side effect may evoke panic ("What is happening to my body?") and then rage ("What have you done to my body?"). Litigation thus becomes a means of venting the patient's feelings of helplessness and betrayal in the face of an unanticipated outcome.

Another common emotional ground for litigation is the feeling of abandonment by the physician. No matter what the outcome or the degree of injury that results, the experience of being left alone with a bad outcome and bad feelings about it can be devastating. Not uncommonly, in this context, the patient turns to litigation as a way of forcing the physician into an empathic relationship. It is as though the patient were saying, "I feel so bad and so wronged by what has happened that I will sue you to make sure you understand by direct experience just how wronged and bad I feel." While a malpractice lawsuit may be many things to many people, largely depending on their role in it, a reality of such litigation often goes unnoticed: namely, that a lawsuit is a relationship, and a very intense one at that. Thus, in this curious manner, litigation is used to counter the experience of being alone with one's calamity.

This list of bad feelings that may trigger litigation is not intended to be exhaustive; many other feelings can lead to claims of malpractice. Nor are we making any statements about the justifiability of these feelings. What people feel after a tragic outcome is the result of a host of influences. In the experience of expert witnesses, however, the feelings we have noted are among those most commonly expressed through legal actions.

These bad feelings are most likely to occur in the absence of a therapeutic alliance between physician and patient. Sometimes, for example, the clinician employs a legalistic approach to the patient to avoid coming to grips with that person's suffering—what we have elsewhere called the use of legal defenses as ego defenses (12).

To grasp this point, consider that work with the mentally ill, particularly patients with severe or chronic illness or both, requires formidable personal resources in the clinician. Even in the strongest professional, the emotional intensity of such work over time, the raw affects unleashed, and the strains of prolonged empathic involvement in psychotic states of mind may trigger the impulse that Kubie describes as a "retreat from patients" (13).

Clinicians, especially trainees, may find various ways to "retreat," including the adoption of medicolegal pseudo-defenses. For example, the most common form of avoidance is to forsake an alliance with the patient in favor of the law's adversarial posture, that is, to practice defensively (see Chapter 11). Defensive medicine converts the patient into an enemy (potential plaintiff) instead of an ally. Such an approach, of course, jettisons the most vital element of therapeutic success *and* liability prevention: the alliance itself.

Other manifestations of this difficulty abound. When informed consent is limited to a signature on a printed form, the clinician hides behind the wording and the signature, counting on the mere mechanical proffering of the form as a substitute for a frank, joint consideration of the uncertainty inherent in medical practice. The vignette at the beginning of this chapter is an example of defensive practice. The gynecologist recites a litany of risks in lieu of engaging in an open dialogue with the patient. Ironically, a procedure that he believes will protect him from malpractice litigation actually makes him more vulnerable to it.

Another example of defensive medicine is a posture of overly scrupulous neutrality. Instead of recommending a particular course of action, the physician presents the options like a fanned-out deck of cards and invites the patient to pick one. This noncommittal stance leaves the patient alone with the alternatives and unsupported in his or her attempts to come to grips with the risks and benefits of a given intervention.

Defensive clinical practice, in whatever form, eclipses the physician's ethical responsibility to the patient; "first do no harm" is overshadowed by "first protect oneself." Every clinician should know and follow the legal requirements of medical practice, but these must not be used as a substitute for the moral standards of the profession. Simon underscores the distinction between the clinician's legal and moral duties to the patient: the first is framed as a minimum obligation, the second as a maximum. "The difference," Simon notes, "represents the gulf that exists between the human condition and the human spirit" (14).

Once we realize that malpractice suits result from a bad outcome coupled with bad feelings, we can understand the ways in which the informed consent process, in conjunction with the therapeutic alliance, may serve as a preventive or a remedy for these unfortunate results. At the heart of the alliance is the patient's feeling of being joined by the physician in an active collaboration to reduce suffering and restore health or manage illness. The informed consent process, at its best, endorses this collaboration as it fosters the mature responses of anticipation, preparation, and realistic appraisal, while at the same time dispelling any magical expectations of perfection. When the informed consent process and the alliance are successful, patient and physician together face the uncertainty of medical practice. In the wake of a tragic outcome, rage is tempered, grief shared (and mourning thus made possible), surprise diminished, and loneliness assuaged.

REFERENCES
1. Gutheil TG, Havens LL. The therapeutic alliance: contemporary meanings and confusions. Int Rev Psychoanal 1979;6:467–481.
2. Freud S. The psychogenesis of a case of homosexuality in a woman. Standard Edition. 1920;18.
3. Hilfiker D. Facing our mistakes. N Engl J Med 1984;310:118–122.
4. Bursztajn H, Feinbloom RI, Hamm RM, Brodsky A. Medical choices, medical chances: how patients, families, and physicians can cope with uncertainty. New York: Delacorte/Seymour Lawrence, 1981.
5. Reiser SJ, Anbar M. The machine at the bedside: strategies for using technology in patient care. Cambridge, UK: Cambridge University Press, 1984.
6. Appelbaum PS, Lidz CW, Meisel A. Informed consent: legal theory and clinical practice. New York: Oxford, 1987.
7. *Harnish v Children's Hospital Medical Center*, 387 Mass 152 (1982).

8. Gutheil TG, Bursztajn H, Brodsky A. Malpractice prevention through the sharing of uncertainty. N Engl J Med 1984;311:49–51.

9. Gutheil TG, Bursztajn H, Brodsky A. Liability prevention through informed consent: some new approaches for the clinician. Risk Management Found Forum 1986;7:8–9.

10. Gutheil TG, Appelbaum PS. Clinical handbook of psychiatry and the law. New York: McGraw-Hill, 1982.

11. Bowyer EA, Paulson L. Informed consent allegations affect all specialties. Risk Management Found Forum 1986;7:3–6.

12. Gutheil TG. Legal defense as ego defense: a special form of resistance to the therapeutic process. Psychiatr Q 1979;51:251–256.

13. Kubie LS. The retreat from patients. Arch Gen Psychiatry 1971;24:98–106.

14. Simon RI. A clinical philosophy for the (unduly) defensive psychiatrist. Psychiatr Ann 1987;17:197–200.

SECTION III. CLINICAL AND LEGAL ARENAS FOR DECISION MAKING

chapter 5.
INVOLUNTARY COMMITMENT

One of the most difficult decisions that psychiatrists must face is whether or not to petition a court for involuntary commitment of a patient. The dilemma underlying the decision is a classic example of a tragic choice, that is, a choice between two alternatives, both of which may have tragic consequences. Recall that in the introductory case Dr. Newell makes an initial evaluation of the clinical issues presented by Ms. Adams and decides to suggest hospitalization. The patient, however, is steadfast in her opposition to the idea. Dr. Newell then embarks on another, much more difficult course of decision making: should he petition the court for involuntary commitment of Ms. Adams? The route to that decision is complex. Not only must the clinician decide whether the patient meets the local legal standard for involuntary commitment, he must also weigh the risks of hospitalization under these circumstances against the risks of outpatient treatment.

In many respects, the commitment decision can be conceptualized as a choice between protection of the patient's safety and protection of the patient's autonomy. That is, commitment protects the patient from destructive impulses toward self and others, while not petitioning permits (or requires) the patient to exercise autonomous control of these impulses. Yet aside from the ethical and civil libertarian facets of that choice, hospitalization does not offer unadulterated protection. In fact, as Dr. Newell realizes, the very experience of being hospitalized against one's will may increase the risk of suicide by intensifying feelings of helplessness and despair. Many people who are intent on killing themselves do so while in the hospital or shortly after discharge.

Commitment decisions are made more complex by the fact that in many jurisdictions they represent a two-step process. First, the psychiatrist decides whether or not to petition for commitment. If the decision is to petition, then a hearing is held in court, and the presiding judge decides whether or not to grant the petition.

Eisenberg et al. have pointed out the complex clinical issues that may be dramatized by the commitment hearing itself (1). The proceedings are inherently adversarial, with attorneys representing each side (patient and physician), testimony for and against the petition, and cross-examination of witnesses. The confrontational nature of the hearing may damage the therapeutic alliance or the potential for developing such an alliance between the physician and the patient. Especially in the case of a paranoid patient, the commitment process may augment the patient's fear and distrust of the physician.

Paradoxically, however, the patient may view the decision to petition for commitment and the subsequent hearing as signs that the therapist is genuinely concerned and is taking the patient seriously, thus bolstering the patient's trust in the therapist. Moreover, some patients are ambivalent in their refusal and actually wish to be hospitalized involuntarily. That is, they wish to be hospitalized without assuming responsibility for that wish, as when the court opposes their stated preference. This is problematic not only for the clinician but also for the attorney who represents the patient in a commitment hearing.

Eisenberg et al. suggest that the process of seeking commitment offers the possibility of therapeutic benefits as well as dangers (1). In many respects, physician and patient have equivalent roles in the courtroom. In bringing their disagreement to court, they are copartici-pants in the drama played out before the judge, and both must face the uncertainty of the judge's final decision. If that uncertainty can be shared, their experience of awaiting a court decision together may augment rather than erode the therapeutic alliance.

Thus, commitment proceedings can dramatize a host of clinical issues and have far-reaching effects on the therapeutic alliance. The physician facing a commitment decision must be alert not only to the clinical implications of involuntary hospitalization but also to those of the commitment process itself.

STATUTORY STANDARDS

Statutory law concerning involuntary commitment has grown out of two legal traditions: parens patriae and police power. Parens patriae is a term from English law referring to the king's responsibility, like that of a parent, to protect his subjects, or children. Interpreted in the context of civil commitment, parens patriae holds that the state must protect those citizens who are unable to care for themselves. The criterion for commitment on the basis of this principle is the patient's need for treatment.

Police power, the other legal tradition behind commitment stan-dards, holds that the state is responsible for maintaining order in society and for protecting citizens at large from individuals who are dangerous. The commitment criterion that has evolved from the principle of police power is dangerousness, either to oneself or to others.

Parens patriae, which centers on evaluation of the patient's need for treatment, is a standard that is clinically oriented, or at least amenable to the clinical setting. The concept of dangerousness embodied in the police power standard is more problematic in this respect. Although clinicians may lay claim to some skill in evaluating violent behavior and its origins, "dangerousness" is not a clinical concept. It represents a potential for future action—which is, strictly speaking, beyond clinical expertise to predict, even though clinicians are commonly required to do so.

The past several decades have seen significant changes in the statutory requirements for commitment. In the 1940s and 1950s, an era of enthusiasm for the resources of psychiatry in treating mental illness, parens patriae was the predominant or sole standard for civil commitment. In the 1960s civil libertarians expressed concern about patients' rights as citizens and argued that involuntary commitment based on the parens patriae standard gives psychiatrists too much paternalistic discretion in deciding whether to hospitalize patients against their will. According to this perspective, involuntary commitment denies patients their rights as citizens in the same way that criminal incarceration does and should therefore be treated in an analogous way by the courts. That is, a petition for involuntary commitment should be granted only if the patient poses an imminent danger (to self or others). This argument signaled a shift toward tighter restrictions on civil commitment.

Recent years have seen a moderation in this trend, with most jurisdictions seeking some combination of commitment criteria that reflects the concerns of both parens patriae and police power. The actual standard invoked by the courts varies from one jurisdiction to another, but the criteria generally include the following assessments: dangerous to self or others and unable to care for self or "gravely disabled" (hence the need for treatment).

THE PRINCIPAL PLAYERS

Involuntary commitment is an action that evolves from a web of decisions made by three principal players: the patient, the psychiatrist, and the judge. The processes underlying clinical and judicial commitment decisions are triggered by a patient's refusal to be admitted to a hospital or to remain hospitalized on a voluntary basis. Each strand of the web that ensues is spun from a host of subtle influences. The strands are intertwined as each of the players anticipates and responds to the decisions made by the others. Thus, to determine how commitment decisions are made, one must consider several dimensions of decision making and be alert to the intricate interactions among them.

The Program in Psychiatry and the Law at the Massachusetts Mental Health Center has developed an integrated body of research on commitment decisions as they are perceived and constructed by patients, psychiatrists, and judges. These studies trace the individual strands that make up the web of decisions and provide insight into the ways in which the strands are interwoven. The findings and implications of this research are presented here.

Psychiatrists' Commitment Decisions

Do psychiatrists adhere to the statutory criteria in deciding whether to petition a court for involuntary commitment of a patient? Do they consider other, nonstatutory factors? If so, is this appropriate? Although several studies have been conducted to address these controversial questions, they have unfortunately produced conflicting evidence, thus obscuring rather than illuminating the issue. Some observers suggest that psychiatrists are not sufficiently attentive to the statutory grounds for commitment and are strongly influenced by personal, interpersonal, and socioeconomic considerations. Others disagree, claiming that the statutory criteria predominate in psychiatric decision making, with any additional factors playing a secondary part.

The Program in Psychiatry and the Law has conducted a series of studies designed to clarify both the substance and the process of psychiatric decision making with respect to commitment. These studies address three questions. First, do psychiatrists consider the statutory requirements for civil commitment? Second, do they consider any other factors apart from those related to the statutory criteria? Finally, if they do consider other, nonstatutory factors, are these influenced by changing conditions (e.g., changes in social policy, institutional practices, or professional philosophy)? That is, do the standards of the psychiatric community change over time?

The context for these studies is the use of a legal document in Massachusetts that is known as the "three-day paper": a written notice that a voluntarily hospitalized patient intends to leave the hospital, independent of medical advice. The patient must file the paper three days in advance of the requested discharge. Upon receipt of the paper, the psychiatrist has those three days to 1) attempt to persuade the patient to negotiate a mutually planned discharge and retract the paper; 2) failing that, decide whether to petition the court for a commitment of up to six months; or 3) simply honor the paper and allow the patient to leave the hospital in three days at the paper's expiration. In Massachusetts the legal standard for commitment is the presence of serious mental illness in combination with the likelihood of serious harm from one or more of the following: dangerousness to self, dangerousness to others, or inability to care for self.

Note that, all other considerations aside, the use of the three-day paper represents an intrinsically anti-alliance device. The patient who uses it has elected not to negotiate or plan for a reasoned, deliberate discharge. Instead, the patient has retreated to a legalistic formalism or, figuratively, has intruded a lawyer into the doctor-patient relationship.

Do Psychiatrists Adhere to the Statutory Criteria?

To answer this question, the Program in Psychiatry and the Law studied commitment decisions made by clinicians (most were residents in psychiatric training) at the Massachusetts Mental Health Center whose patients had requested discharge by filing a three-day paper. The study was conducted over a seven-month period, from October 1979 through April 1980 (2).

Participants were asked to fill out a questionnaire once they had decided how to respond to the patient's discharge request. If a patient retracted the paper during the three-day waiting period, the clinician was asked to respond to the questionnaire as if the patient had not withdrawn the request for discharge. In addition to stating their decisions (to petition for commitment or to honor the discharge request), the participants were asked to rate the patients on a scale from 1 to 7 with respect to the three statutory criteria for commitment, as well as various social, clinical, and interpersonal factors that we believed might be relevant to the commitment decision (Table 5.1).

Analysis of the questionnaire responses showed that the clinicians' ratings of the three statutory criteria for commitment—danger to self, danger to others, and ability to care for self—were all significantly correlated with the decision to petition for commitment or honor the patient's discharge request. Furthermore, when the variables were grouped, the statutory criteria demonstrated a greater contribution to the commitment decision than clinical judgments, psychosocial judgments, or interpersonal factors, although clinical and psychosocial judgments made a secondary contribution to the commitment decision. Thus, the results of this study suggest that the answer to our first question—whether psychiatrists consider the statutory standards for commitment—is yes. Clinicians clearly attend to the requirements of the law in making decisions about involuntary commitment.

These findings were replicated in two subsequent studies. One was conducted over a substantially longer period of time (November 1980 through August 1983) at the same center (3). The other took place during a four-month period in 1982 at the Payne Whitney Clinic in New

Table 5.1.
Patient Characteristics

Judicial Variables	Extrajudicial Variables (*Continued*)
Danger to others	Psychosocial judgments (*Continued*)
Danger to self	Poor/rich
Unable to care for self	Cares for others
Extrajudicial Variables	Family for commitment
Clinical judgments (diagnostic)	Interpersonal factor judgments
Crazy/sane	Frustrating
Acute/chronic	Likable
Needs treatment	Verbal
Well/ill	Discouraging
Psychotic thought	Frightening
Psychotic behavior	Gratifying
Clinical judgments (predictive)	Seductive
Reliable outpatient	Intelligent
Reliable with medications	Argumentative
Psychosocial judgments	Depressing
Place to live	Appearance
Age	Disruptive on ward
Support on outside	Miscellaneous judgments
Able to work	Well known to doctor
	Of academic interest

York (4). Like Massachusetts, New York requires a three-day waiting period following a patient's request for discharge, although that requirement applies only in cases where "there are reasonable grounds for belief that the patient may be in need of involuntary care and treatment" (4). The statutory criteria for civil commitment in New York are also similar to those in Massachusetts.

In sum, the results of these studies suggest that clinicians do indeed give careful consideration to the statutory criteria in deciding whether or not to petition a court for commitment of a patient.

Do Psychiatrists Consider Nonstatutory Factors?

Aside from the statutory criteria, do clinicians consider other factors when they face the decision whether or not to petition a court for commitment of a patient? If so, what are those factors, and what role do they play in the decision-making process?

This is a more complicated question than the initial one (whether clinicians consider the statutory requirements for commitment), since it requires both a broader scope of investigation and one that probes at a deeper level of decision making. The first question could be answered fairly directly by seeking significant correlations between the commitment decision and the clinician's rating of the patient according to the characteristics listed in Table 5.1. This type of analysis is designed to relate inputs (in this case, patient characteristics, including the three statutory criteria) to outputs (the decision to petition or not petition for commitment). It is known as a "black box" analysis, because the decision-making apparatus—the process by which the inputs and outputs are related—is concealed (in the box, so to speak).

Since the black box approach does not explore the relationship between inputs and outputs, it falls short of the challenge posed by our second question, which calls not simply for a yes or no answer but for a fuller explanation of how and why. To determine whether nonstatutory factors contribute to the psychiatric commitment decision and, if so, how they are related to the statutory criteria, we need to design an analysis that can penetrate the interior of the black box—in this case, the introspective dimensions of decision making.

To meet this research challenge, the Program in Psychiatry and the Law developed a second scale (5). Whereas the first scale asks the clinician to rate the patient according to various characteristics, the second scale probes the clinician's perception of the influence that each characteristic has on the commitment decision. The clinician is asked to report the impact of that characteristic by assigning it a weight ranging from -100 to $+100$, with -100 indicating a very strong contribution to the decision to release the patient, 0 no contribution in either direction, and $+100$ a very strong contribution to the decision to seek commitment. We call this impact rating a "grey box" approach to the study of decision making (5), because it is designed to illuminate the interior of the black box, which in this case is the introspective process that culminates in the final decision. Exploration of the second question—whether nonstatutory considerations contribute to psychiatrists' commitment decisions—also calls for some modification of the list of patient characteristics in order to give additional focus to the kinds of clinical judgments that may enter into such decisions. Specifically, the category of clinical characteristics in the modified questionnaire includes diagnostic considerations (acute, needs treatment, ill, psychotic thought, psychotic behavior) and predictive considerations (reliable outpatient, reliable with medications).

In the study conducted from 1979 to 1980, described above, we asked the clinicians to use the impact scale to indicate which nonstatutory factors, if any, influenced their decisions, how, and to what extent (2). The responses provided clear evidence that various factors other than those required by the law figure in psychiatric commitment decisions. Some of these nonstatutory criteria—for example, whether or not the patient strikes the clinician as frightening—may represent certain facets of the statutory considerations—in this case, dangerousness to others.

As a group, the clinical judgments were most prominent among the nonstatutory factors reported to influence commitment decisions. Psychosocial considerations (e.g., place to live, support on outside) played a somewhat smaller role. Certain interpersonal factors (e.g., frightening) also contributed to the decision, but as a group they were the least important. These results were also corroborated by subsequent studies (3, 4). As a further probe, we performed an analysis to determine whether any of the nonstatutory factors made a unique additional contribution to the commitment decision, over and above the contributions of the statutory criteria. Three clinical factors were found to exert a significant influence that was independent, statistically speaking, of the statutory considerations. All three fell into the category of diagnostic clinical judgments: needs treatment, ill, and psychotic behavior.

Thus, psychiatrists do appear to consider other factors in addition to the statutory requirements for commitment. Furthermore, some of the diagnostic clinical factors they consider contribute to the commitment decision beyond their association with the statutory criteria.

These findings can be interpreted in several ways. Clinicians may use nonstatutory factors to gauge the severity of illness, which is a parens patriae criterion and one element of the legal standard (in Massachusetts and many other jurisdictions), in addition to the dangerousness criteria.

It is also possible that clinicians consider nonstatutory criteria as an initial step in deciding whether or not to petition for commitment. Like Dr. Newell, in his evaluation of Ms. Adams, the clinician may first weigh the risks and benefits of involuntary hospitalization, attending largely to the clinical factors involved. If the benefits of commitment appear to outweigh its risks, then the clinician must decide whether to petition for commitment, a process guided by the statutory criteria.

Note that commitment statutes mandate when psychiatrists may petition but not when they must do so. Thus, whereas the decision to petition should and, as we have shown, does have a statutory basis, the decision not to petition may well have a nonstatutory (clinical) basis, at least initially. Even the decision to seek commitment, however, is influenced to some degree by nonstatutory factors. Moreover, when a commitment decision becomes the focus of malpractice litigation, the courts often examine clinical as well as statutory considerations in determining liability. In the wake of a tragic outcome, psychiatrists have been sued for negligence in failing to commit a patient, yet they have also been sued for false imprisonment in pursuing commitment against the patient's will. Whereas the latter case would clearly hinge on the clinician's attention to the judicial criteria for commitment, the former case might center on the reasonableness of the decision not to petition, with the customary practices of the professional community forming the basis for a determination of liability.

A third explanation for the independent consideration of clinical factors is that they may help the therapist probe his or her intuitive understanding of the statutory criteria as they apply to a particular case. For example, consideration of a patient's psychotic behavior may illuminate facets of that patient's condition that are not revealed by a simple assessment of dangerousness to self or others. From this perspective, the nonstatutory criteria act as heuristic devices in the clinician's subjective assessment of the three legal requirements for commitment. The simple phrase, "dangerous to self," for example, may not call to mind all the factors that are actually relevant to a patient's dangerousness to self. By asking a variety of questions, one may be able to illuminate different perspectives and different parts of one's consciousness and experience, thus broadening and deepening the assessment. Known as "triangulation," this process can help reduce errors in decision making.

Of course, these interpretations need not be mutually exclusive. Any or all of them may characterize the multidimensional cognitive process that clinicians engage in when facing commitment decisions. What our studies make clear, however, is that clinicians use multiple cues and indicators in deciding whether or not to petition for commitment. While attending to the three statutory requirements, they also consider a range of clinical, psychosocial, and interpersonal factors that are intricately woven into the cognitive process underlying commitment decisions.

Do the Standards of the Psychiatric Community Change Over Time?

The studies described above suggest that clinicians are appropriately alert to both the dangerousness and parens patriae standards expressed in the statutory requirements for civil commitment. In addition, they report that certain nonstatutory factors, especially diagnostic clinical judgments and psychosocial considerations, enter into the process of making commitment decisions. Does this process change over time, in response to changing conditions? That is, are the nonstatutory factors that clinicians consider subject to external temporal influences?

To answer this question, the Program in Psychiatry and the Law compared data from the two studies conducted at the Massachusetts Mental Health Center during different periods of time: October 1979 through April 1980 (2) and November 1980 through August 1983 (3). The hypothesis underlying this analysis was that changes occurring over time in the psychiatric community influence clinicians' perceptions of the process by which they arrive at commitment decisions. Specifically, changes in the norms, resources, and training of the psychiatric community in the early 1980s interacted with the statutory requirements for commitment and thus altered the context of decision making with respect to involuntary commitment.

A comparison of responses to the questionnaires in the two study periods bore out this hypothesis. In both periods clinicians were alert to the statutory criteria for commitment while also considering other, extrastatutory factors. From the first to the second period, however, there was a shift in emphasis from patient characteristics that were primarily psychosocial (e.g., place to live, support on outside) and interpersonal (e.g., likable, frustrating, discouraging) to more descriptive clinical characteristics (psychotic thought, psychotic behavior, reliable with medications).

This shift in the extrastatutory factors that clinicians considered when making commitment decisions paralleled several changes that occurred in the psychiatric community from the first to the second study period. One such change was the 1980 publication of the third edition of the *Diagnostic and Statistical Manual of Mental Disorders* (DSM-III) (6), which provides clinical and diagnostic classifications that are more objective-descriptive (external) and less psychodynamic (internal) in tenor than those published in earlier editions. The early 1980s saw a growing acceptance of the guidelines established in DSM-III.

Several socioeconomic and institutional changes also occurred over the years of the two studies. Public funding for institutional psychiatric care was considerably reduced. In addition, a policy of deinstitutionalization was implemented in favor of community-based care, with short-term hospital treatment reserved for the most seriously ill patients.

In 1981 the Massachusetts Mental Health Center, where these studies took place, underwent an extensive reorganization (7). Two day hospitals and an intensive care unit replaced the previous inpatient services, and a "dormitory/inn" was established for day hospital patients in need of temporary transitional housing. The reorganization was designed to emphasize day treatment, with the inpatient unit and dormitory/inn functioning as backup services. Under the new system, all patients are admitted to one of the two day hospitals. A patient experiencing an acute episode of illness is hospitalized in the intensive care unit and returned to the day hospital as soon as his or her condition has been stabilized.

As a result of deinstitutionalization, changes in the delivery of institutional services, funding constraints, and cost-containment pressures, clinicians must now evaluate and treat hospitalized patients in a much shorter period of time. Previously trained to get to know their patients in terms of such psychodynamic and interpersonal traits as likable, frustrating, or seductive, clinicians are now schooled in the descriptive language of DSM-III, which may indeed be more amenable to the exigencies of short-term hospital treatment, with its emphasis on what meets the eye first.

In some respects, however, these temporal changes in the factors that influence commitment decisions may reflect subtle shifts in the introspective style of clinical decision making more than alterations of its substance. For example, the clinician who reports being influenced by the patient's likability (an interpersonal judgment) in making a commitment decision is not simply revealing a personal bias. Instead, a sense of whether or not the patient is likable provides an indirect clue to the depth of his or her social supports outside the hospital. If the therapist finds it difficult to like the patient, perhaps those outside the hospital (family, friends, and human services agencies) have the same difficulty, which may interfere with their ability to be genuinely supportive of the patient. A focus on psychotic behavior (a descriptive clinical judgment) may elicit the same kind of information, since a patient who is acting psychotically is probably less likable than one who is not, with the same implications for social supports. On the other hand, a likable person who is psychotic may have a solid social support network, allowing for continued autonomy and treatment on an outpatient basis.

In any case, it seems clear that clinicians not only use a range of cues in making commitment decisions but also adapt their choice of cues to changes in the patient population and the availability of resources. Thus, the decision-making process is influenced by the clinical setting, which in turn is influenced by changing social, economic, and political currents.

The "Thank You" Theory of Commitment

So far we have considered the physician's role in decisions concerning involuntary commitment, and in a later section we will examine the role of the judge who hears a petition for commitment, but what about the most important player in the drama—the patient? Recall that in the introductory case the entire sequence of decision making with respect to involuntary hospitalization was triggered by Ms. Adams' refusal to be hospitalized voluntarily. Likewise, a three-day paper represents a patient's decision to leave the hospital, independent of (or even against) medical advice. These situations should remind us that clinicians' commitment decisions evolve from an interactive process comprising both the clinician's and the patient's perspective on the need for hospitalization.

The parens patriae standard has occasionally been labeled the "thank you" theory of commitment (courtesy Alan A. Stone, M.D.) because of its implicit view that the patient who is temporarily unable to make a life-sustaining choice will ultimately be thankful that the physician has intervened and set in motion the process to hospitalize the patient against his or her will. To return to the parent-child analogy on which parens patriae is based, the theory is that the child who today rebels against the parent's protective action will some day, as an adult, realize that the action was in his or her best interests.

The three-day paper offers a particularly rich context for examining the way in which the perspectives of patient and physician interact when commitment decisions must be made. During the three days that follow formal notification of the patient's intention to leave the hospital against medical advice, both the patient and the physician have time to step back and reconsider their respective views of the situation. In many cases the patient decides to retract the paper during the three-day waiting period, relieving the therapist of the need to make a commitment decision. For example, between November 1980 and August 1983, 79% of patients at the Massachusetts Mental Health Center (56 of the 71 whose therapists completed questionnaires) were reported to have withdrawn their discharge requests (3). The proportion was similar in the New York study (73%) (4). Retraction of the paper may reflect the patient's agreement that continued hospitalization is necessary, or at least a willingness to accept the physician's perspective on the need for hospital care. On the other hand, the patient who files and then retracts the paper may be deeply ambivalent about asking for and accepting help or may be testing the clinician's commitment to taking care of the patient.

Which patients decide to retract the three-day paper? Our research indicates that patients who are most likely to retract their requests for release are those who, according to their physicians, are most in need of treatment, are least able to care for themselves, and demonstrate psychotic thought and behavior (3). Other patient characteristics that tend to be related to retraction include danger to self, acute (rather than chronic) illness, and ill (rather than well). Thus, patients who retract their requests for discharge are also more likely to be suicidal and acutely ill.

There are several possible explanations for the relationship between these characteristics and retraction of the discharge request. Some patients, especially those with paranoid tendencies, may decide to comply with rather than challenge medical advice, preferring to let the clinician assume responsibility for the commitment/discharge decision. Others, anticipating that the psychiatrist will petition for commitment, may decide to "give up" rather than go to court. It is also possible that patients are instinctively inclined to act in their own best interests, even—perhaps especially—those who are seriously ill. Of course, various elements of the conflict between physician and patient may change during the three-day waiting period. For example, the discharge request may reflect an ambivalence in the patient that is resolved in the therapeutic relationship before the three days have elapsed, or the therapist may be able to persuade the patient that continued hospitalization is the best course. (By the same token, the patient may be able to persuade the clinician not to seek commitment.)

In some cases, a patient's decision to retract the discharge request may influence the clinician's responses to the questionnaire (ratings of patient characteristics or the hypothetical commitment decision or both). Identification with a patient's wish to be healthy, for example, could color the clinician's perception of that patient.

Nevertheless, the general impression is that patients act prudently on their own behalf: those with the greatest need for continued hospitalization are most inclined to retract their requests for release. This "prudent patient" pattern appears to be influenced not only by the degree of the patient's need but also by the clinician's commitment decision. Our study indicated that for the group of patients whose physicians decided to seek commitment, the more dangerous or seriously ill patients were more likely to retract the discharge request. For patients whose physicians decided not to seek commitment, the relationship between dangerousness or illness and the patient's retraction decision was weakened or even reversed (that is, the less dangerous or ill patients were more likely to retract the request).

Thus, the patient's retraction decision is clearly influenced by the physician's commitment decision, even when the petitioning option is not exercised. Perhaps the most important message these patterns convey is that the three-day paper is part of an interactive process of decision making in which patient and clinician engage.

Judges' Commitment Decisions

The final stage in commitment decisions is the judge's ruling. How do judges approach the question of involuntary commitment? Is the decision-making process in which they engage similar to that of psychiatrists?

Research on judges' decision-making behavior has generally focused on the outcome of that behavior rather than on the process underlying it. For example, as part of an evaluation of the 1970 revision of the Massachusetts civil commitment statute, Lelos reported the results of a courtroom observation study, in which observers recorded and rated the performance of psychiatrists, attorneys, and judges (8). The purpose of the study was to evaluate the courtroom application of revised statutory criteria for commitment. Lelos concluded that commitment decisions were sometimes based on inadequate testimony and evidence, in terms of the revised criteria, especially those concerned with dangerousness. The judges reportedly were not influenced in their rulings by the patient's race, sex, physical size, or history (e.g., previous psychiatric hospitalization). These conclusions were based entirely on observation of behavior in the courtroom and the outcomes of the hearings.

In another observation study Maisel examined the behavior of judges during commitment hearings in California (9). He was particularly struck by the speed with which decisions were made (typically, eight to ten minutes) and the unanimity of opinion, which represented a predominantly psychiatric rather than judicial perspective. Maisel (writing in 1970, before the policy of deinstitutionalization had been implemented throughout the United States) expressed concern that civil commitment hearings might well provide a forum for social control of a wide range of deviant behavior labeled "mental illness," rather than for "careful judicial review of cases where mental illness is suspected, alleged, or asserted" (p. 360).

Other investigators have studied commitment decisions retrospectively. For example, Rothman and Dubin analyzed commitment forms and psychiatric evaluation records over a two-year period for a population of patients seen at a hospital crisis center in Philadelphia (10). Their data, retrieved from the documents, included demographic information about the patients, their psychiatric history, diagnosis, and treatment and disposition. The authors concluded that committed and released patients were distinguishable primarily on the basis of the diagnosis. Those who were committed tended to be psychotic and seriously disturbed, typically with a diagnosis of schizophrenia, whereas among released patients the diagnosis was more commonly neurosis, personality or affective disorder, or substance abuse. This study provided descriptive information about patient populations evaluated for commitment, but it did not examine the nature of the commitment decision, the role of the decision maker (whether psychiatrist or judge), or the process used to arrive at the decision.

Hiday undertook a narrower but more penetrating examination of judges' commitment decisions by focusing on judicial discretion in applying the dangerousness criteria to such decisions (11). This was an observation study in which researchers recorded references to dangerousness made by lawyers, judges, and witnesses during commitment hearings.

One of the most interesting aspects of Hiday's investigation was her attempt to probe the role of dangerousness as a multidimensional concept in civil commitment. As she notes, many jurisdictions do not define dangerousness in explicit terms. Although some statutes specify overt behavior that is likely to result in substantial harm, they fall short of defining these terms or addressing the problems of predicting dangerous behavior. Hiday attempted to bring some clarity to this issue by looking at five dimensions of courtroom references to dangerousness: the type of behavior (e.g., actual or threatened attack, physical or property attack), its frequency, recency, severity, and target (self, others, or both). The first dimension, type of behavior, attempts to gauge the degree of harm. Frequency and recency provide clues to the likelihood of future harm. According to this reasoning, a single harmful action might signify better self-control on the part of the patient than repeatedly dangerous behavior. Similarly, the more time that has elapsed since the behavior in question, the more likely that the patient has regained self-control.

In hearings that alluded to dangerous behavior, Hiday found that, in general, the more severe, recent, and recurrent the behavior, the more likely the decision to commit rather than release the patient. In addition, harm directed at others was more closely associated with commitment than harm directed at oneself. However, Hiday found considerable variance in the commitment decisions. Moreover, in over a third of the cases the courtroom hearing did not include any discussion of the patient's dangerousness, even though in most of those cases the psychiatrist's affidavit mentioned one or more types of dangerous behavior. Thus, as Hiday points out, there was a tendency for both counsel and judge to accept the affidavit at face value rather than subject it to a critical examination in court. She concludes that dangerousness should be defined in terms of explicit behavioral criteria and that these criteria should be addressed in testimony during the commitment hearing, in order to ensure an explicit, critical application of the dangerousness standard in the courtroom.

The Process of Judicial Decision Making

To explore the commitment decisions that judges make, the Program in Psychiatry and the Law undertook a form of in-process examination that has not been described before (12). Five district court judges in Massachusetts participated in this preliminary empirical study (from an estimated total of 20 to 30 judges who rule on commitments in that state). The judges filled out a four-part, anonymous questionnaire (see Appendix 5.1) after each commitment hearing that they presided over during the four-month period of the study. The questionnaire contained rating and impact scales that paralleled those used to study psychiatrists' decisions. In addition, the judges were asked to rate the ease with which they had made each decision.

The five judges heard a total of 41 cases and decided to grant the commitment petition in 34 cases (a commitment rate of 83%). The other six cases were continued (i.e., held over for consideration at a later date). Thus, none of the petitions were denied outright, and almost all of them were granted.

For the most part, the judges did not report any difficulty in arriving at their decisions. Factors related to compliance or competence, as well as parens patriae considerations, tended to figure more prominently in judicial decision making than those concerned with dangerousness, even though the latter represent statutory criteria for commitment. The three factors that had the greatest impact on the rulings were the degree to which the psychiatrist's opinion was convincing, whether the patient would be reliable as an outpatient, and the patient's ability to take care of himself or herself. Subjective factors such as whether the patient seemed likable or frightening, which psychiatrists are likely to consider in arriving at a commitment decision (see earlier discussion), appeared to have comparatively little influence on judicial decisions.

When considering the implications of these findings, it is important to keep their social context in mind. In the United States both the medical and legal systems prefer voluntary to involuntary hospitalization, so that, all other things being equal, the decision is weighted against commitment. For these and other reasons, commitment is not a frequent event.

There are several possible explanations for the high commitment rate in this study. First, the sample of judges was small and may have been unrepresentative; that is, those who were willing to participate in the study were perhaps more receptive to clinical reasoning than the majority of their peers. Another possible factor is time: there is usually about a week's delay between the petition and the hearing. During that time the patient's condition or relationship with the physician often improves to the extent that the physician withdraws the petition or the patient withdraws the request for discharge. Thus, the cases that come to court tend to reflect the most severe illness and the greatest impairment of the therapeutic relationship.

Whatever the explanation, it is surprising to find that nearly all the petitions heard by the five judges were granted and that none were denied outright. The very low frequency of petitions, combined with the very high rate at which they are granted, suggests a reciprocity—perhaps even an implicit collusion, whether conscious or unconscious—between psychiatrists and judges as they make decisions about commitment. Psychiatrists are generally reluctant to go to court to retain a patient and may do so only when they feel certain that the petition will be granted. They may preselect patients who are so severely ill that there is little question of the statutory grounds for commitment, instead of petitioning when they feel that the ambiguous clinical grounds justify presenting the case in court. The judges, in turn, hearing only the most severe cases (i.e., those that have been clinically filtered), may come to rely on the psychiatric assessment that resulted in preselection as they make their rulings on commitment petitions. If judges are hearing only cases involving intractable conditions and irreconcilable differences between patient and physician, it is not surprising that they report having little difficulty in arriving at their decisions. Their narrow exposure to the most serious cases is cause for some concern, however, since in a sense it foreshortens the judicial decision-making process, eliminating the need for judges to consider—and to practice assessing—different degrees of dangerousness or need for hospitalization and treatment.

In some respects, the reciprocity reflected in commitment decisions made by psychiatrists and judges—the fact that psychiatrists tend to second-guess judges and judges tend to rely on psychiatric opinion—can be seen as a type of role-switching. Our studies suggest that in approaching commitment decisions, clinicians assume a judicial role by anticipating the judge's ruling on a case, and judges assume a clinical role by relying on the psychiatric evaluation and on extrastatutory factors concerned with compliance.

Perhaps clinician and judge tend to switch roles in response to the inherent tension between the two legal traditions reflected in commitment criteria: police power and parens patriae. The doctrine of police power is concerned with maintaining social order and control, for the good of the people, while parens patriae emphasizes protection and treatment of the patient, for the good of that individual. The criterion of dangerousness, associated with police power, is much more at home in the legal domain, whereas need for treatment, suggested by parens patriae, is more comfortably addressed in the clinical domain. Yet, both kinds of criteria must be brought to bear on commitment decisions as they are made in the two domains. The psychiatrist and the judge may each overcompensate for the criteria representing the less familiar domain, their mutual overcompensation expressed as role-switching.

TOWARD A COMMON GROUND

The implications of the tendency for psychiatrist and judge to switch roles, or at least to anticipate and second-guess one another, are not all negative. Each, after all, must find a way to bridge the gap between medical and legal concerns when considering involuntary hospitalization. Clinicians must consider the statutory criteria in deciding whether or not to petition for commitment. The dangerousness criteria are particularly problematic in psychiatric decision making, since they have no strict clinical meaning. Judges, in turn, must weigh the complexities of psychiatric conditions within the legal arena. The ability to "try on" the other perspective is essential for both psychiatrist and judge, as they engage in decision-making processes that are, by their very nature, extradisciplinary and multidimensional.

Thus, both clinicians and judges are alert to the statutory standards for commitment and appear to use clinical indicators to interpret and apply those standards. Even if parens patriae criteria were eliminated from the statutes, leaving only the dangerousness criteria, it seems likely that concerns about the ability of patients to care for themselves and their need for treatment would continue to inform both clinical and judicial decisions about commitment.

REFERENCES

1. Eisenberg GC, Barnes BM, Gutheil TG. Involuntary commitment and the treatment process: a clinical perspective. Bull Am Acad Psychiatry Law 1980;8(1):44–55.
2. Bursztajn H, Gutheil TG, Hamm RM, Brodsky A, Mills MJ, Levi LM. Transitions in clinicians' self-reports of the assessment of committability. Int J Psychiatry Law; in press.
3. Bursztajn H, Gutheil TG, Hamm RM, Brodsky A, Mills MJ. Parens patriae considerations in the commitment process. Psychiatr 1988;59(3):165–181.
4. Schwartz HI, Appelbaum PS, Kaplan RD. Clinical judgments in the decision to commit. Arch Gen Psychiatry 1984;41:811–815.
5. Hamm RM, Bursztajn H, Mills M, Appelbaum P, Gutheil TG. Regression and introspection in the analysis of clinical decision making: the case of the three-day paper. Presented at the First International Congress for Psychiatry, Ethics, and the Law, Haifa, Israel, 1983.
6. American Psychiatric Association. Diagnostic and statistical manual of mental disorder. 3rd ed. Washington, D.C.: American Psychiatric Association, 1980.
7. Gudeman JE, Shore MF, Dickey B. Day hospitalization and an inn instead of inpatient care for psychiatric patients. N Engl J Med 1983;308:749–753.

8. Lelos D. Courtroom observation study of civil commitment. In: McGarry AL, Schwitzgebel RK, Lipsitt PD, Lelos D, eds. Civil commitment and social policy: an evaluation of the Massachusetts Mental Health Reform Act of 1970. Rockville, MD: National Institute of Mental Health (DHHS Publication No. (ADM) 81-1011), 1981:102–125.

9. Maisel R. Decision-making in a commitment court. Psychiatry 1970;33:352–361.

10. Rothman M, Dubin WR. Patients released after psychiatric commitment evaluation: comparison with the committed. J Clin Psychiatry 1982;43(3):90–93.

11. Hiday VA. Reformed commitment procedures: an empirical study in the courtroom. Law Soc Rev 1977;11:652–666.

12. Bursztajn H, Gutheil TG, Mills MJ, Hamm RH, Brodsky A. Process analysis of judges' commitment decisions: a preliminary empirical study. Am J Psychiatry 1986;143:170–174.

Appendix 5.1: Judicial decision-making study

This questionnaire has four parts and should not take more than a few minutes to fill out. Please complete as soon as possible after the commitment hearing. Return all questionnaires to Judge _____; [he/she] will ensure complete anonymity for individual respondents.

Judge's code number _____.

Part I: Demographic Data

1. Facility: Public ____ Private ____

2. Patient hospitalized previously? yes____ no____

   First commitment hearing? ____ Recommitment hearing? ____

3. Marital status (check one):

   never married ____ married ____ separated ____

   divorced ____ widowed ____

4. Time since last steady employment or functioning (check one):

   a week ____ a month ____ 6 mos. ____ a year ____ 2+ years ____

5. Did patient appear for hearing? yes ____ no ____

6. If not, did he/she decline to appear? yes ____ no ____

7. Did patient speak for self? yes ____ no ____

8. If patient spoke, was it with attorney's approval? ____

   Over attorney's objection? ____

9. Procedural requirements in hearing: met ____ not met ____

10. Was continuance granted for reasons OTHER THAN availability of witnesses, counsel, or court personnel?

11. To judge: how often per month do you perform civil commitment hearings? ____

12. Psychiatric diagnosis? _____

13. Petition granted? ____ Petition denied? ____ Continued? ____

14. Judicial experience: Number of years ____

Part II: Questionnaire on Patient Characteristics

Please rate the patient whose hearing you have just completed, according to the categories below; please rate every characteristic, no matter how feebly it seems to fit this particular patient. Indicate your rating by circling a number from 1 to 7, where 4 is the half-way point. Please don't use the blanks on the right just yet.

1. well known to you   not well known to you
   1   2   3   4   5   6   7 _____

2. has adequate place to live   no adequate place to live
   1   2   3   4   5   6   7 _____

3. family or friends   family or friends
   favor release   favor commitment
   1   2   3   4   5   6   7 _____

4. disheveled-looking   appears well-groomed
   1   2   3   4   5   6   7 _____

5. seriously disturbed   composed
   1   2   3   4   5   7 _____

6. many security guards   few security guards
   appear with patient   appear with patient
   1   2   3   4   5   6   7 _____

7. cooperative in hearing   uncooperative
   1   2   3   4   5   6   7 _____

8. able to take care of self   not able to take care of self
   1   2   3   4   5   6   7 _____

9. psychiatrist's opinion is   psychiatrist's opinion is
   convincing   not convincing
   1   2   3   4   5   6   7 _____

10. frightening   not frightening
   1   2   3   4   5   6   7 _____

11. capable of work   not capable of work
   1   2   3   4   5   6   7 _____

12. acts of extreme physical   no more than
   violence done   verbal threats
   1   2   3   4   5   6   7 _____

13. dangerous to others   not dangerous to others
   1   2   3   4   5   6   7 _____

14. would be a reliable outpatient
would not be a reliable outpatient
1   2   3   4   5   6   7 _____

15. recent past evidence of violent behavior
only remote past evidence of violent behavior
1   2   3   4   5   6   7 _____

16. extreme self-destructive behavior
only threats of self-destructive behavior
1   2   3   4   5   6   7 _____

17. can count on patient to take medications
cannot count on patients to take medications
1   2   3   4   5   6   7 _____

18. recent past evidence of self-harm
remote past evidence of self-harm
1   2   3   4   5   6   7 _____

19. prognosis good
prognosis poor
1   2   3   4   5   6   7 _____

20. dangerous to self
not dangerous to self
1   2   3   4   5   6   7 _____

21. likable
not likable
1   2   3   4   5   6   7 _____

22. patient in great suffering
not suffering
1   2   3   4   5   6   7 _____

23. patient seems competent
patient seems incompetent
1   2   3   4   5   6   7 _____

24. patient predictable
patient unpredictable
1   2   3   4   5   6   7 _____

25. quality of care in referring institution good
quality of care in referring institution poor
1   2   3   4   5   6   7 _____

Part III: Weight of Patient Variables in the Decision

Please say how important each of the above factors (Part II) is in making your decision. To the right of each characteristic is a blank. Put a number from minus 100 (− 100) to plus 100 (+ 100) there, where the number − 100 means that this fact about the patient was strongly *against* commitment in your thinking, and + 100 means that the fact is strongly *for* committing the patient, and 0 means the fact has no bearing at all on your decision. Please go back now and fill in your numbers.

Part IV: Difficulty

How much difficulty did you have in reaching your decision?

no difficulty   much difficulty

1   2   3   4   5   6   7

chapter 6.
MAKING TREATMENT DECISIONS

A young male college student was brought into a psychiatric clinic on a weekend by the police and left handcuffed to a chair. The resident who was on call that night observed that the man was well-dressed and sitting quietly. Upon finding that there was no available information about the student, the resident tried to talk to him. The man refused to talk, however, unless his handcuffs were taken off. The resident explained that he would first like to find out why the student had been brought to the clinic. Again the man refused to talk while handcuffed. Although sympathetic, the resident was reluctant to release the student, realizing that he had been brought in handcuffed by the police and that security might be inadequate, should he try to escape. Trying to convince the student to communicate, the resident explained that he would not agree to remove the handcuffs until they had talked, because he did not know whether the student could control himself. The student still insisted on having the handcuffs taken off first. As a last resort, the resident said that it was the student's responsibility to demonstrate, by first talking to the resident, that he would be able to control himself. The man refused and was hospitalized.

◆

Both patients and clinicians find it difficult to acknowledge the uncertainty inherent in illness and its treatment. In the above example, the resident and the patient faced complex decisions in a situation that was fraught with uncertainty for each of them. The resident had to decide whether or not to trust the patient's apparent self-control. Premature removal of the handcuffs might have put both patient and resident in danger, but unnecessary use of restraint would have robbed the man of his right to bodily freedom. The resident's decision posed an equally difficult choice for the patient: whether to insist on his right to be free of restraints before talking or give up that right long enough to demonstrate his self-control to the resident's satisfaction. The resident had to reckon with the uncertainty of external control as a barometer of internal control, the patient with the uncertainty of a promise as a reflection of intention. For both patient and physician, the uncertainty centered on a relationship that demanded trust between two strangers.

Unconscious wishes for certainty and perfection in medical care often foster unrealistic hopes in both patient and physician. The

Presented at the Society for Medical Decision Making meetings, November 1983, Toronto, Canada. (Published in abstract form: Med Decis Making 1983;3:539.)

patient, wishing to be cured, hopes to receive perfect care, and the physician, wishing to cure, hopes to provide perfect treatment. If they fail to acknowledge the uncertainty that characterizes all human transactions, including medical care, these hopes will solidify into expectations and are bound to be disappointed. Malpractice litigation and defensive medical practice represent the failed expectations of patient and clinician, respectively.

In reality, treatment always carries potential risks as well as benefits. Every difficult treatment decision is a tragic choice; that is, a choice between two alternatives, both of which may have tragic consequences. In the above example, release of the patient might have resulted in serious harm or even death (to the patient or others). Hospitalization deprived the patient of his freedom and his right to decide for himself; it also carried the risk of adverse emotional consequences (e.g., regression).

In the previous chapter we examined the ways in which clinicians, patients, and judges frame decision making with respect to involuntary commitment, which represents a tragic choice between autonomy and protection. Here we consider decisions about treatment in a similar light. First, how do clinicians and judges weigh the risks and benefits of treatment in relation to the tragic choice posed by a decision about the use of neuroleptic (antipsychotic) medications? Second, how is the principle of triage (allocation of limited medical resources) used and misused in making decisions about "difficult" patients, where continued hospitalization and discharge may have equally tragic consequences? Third, why do some patients decide to refuse treatment, and what are the clinical implications of validating or challenging treatment refusal, in light of the tension between protection and autonomy? In discussing these topics, we will pay special attention to the influences—professional, social, linguistic, systemic, etc.—that impinge on treatment decisions.

RISK PERCEPTION AND DECISIONS ABOUT TREATMENT

The use of neuroleptic medications in the treatment of serious mental illness, such as schizophrenia, presents a difficult problem in medicolegal decision making. Whether one views schizophrenia and other thought disorders as primarily physiological or psychological in nature, most studies have confirmed the value of neuroleptics in decreasing psychosis associated with these disorders and, perhaps more important, shortening the length of stay in the hospital. Unfortunately, neuroleptics do not provide a cure, and they often have side effects, some of which may be permanent. The use of neuroleptic medications to ameliorate psychosis thus poses a complex treatment decision for clinicians. In some circumstances, judges may also have to weigh the risks and benefits of neuroleptic treatment—for example, if a patient refuses treatment that the clinician believes is necessary and a judge must rule on the matter, or if a poor outcome prompts a malpractice claim that is brought to court.

Clinical and Judicial Perceptions of Risk

How do clinicians and judges evaluate the risks and benefits of neuroleptic treatment for psychotic patients? In other words, how do the two professions estimate the risk associated with neuroleptic drugs, and how much risk is considered acceptable? To answer this question, the Program in Psychiatry and the Law designed a study to compare the ways in which clinicians and judges perceive risks (1). We hypothesized that, because of differences in training and perspective, the two professions would evaluate the benefits and risks of treatment differently. Specifically, we expected that judges would assign a greater weight to the risks associated with neuroleptic medications, as compared with psychiatrists. In addition, we hypothesized that the language used to frame the treatment question would influence the perception of risk.

To test these hypotheses, we presented psychiatrists and judges (who were attending seminars on medicolegal issues) with the following clinical vignette concerning a common problem in neuroleptic treatment:

A [20/40/70]-year-old patient of yours becomes violently psychotic when taking any less than a neuroleptic equivalent of 400 mg of Thorazine (a commonly prescribed antipsychotic medication). As you know, Thorazine is effective in reducing psychotic behavior, but its continuing use is associated with tardive dyskinesia (involuntary muscle spasm).

We then asked two questions about this case:

1. What probability of tardive dyskinesia would you [risk/accept] to prevent recurrence of psychosis in this [20/40/70]-year-old patient?
2. What is the probability that this patient will get tardive dyskinesia if continued on medication?

The brackets in the vignette and in Question 1 indicate different versions of the questionnaire given to subgroups of respondents. We expected the respondents to perceive the risks differently according to the age of the patient (20, 40, or 70 years old), since the relationship between advancing age and an increased prevalence of tardive dyskinesia is well-documented (2, 3).

We also expected the variation in language ("What probability of tardive dyskinesia would you risk/accept?") to influence the perception of risk.

From the responses to these questions we obtained three dependent variables. The first was a percentage measure (0 to 100%) of the respondent's willingness to prescribe the drug, given the risk of tardive dyskinesia (Question 1). The second variable was the respondent's estimate of the actual probability (0 to 100%) that the drug would induce tardive dyskinesia (Question 2). By subtracting the value for the second variable from the value for the first, we obtained an adjusted value representing the inferred treatment decision, given the perceived risks and benefits of the medication. A positive value meant that the respondent believed the benefits outweighed the risks, implying a decision to recommend treatment with Thorazine. A negative value reflected the respondent's perception that the risks outweighed the benefits, justifying a decision not to recommend Thorazine.

We gave the questionnaire to a total of 70 psychiatrists and 41 judges. The two groups generally agreed in their opinions about an acceptable level of risk (Question 1). On average, the psychiatrists felt that a 51% risk of tardive dyskinesia was acceptable for treatment that would prevent recurrent psychosis; the judges reported a risk threshold that was only slightly lower, at 48%. However, the two groups differed greatly in their estimates of the probability that tardive dyskinesia would occur with continued medication (Question 2). The psychiatrists gave an average estimated probability of 25%, as compared with 63% for the judges.

These responses were then used to calculate the adjusted expressions from which we inferred the respondents' treatment decisions. A positive adjusted value suggested a positive treatment decision (i.e., a decision to prescribe Thorazine); a negative adjusted value suggested a negative decision (a decision not to prescribe the drug). For example, if a respondent would accept a 50% chance of complications (Question 1) and believed that use of neuroleptic medication carried a 30% risk of tardive dyskinesia (Question 2), the adjusted expression had a value of $+20$ ($50 - 30$), suggesting that this individual considered the benefits of Thorazine to outweigh its risks. In the case of a respondent whose level of acceptable risk was 45% and who estimated a 60% risk of tardive dyskinesia, the adjusted expression had a value of -15 ($45 - 60$), indicating a perception that the risks outweighed the benefits of treatment.

These two examples roughly correspond to the average responses given by the psychiatrists and judges, respectively, who participated in our study. The data show that 87% of the psychiatrists (59 of 68) had a positive adjusted expression, representing a risk-benefit analysis that would justify treatment with Thorazine. In contrast, only 41% of the judges (14 of 34) had a positive adjusted expression, whereas 59% (20 of 34) had a negative adjusted expression, reflecting a risk-benefit analysis that would not justify neuroleptic treatment. (Nine subjects were dropped from the analysis because they failed to answer both questions.)

Thus, although the judges and psychiatrists had similar views on what constitutes an acceptable risk, they had quite different views on the actual magnitude of the risk associated with the use of neuroleptics, suggesting a disparity in the treatment decisions that the two groups might be expected to make.

In designing this study, we attempted to measure two elements of decision making with respect to neuroleptic treatment: the level of risk considered acceptable in order to obtain the benefit of treatment and the actual level of risk thought to be associated with treatment. Both elements are largely subjective, filtered through an individual's unique faculties of perception, yet the second—the actual risk—is at least potentially more susceptible to empirical adjustment than the first. It was this second element, not the first, that differentiated clinical and legal perspectives on the appropriate use of neuroleptic treatment. Psychiatrists and judges generally agreed on the level of risk that they would tolerate in order to prevent psychosis, but they parted ways on the actual risk that neuroleptic agents pose.

Various clinical studies have reported a 5 to 20% probability of tardive dyskinesia as a complication of neuroleptic treatment, yet the judges in our study gave an average estimate of 62%. In a risk-benefit analysis this sizable overestimate would be likely to tip the scales toward a decision not to use neuroleptics.

Of course, in many judicial hearings expert witnesses can report the probability range established by empirical research, giving the judge an opportunity to correct an intuitive overestimate. Nevertheless, studies conducted by cognitive psychologists suggest that people are often reluctant to revise their initial probability estimates (4, 5). Moreover, if the occasion for the judicial hearing is a malpractice claim in the wake of a tragic outcome, hindsight bias may tend to make the negative outcome seem inevitable in retrospect (6).

The data from our study suggest that perceptions of risk—and, consequently, decisions about treatment—are affected by occupational perspective. Differences between medical and legal perspectives on the risks of treatment become problematic when treatment decisions enter the legal arena. If psychiatrists and judges perceive the risks of neuroleptic treatment so differently, as the data from our study imply, then they may well end up on opposing sides of a treatment decision.

Moreover, judicial assessments of risk are subject to an obvious but often overlooked structural element of the litigation: no one seeks legal action for a benefit. Like many other forms of litigation, malpractice focuses on harms—that is, the negative consequences of a risk—not on benefits. Thus, the courts tend to be more attuned to the potential harm of treatment than to its benefits.

In addition to these influences, courts face an asymmetry native to the particular tragic choice of neuroleptic treatment for schizophrenia: the "harms of treatment" are concrete, whereas the "harms of no treatment" are abstract. The harms of tardive dyskinesia can be demonstrated by bringing the patient into the courtroom and pointing out the abnormal movements that characterize the disorder. It would be difficult and perhaps unethical, however, to do the same with untreated psychosis. Moreover, a courtroom demonstration would fail to point out many of the harms of serious mental illness that goes untreated, including severe stigma, social alienation, loss of employment, homelessness, and unnecessarily long hospital stays. The drama of the concrete overwhelms the abstract.

The same problem occurs in trying to demonstrate the benefits of treatment as compared with its risks. Again, the harmful consequences of a treatment risk (tardive dyskinesia) can literally be brought before the court, but the benefit of treatment—say, ten years of untroubled life in the community without rehospitalization—is not comparably demonstrable.

To complicate matters further, neuroleptic treatment has figured prominently in recent malpractice litigation, and many physicians have begun to revise their perception of the risk associated with neuroleptics. These drugs are now perceived as posing a dual risk: the clinical risk of tardive dyskinesia for the patient, and the legal risk of a malpractice claim for the physician. Fearful of the legal risk, some physicians may be tempted to make treatment decisions on the basis of what they believe a judge (or jury) would consider appropriate medical practice. In other works, they may gauge the risks of neuroleptic treatment by a legal, not a clinical, measure. Ironically, by allowing their own legal interests to eclipse the medical interests of their patients, these physicians actually make themselves more rather than less vulnerable to malpractice litigation (see Chapter 11).

The Effect of Language on Risk Perception

Our study also suggests that treatment decisions are affected by the use of language. What we are willing to risk and what we are willing to accept are not necessarily the same. Each term has a range of connotations, which take on different shadings of meaning according to the situation and the person. Distinctive orientations influenced by language may, in turn, foster different patterns of responses to the uncertainty surrounding decision making.

In our study the term "accept" was associated with a more conservative approach to treatment decisions than the word "risk." A comparison of the questionnaire responses by language subgroup (i.e., the group of subjects who were asked what probability of tardive dyskinesia they would accept and the group asked what probability they would risk) showed that the "risk" group tended to have a higher risk threshold than the "accept" group. On average, subjects in the first group would risk a 57% probability of tardive dyskinesia, whereas those in the second group would accept only a 44% probability. The actual probability estimates given by the two groups were 40 and 35%, respectively. Again, by subtracting the probability estimate from the risk threshold, we arrived at the inferred treatment decision. Although both groups had positive adjusted expressions, suggesting a decision to prescribe Thorazine, the value for the risk group was twice as high as the value for the accept group (17% versus 8%, respectively).

A possible explanation for this difference in responses is that the word "risk" is more likely to elicit an awareness of all the potential problems in a situation. The decision maker who is aware of these problems can then consciously consider them and explore options that might reduce the risk involved, leading to a greater sense of safety and control in arriving at a decision. In contrast, the term accept may function as a euphemism, allowing the decision maker to avoid confronting the uncertainty that is an inevitable part of any treatment decision.

This explanation is only conjectural, of course. The important point is that language influences perceptions of risk. Thus, a treatment decision may hinge not only on the conceptual approach that one uses to frame the risks and benefits of the treatment but also on the linguistic terms in which they are framed. No analysis of risks and benefits is impervious to the bias of language. Even quantitative expressions of probability are rooted in a linguistic formulation of the problem to be solved and the elements of that problem.

In view of our findings, clinicians and judges making difficult treatment decisions might do well to articulate the choices they face in more than one way (e.g., "What probability of a particular side effect or outcome am I willing to risk? What probability am I willing to accept?"). Any disparity in the answers may reveal a tendency either to overemphasize the extent of one's control in an uncertain situation or to retreat from the limits of that control.

In the next section we extend this discussion of risk perceptions to the use of triage in making treatment decisions.

TRIAGE AND PSYCHIATRIC TREATMENT DECISIONS

A French word meaning "sorting" or "choice selection," triage refers to a process of allocating limited medical resources to a large numbers of patients (7). The concept of triage originated on the battlefield. According to a NATO handbook entitled *Emergency War Surgery:*

[Triage] is based on the principle of accomplishing the greatest good for the greatest number of wounded and injured men in the special circumstances of warfare at a particular time. The decision which must be made concerns the need for resuscitation, the need for emergency surgery and the futility of surgery because of the intrinsic lethality of the wound. Sorting also involves the establishment of priorities for treatment and evacuation. (8)

Patients are generally sorted into three categories: those with minimal injuries that do not require immediate attention, those with severe injuries and a poor chance of survival even with treatment, and those whose survival may depend on immediate treatment (8).

Triage has become an established approach to medical decision making in hospital emergency rooms and other general medical settings where the need for emergency care may outstrip the available resources in the event of a disaster. The concept has also been applied to the many underfunded mental health centers where staff are besieged by the sheer numbers of patients in need.

Although the triage model may be quite useful under these circumstances (9), it does pose special clinical and ethical pitfalls because of the emotional exchange between clinician and patient, which plays a vital role in the treatment of mental illness. The following case exemplifies some of these pitfalls:

A 29-year-old man has been hospitalized for eight months on the crowded inpatient unit of a state-funded mental health center. The patient is chronically ill, recalcitrant, and often assaultive to other patients and staff. As a child, he was neglected by his mother, who was preoccupied with the patient's congenitally disabled twin brother, and beaten by his father.

Problems with this patient have dominated the discussions at many staff meetings. Members of the staff who care for the patient feel overwhelmed, depleted, and angry. At one of these meetings, a resident involved in the case asks whether the patient should continue to be treated "at the expense of other patients," especially in light of the limited resources available on the inpatient unit. The staff members agree that the patient is resistant to treatment and jeopardizes the care of the other patients on the unit. They feel he should be transferred to the state hospital, which is better equipped to provide the care that he requires.

Clinical Implications of Triage

Caught up with the triage question posed by the resident (i.e., allocation of scarce resources where they can do the most good), the staff fails to consider the interaction between the patient's pathology and the use of triage to justify a treatment decision. Instead of exploring the interpersonal dynamics of the case (e.g., the way in which the patient reenacts on the ward his earlier rejection at the hands of his parents), they conclude prematurely that the patient has a damaging "environmental impact" and should be transferred elsewhere.

Group dynamics frequently come into play in the use of triage to make a treatment decision. Attempts to expel a member of a group are common in the face of perceived scarcity. The individual chosen for expulsion may be unable to resist the role of scapegoat or may even, perhaps unconsciously, invite it. Unfamiliarity and uniqueness tend to provoke anxiety in a group, and the scapegoat is often a newcomer; a member who is on the fringes of the group, behaviorally or otherwise; or someone who has distinguishing characteristics that become repugnant to the group.

From an ethological perspective, mental illness is the consequence of an intrafamilial struggle for existence (10). An individual who has been singled out by the family as the cause of its problems may provoke the same unintentional scapegoating in other social contexts. Estranged from the family and from society, the mentally ill patient recreates this familiar experience in the hospital. In a complementary manner, a difficult patient who provokes anxiety, anger, and blame in the staff may be perceived as threatening and hopeless, the embodiment of all the problems on the unit that the staff feels powerless to solve.

The institutionalized mentally ill are particularly susceptible to these prejudicial implications of triage. Indeed, unlikability and estrangement can function in practice as a partial definition of mental illness. Studies have shown that patients reported to be unlikable by residents also tend to be judged in need of commitment (11) and that patients who elicit negative reactions are more likely to commit suicide than those evoking positive reactions (12, 13).

In view of the close link between unlikability and pathology, the use of triage to make treatment decisions about institutionalized patients should be examined as a possible response to the negative feelings that such patients may provoke in the hospital staff. Feelings of helplessness and frustration in treating the chronically ill or anxiety about safety in caring for violent patients may be blamed on lack of external resources. Similarly, if not acknowledged, overidentification with a patient's feeling of helplessness may be perceived as an external crisis in the milieu. Under these circumstances, triage offers a back door out of the decision-making process, preempting a thorough exploration of the possible options for treatment.

Triage may also be invoked as a way of avoiding full therapeutic engagement with patients seen as too difficult or sick to treat. By casting the problem in terms of selective use of scarce resources, triage offers an acceptable outlet for the uncomfortable feelings that such resistance evokes in the clinician (14).

Even when the shift from clinical considerations to a patient's "environmental impact" is made on reasonable grounds, losses are suffered in the process. In focusing on the well-being of the unit or institution as a whole, staff members may inadvertently distance themselves from the patient in question, exacerbating that individual's difficulty in learning the basic human skill of survival through cooperation.

Moreover, the transfer of a patient deemed untreatable or dangerous to other patients results in a discontinuity of care that carries large costs of its own. Such patients are generally transferred to less stimulating settings (e.g., a locked ward for chronically ill patients or a maximum security hospital). However scrupulous the staff is in preparing for a transfer, the patient is likely to feel rejected and abandoned. In view of the inherent costs of referral or transfer, such a course of action should be undertaken only after a careful evaluation has shown that these costs are justified by the benefits (15).

Group theory suggests that when one member of the group is expelled, that individual is not the only one who suffers. The initial relief that the group experiences after eliminating the difficult member is replaced by guilt and by regret at the missed opportunity to resolve the conflicts that the individual has provoked. The indiscriminate use of triage in the mental health setting may have similar effects on both patients and staff.

In practice, of course, psychiatry, like politics, is the art of the possible, and limited resources certainly play a critical part in determining what is possible. Moreover, every treatment team has its limits of tolerance under pressure. The point that we want to stress is that triage is sometimes used prematurely, which precludes a multidimensional examination of the interactions between patient and staff.

Ethical Implications of Triage

Treatment decisions made by triage have ethical as well as therapeutic and practical implications. Triage represents a modified version of a simple rule: the greater the need, the greater the resources to be applied. Decision making by triage follows this reasoning up to the point where a patient's ability to survive (or to benefit from treatment) is questionable. At that point, the principle of triage calls for "fewer" rather than more resources to be applied to the care of the patient. Thus, a patient in extremis might be denied treatment on the grounds that a disproportionate expenditure of limited resources to save one patient would cause more damage to other patients (in the aggregate) than would be prevented by saving the single patient in question. In a sudden disaster, such as an earthquake or fire involving large numbers of casualties and limited available resources, the need for such tragic choices is incontestable (16). When used in a stable mental health setting to justify decisions about patients viewed as difficult, dangerous, or untreatable, however, triage raises serious ethical questions (17–20).

First, the judgment that a patient is beyond help is inevitably a probabilistic one (see the discussion of probability in Chapter 2). Like any other clinical judgment, it is a question not of absolute certainty but of a greater or lesser degree of probability (21). Decisions made by triage are based on such implicitly probabilistic judgments—for example, that there is a 90, 95, or 99% probability that a patient will not survive or improve. Balancing such estimates against the probabilities of saving other patients, as well as comparing the value of the lives saved, is a delicate matter.

Moreover, while the anticipated outcome (i.e., death or lack of improvement) is not absolutely certain to occur, the assumption that it will occur may become a self-fulfilling prophecy. The decision to treat a patient as hopeless may itself (for whatever organic and psychological reasons) close the gap from, say, a 95% probability of a tragic outcome to a 100% probability. Just as in Paris before World War I the word "triage" meant "the sorting out and throwing away of wilted or 'dead' produce" (22), today there is cause for concern that the labeling of people as dead (or incurable) will leave them fit only for discard. The psychology of survival during the Holocaust confirms that people who are labeled as dead either by themselves or by others tend to engage in a powerful form of self-fulfilling prophecy (23–25).

Finally, we need to ask whether our moral responsibility toward individual patients extends beyond "accomplishing the greatest good for the greatest number" (8). Although this may be a useful decision rule, it is not fully sufficient in a society that values the rights of minorities, including the smallest minority—the individual. As a society, then, we must judge psychiatric and other health care institutions not only by how well they serve patients in the aggregate but also by how well they discharge their special duties on behalf of those individuals who are worst off, the most unfortunate.

Safeguards for Using Triage

Triage can be a valuable decision rule under certain circumstances, but it must never be used as a camouflage for giving up on difficult patients. Where resources are severely limited, we need decision rules that (when necessary) take these limits into account, but we must safeguard against the automatic resort to triage reasoning. Triage must be used consciously and critically when making treatment decisions that concern "difficult" patients. The best antidote to the uncritical use of triage is a high degree of precision in framing the choices involved. This, in turn, requires self-knowledge and self-scrutiny with respect to the feelings that difficult patients arouse.

Triage is not a moral principle but rather a strategy for serving the larger purpose of healing and reducing suffering in emergencies when resources are limited. Transplanted to the psychiatric setting, triage must be used with great care. Three moral principles that can help frame the ethical use of triage are beneficence, respect for persons, and justice.

The principle of beneficence suggests avoiding harm to others and helping them whenever possible. In the mental health setting, vigilance is needed to prevent avoidance of difficult clinical issues under the guise of "limited resources." It is essential to specify the way in which resources expended on one patient will detract from the care of other patients and to determine whether that view has a counterpart in clinical reality.

Similarly, the claim that a patient is untreatable must be subjected to the same scrutiny under conditions of triage as in any other clinical situation, since countertransference operates in all clinical interactions, including triage.

The principle of respect implies that persons should be treated as ends in themselves rather than simply as means to the achievement of an end (e.g., the welfare of others) or units in a cost-benefit equation. Although triage is commonly assumed to be equivalent to cost-benefit analysis, it is more accurate to think of it as an attempt to resolve the tension between two sets of rights: the right of an individual patient to receive treatment and the right of other patients not to have that treatment proffered at their expense.

The principle of justice, which refers to a fair distribution of benefits and burdens within a community, requires that an unequal allocation of clinical resources be justified in terms of the welfare of the least fortunate patients. One rule of thumb is to ask how a treatment decision will alter the resources available not only for the care of the average patient but also for the care of the most unfortunate or most difficult patient. To avoid the pitfall of overidentification with the interests of the healthier patients on the ward, the staff might ask themselves whether they would make the same triage decision if they were playing a lottery in which one possible outcome was that they would each share the fate of the difficult patient in question (26).

To summarize, triage was designed as a last resort strategy for making treatment decisions where the need for care overwhelms the resources available to provide it. In the mental health setting triage presents special clinical and ethical problems that must be examined carefully. The ethical principles outlined above, combined with clinical vigilance and practical caution, should help safeguard the use of triage as a justification for making treatment decisions about difficult patients.

So far we have examined a variety of issues surrounding the treatment decisions that a clinician or clinical staff makes. In the next section we consider the patient's decision to refuse the treatment that has been recommended by the clinician.

TREATMENT REFUSAL

Despite the clinician's efforts to choose the best treatment for the patient, using a careful cost-benefit analysis, the patient may refuse the recommended treatment. In some cases, the patient simply disagrees with the clinician's assessment of costs and benefits (e.g., regarding side effects); in other cases, the patient's expectations of the treatment differ from the clinician's because of different cultural, religious, or other perspectives. Sometimes, however, the patient's refusal has clinical underpinnings. For example, the patient may be too psychotic or paranoid to form the alliance necessary for a realistic appraisal of the treatment decision. Moreover, some patients are unable to accept the reality of their illness and the need for treatment. Indeed, in Chapter 1, Ms. Adams was, in effect, a treatment (or treatment recommendation) refuser.

Clinical Perspectives

If a patient refuses treatment, the clinician can, of course, petition a court to resolve the matter. However, viewing a patient's treatment refusal as purely a legal problem may compromise future therapeutic efforts (27). It is important to examine the clinical issues underlying the patient's refusal. Consider the following example:

A patient who had been taking neuroleptic medication for the previous eight months was told by her therapist that he was leaving the clinic and must terminate therapy with her. At the next session the patient told him that the medication was not working because it did not make her feel good. She said that she would only take pills that would make her happy. The therapist explained that no pills would make her feel happy because what she felt was depression over the imminent termination; all her medication did was make her think more clearly. She reluctantly acknowledged that she was thinking more clearly on the medication but that she still felt bad. When the therapist suggested that she was feeling that way because she did not want to lose him, she started to cry. They spent the rest of the session exploring her feelings of loss, and at the end of the hour she agreed to continue taking the neuroleptic.

If the therapist had gone directly to the courts to deal with his patient's refusal of treatment, he would have missed a valuable opportunity to explore the clinical issues threatening the alliance—in this case, the patient's reaction to the therapist's impending departure. Moreover, a premature legal resolution of the problem might well have jeopardized future therapeutic work with the patient.

Before resorting to legal means for circumventing a patient's treatment refusal, the clinician should consider the reasons behind the refusal. Factors that might lead to a refusal of treatment include realistic concerns (e.g., about side effects or autonomy), religious or cultural beliefs, idiosyncratic meanings of treatment for the patient, the effects of transference or countertransference, and familial factors (27).

A patient's refusal of treatment may be motivated by fear of side effects. Most patients have some negative side effects from neuroleptic medications. Tardive dyskinesia is certainly one of the most serious, but a host of others—for example, dystonia (impaired muscle tone), akathisia (motor restlessness), sexual dysfunction, even the possibility of weight gain—may prompt a patient to refuse treatment. All these concerns, however embarrassing or seemingly minor, should be addressed.

Religious or cultural beliefs that might affect the patient's feelings about treatment should also be discussed. Although the views of the Christian Science Church with respect to medication are fairly well-known (and the courts recognize the right of a Christian Scientist to refuse medication), clinicians may not be aware of other deep-seated religious beliefs about medical treatment. Similarly, particular cultural perspectives may be at odds with the recommendation for treatment, which after all is itself embedded in the specific cultural context of Western views on science, medicine, and health care. Thus, the patient's cultural or religious values may lead to an interpretation of treatment benefits and risks that is quite different from the clinician's interpretation.

Some patients refuse treatment because of their feelings about the therapist. For example, a refusal may be prompted by fear that the therapist is trying to invade the patient's body or that acceptance of the medication would be a sign of submission to or merger with the therapist. The patient may respond to the therapist as an intrusive parent trying to dominate the patient-child. Even a vacation by the therapist may elicit responses that lead to treatment refusal.

Countertransference may also prompt a refusal of treatment. For example, a patient may start to refuse medication if the therapist is repeatedly late or cancels appointments. Sensing that the therapist is angry or has lost interest, the patient uses refusal as a way to retaliate.

Preservation of the sick role can be a strong motive in the psychotic patient's refusal of psychotropic medication. Under stress, the patient may take refuge in the defenses that psychosis provides or seek escape in manic behavior. To return to the case example provided earlier, medication made the patient think more clearly, but clearer thinking gave her less protection from the uncomfortable feelings that her therapist's imminent departure had stirred in her.

In some cases, the patient's family plays an important role in treatment refusal. Families with symbiotic relationships may have an unconscious need to keep the patient ill. For example, a parent who feels ambivalent about separating from an adult child might discourage the use of medication because it represents the child's diminishing dependence on the parent.

In summary, many factors can contribute to a patient's refusal of treatment. The clinician should consider these factors carefully before seeking a legal resolution to the problem of treatment refusal. The courts play an important role, especially in emergencies, but a premature legal solution to a clinical problem of treatment refusal may sacrifice long-term therapeutic gains for a short-term fix.

Legal Perspectives

The right to refuse treatment is based both in common law and in constitutional law. Common law holds that treatment without consent is a form of illegal touching, which is a civil wrong, or tort. Yet until recent decades, involuntary treatment of hospitalized psychiatric patients was acceptable practice. The letter of the law on this point was ignored both by the psychiatric profession and by the courts (28).

The civil rights movement in the 1960s brought attention to the rights of patients, among them the right to refuse treatment. In 1964 the U.S. Supreme Court ruled that the Bill of Rights includes a right to privacy (29). Patient advocates argued that involuntary administration of neuroleptic drugs, for example, violated the privacy of the patient's body and person (28). *Rennie v Klein* invoked this interpretation of involuntary treatment, citing a constitutional basis for the patient's right to refuse treatment (30).

In *Rogers v Okin* the court relied on a more problematic interpretation, ruling that involuntary treatment is a violation of the constitutional right to freedom of speech and thought (31). According to this line of reasoning, neuroleptic drugs alter the mind, and involuntary administration of such drugs interferes with the First Amendment right to freedom of thought (28). The clinical evidence on how neuroleptic agents operate, however, does not support their depiction as mind-altering drugs in this sense (32–35).

Particular legal interpretations aside, the right to refuse treatment is clearly established in law, and most people would agree that such a right is essential in our society, which places a high value on individual autonomy and privacy. Where the right to refuse treatment engenders complex medicolegal dilemmas is at its periphery—where rights come face to face with needs. For example, treatment refusal by a competent, otherwise healthy individual who is offered antidepressant medication for mild depression poses no serious clinical or legal problems. That person is exercising his or her right to refuse treatment in a competent and presumably reasonable manner. However, treatment refusal by a severely psychotic, paranoid patient, who is convinced that the neuroleptic medication recommended by the clinician is actually a deadly poison, presents a difficult problem. On the one hand, this patient, like the first, is exercising the right to refuse treatment. On the other hand, the patient is desperately in need of that treatment. Should the need overpower the right in this case? The question is even more complex if one considers that the patient's refusal is motivated by paranoia, which is part of the very illness that the treatment would help ameliorate.

One of the guideposts marking the periphery of rights in relation to needs is the medical urgency of a particular situation. In the eyes of the law, need takes precedence over right in an emergency. Thus, if a patient's life is in danger, the clinician not only can but must provide immediate treatment, overriding the informed consent procedure, if necessary, and the patient's right to refuse treatment. Unfortunately, however, even this presumably clear delineation between rights and needs can be murky, since the legal definition of an emergency may not coincide with the clinical definition (36).

Another guidepost is competence. In the examples given above, the first patient is competent to accept or refuse treatment and to assume responsibility for that decision. The second patient has been rendered incompetent by psychiatric illness, making it necessary to find a competent surrogate to accept or refuse treatment on behalf of the patient. This, however, does not resolve the dilemma; it simply passes it along to the vicarious decision maker. The next chapter explores some of the clinical and legal complexities of guardianship under these circumstances.

The fundamental problem with legislation and litigation concerning the right to refuse treatment is that they legalize an important area of negotiation between doctor and patient. The focus of interaction is shifted from a medical setting to the courtroom, and the relationship is formally established as adversarial. Ironically, although patients' rights advocates argue that litigation concerning the right to refuse treatment promotes a dialogue between physician and patient, in fact just the opposite occurs. All too often, the legal procedures for resolving the issue are cumbersome and time-consuming. Since the physician whose patient refuses treatment must spend considerable time filling out forms, meeting with attorneys, and going to hearings, less rather than more time is devoted to engaging in a dialogue with the patient.

At a more subtle level, the adversarial nature of right to refuse treatment proceedings may alienate the physician from the patient, undermining attempts to establish or maintain a therapeutic alliance. The relationship between physician and patient may become oppositional even though both wish to reach a reasonable solution. According to one study of inpatients (37), for example, patients may use treatment refusal as a vehicle for expressing feelings of anger or fear. By prematurely seeking a legal solution to the dispute, the physician bypasses an opportunity to explore the underlying clinical issues, as well as resolve the dispute itself through discussion and negotiation with the patient.

In dealing with treatment refusal, physicians may also feel "caught between torts," as one resident described it. On one side are laws that protect patients from being treated against their will. On the other side are laws that protect patients from negligence caused by lack of treatment. Counterposed against the right to refuse treatment is the right to treatment. A recent study, for example, found that failure to treat psychosis was the fourth leading malpractice claim among all psychiatry claims that were closed between 1980 and 1984 (38).

Case law on the right to refuse treatment in large part reflects this polarity, having swung back and forth between a deference to medical judgment and aggressive judicial intervention. In two cases that bear at least indirectly on the question of treatment refusal (39, 40), the U.S. Supreme Court has indicated its willingness to defer to medical opinion as long as it is clearly and demonstrably being exercised in the matter at hand. At the lower court level, however, the pendulum has swung both toward and away from this position. As Miller and associates have pointed out (41), the recent trend among state courts is to establish greater judicial oversight and more restrictive procedures for treating patients against their will.

In *Project Release v Prevost* (42), for example, a federal circuit court in New York found that New York's medically based two-physician model for ruling on treatment refusal represented adequate due process to protect the patient. At the state level, in contrast, the New York Court of Appeals essentially overturned this ruling in *Rivers v Katz* (43) by setting a judicially based standard in place. Similarly, in Wisconsin a federal district court ruled in the important case of *Stensvad v Reivitz* (44) that a committed patient could be treated involuntarily because "[n]on-consensual treatment is what involuntary commitment is all about." A subsequent case at the state level, *Jones v Gerhardstein* (45), knocked the pendulum back the other way by establishing a more restrictive judicial standard and, in effect, again separating treatment from commitment.

It may be impossible to draw any firm conclusions in a field that is so dramatically in flux. Decisions made within one or two years of each other can turn an entire line of reasoning, buttressed by both philosophical justification and existing case law, completely on its head by posing equally plausible but conflicting philosophical tenets and legal precedent. Perhaps, then, this is the conclusion: there are many possible concepts of how best to address treatment refusal in a just and humane way, and many different procedural approaches to this question have satisfied decision makers of equal good will. No one approach is set in stone. It remains essential, however, that the physician exhaust every clinical approach to resolving the issue of treatment refusal before resorting to a legal resolution, whatever the prevailing judicial perspective at the time.

REFERENCES
 1. Bursztajn H, Chanowitz B, Kaplan E, Gutheil TG, Hamm RM. Contrasting risk perceptions between medical and legal professionals regarding use of antipsychotic medication. Unpublished paper, August 1986.
 2. Mukherjee S, Rosen AM, Cardenas C, Varia V, Olarte S. Tardive dyskinesia in

psychiatric outpatients: a study of prevalence and association with demographic, clinical and drug history variables. Arch Gen Psychiatry 1982; 39:466–469.

3. Kane JM, Smith JM. Tardive dyskinesia: prevalence and risk factors, 1959 to 1979. Arch Gen Psychiatry 1982; 39:473–481.

4. Kahneman D, Tversky A. Prospect theory. Econometrica 1979; 47:263–292.

5. Edwards W. Conservatism in human information processing. In: Kleinmutz B, ed. Formal representation of human judgment. New York: Wiley, 1968.

6. Fischhoff B, Lichtenstein S, Slovic P, Derby SL, Keeney RL. Acceptable risk. Cambridge, UK: Cambridge University Press, 1981.

7. Adapted from Bursztajn H, Gutheil TG, Barnard D, Brodksy A, Levi LM. Medical decision making by triage: lessons from in-patient psychiatry. Unpublished paper, July 1986.

8. Sorting of casualties. In: Emergency war surgery (U.S. issue of NATO handbook for medical personnel). Washington, D.C.: U.S. Government Printing Office, 1975, p. 153.

9. Edelwich J, Brodsky A. Burnout: stages of disillusionment in the helping professions. New York: Human Sciences Press, 1980.

10. Sloman L. Intrafamilial struggles for power: an ethological perspective. Int J Fam Psychiatry 1981; 2:13–33.

11. Hamm RM, Bursztajn H, Appelbaum PS, Gutheil TG, Mills MJ. Regression and introspection in the analysis of clinical decision making: the case of the three-day paper. Presented at the First International Congress for Psychiatry, Ethics, and the Law, Haifa, Israel, 1983.

12. Motto JA, Heilbron DC, Juster RP, Bostrom AG. Suicide risk assessment: development of a clinical instrument. In: Proceedings of the 14th Annual Meeting of the American Association of Suicidology, Albuquerque, New Mexico, 1981, pp. 11–14.

13. Havens LL. The anatomy of a suicide. N Engl J Med 1965; 272:401–406.

14. Kubie LS. The retreat from patients. Arch Gen Psychiatry 1971; 24:98–106.

15. Edelwich J, Brodsky A. Sexual dilemmas for the helping professional. New York: Brunner/Mazel, 1982.

16. Calabrese G, Bobbit B. Tragic choices. New York: Norton, 1978.

17. O'Donnell TJ. The morality of triage. Georgetown Med Bull 1960; 14:68–71.

18. Lucas GR, Jr., ed. Triage in medicine and society. Vol. III: Inquiries in medical ethics. Houston: Institute of Religion and Human Development, 1975.

19. Childress JF. Rationing of medical treatment. In: Reich WT, ed. The encyclopedia of bioethics. New York: The Free Press, 1978: 1414–1419.

20. Winslow GR. Triage and justice. Berkeley: University of California Press, 1982.

21. Bursztajn H, Feinbloom RI, Hamm RM, Brodsky A. Medical choices, medical chances: how patients, families, and physicians can cope with uncertainty. New York: Delacorte/Lawrence, 1981.

22. Rund DA, Rausch TS. Triage. St. Louis: Mosby, 1981.

23. O'Keefe DL. Stolen lightening: the social theory of magic. New York: Random House, 1982.

24. Bettelheim B. The informed heart. Glencoe, IL: The Free Press, 1960.

25. Des Pres T. The survivor: an anatomy of life in the death camps. New York: Pocket Books, 1977.

26. Rawls J. A theory of justice. Cambridge, MA: Belknap Press of Harvard University Press, 1971.

27. Appelbaum PS, Gutheil TG. Clinical aspects of treatment refusal. Comp Psychiatry 1982; 23(6):560–566.

28. Stone AA. The right to refuse treatment: why psychiatrists can and should make it work. Arch Gen Psychiatry 1981; 38:358–362.

29. *Griswold v Connecticut,* 381 US 479 (1965). Cited in Stone AA. The right to refuse treatment: why psychiatrists can and should make it work. Arch Gen Psychiatry 1981; 38:358–362.

30. *Rennie v Klein,* 462 F Supp 1131 (D NJ 1979). Cited in Stone AA. The right to refuse treatment: why psychiatrists can and should make it work. Arch Gen Psychiatry 1981; 38:358–362.

31. *Rogers v Okin,* No. 79–1648, 79–1649 (1st Cir 1980). Cited in Stone AA. The right to refuse treatment: why psychiatrists can and should make it work. Arch Gen Psychiatry 1981; 38:358–362.

32. Spohn H, Lacoursiere RB, Thompson K, Coyne L. Phenothiazine effects on psychological and psychophysiological dysfunction in chronic schizophrenics. Arch Gen Psychiatry 1977; 34:633–644.

33. Chapman LJ, Knowles RR. The effects of phenothiazine on disordered thought in schizophrenia. J Consult Psychol 1964; 28:165–169.

34. Meadow A, Donlan PT, Blacker KH. Effects of phenothiazines on anxiety and cognition in schizophrenia. Dis Nerv System 1975; 36:203–208.

35. Hymowitz P, Spohn H. The effects of antipsychotic medication on the linguistic ability of schizophrenics. J Nerv Ment Dis 1980; 168:287–296.

36. Eisenberg GC, Hilliard JT, Gutheil TG. Ethical aspects of the right to refuse medication: a clinicolegal dilemma for the psychiatrist and patient. Psychiatr Q 1981; 53(2):93–99.

37. Appelbaum PS, Gutheil TG. Drug refusal: a study of psychiatric inpatients. Am J Psychiatry 1980; 137(3):340–346.

38. Malpractice claims for suicides top list. Psychiatric News, April 3, 1987, p. 11.

39. *Parham v JR,* 442 US 584 (1979).

40. *Youngberg v Romeo,* 102 SCt 2452 (1982).

41. Miller RD, Rachlin S, Applebaum PS. Patients' rights: the action moves to state courts. Hosp Community Psychiatry 1987; 38(4):343–344.

42. *Project Release v Prevost,* 722 F2d 960 (2d Cir 1983).

43. *Rivers v Katz,* 495 NE2d 337 (NY 1986).

44. *Stensvad v Reivitz,* 601 F Supp 128 (WD Wis 1985).

45. *State of Wisconsin ex rel Jones and Galicia v Gerhardstein,* No 85–1718 (Wis Ct App October 28, 1986).

chapter 7.

DECIDING FOR OTHERS: AUTONOMY AND PROTECTION IN TENSION

Decision making in the medicolegal realm poses a host of ethical, professional, and practical dilemmas. Many of these dilemmas center on the tension between two overriding social values: individual autonomy and protection of life (and health). In the introductory case, for example, Dr. Newell had to decide whether to protect Ms. Adams by hospitalizing her or respect her autonomy by letting her go home. The keystone of autonomy is the right to make decisions about one's own life, including decisions about medical and psychiatric treatment. When an individual's decision-making ability is impaired by mental illness, however, someone else must often stand in as a substitute decision maker.

For clinicians the dilemma is compounded by two potentially conflicting ethical obligations in the practice of medicine (1). The first is represented by the phrase, primum non nocere—first, do no harm—which instructs the clinician to take a conservative approach to medical intervention. The second is the obligation to do everything medically possible to help the patient: this principle suggests a radical approach to intervention (1). In recent decades the growth of medical technology has enormously expanded the opportunities for radical intervention, making the conflict between the two ethical principles of medical practice even more acute. The more we can do, the more difficult it is to decide what we should do, particularly when the decision concerns someone else's life.

How does one make crucial decisions about another person's life? Parents, of course, make decisions for their children until they are old enough to assume that responsibility themselves. But how does one make a decision on behalf of another adult without violating the person's fundamental right to direct the course of his or her life? That is the question at the heart of guardianship.

THE EVOLUTION OF GUARDIANSHIP

The earliest form of guardianship, dating back to Roman history, was designed to protect the property of a person deemed incapable of managing his or her own financial affairs. Extended to Anglo-

American law, guardianship allowed the lord of the manor to assume responsibility for the property of any subjects who could not care for themselves, including minors, persons with physical impairments, and the mentally retarded. In medieval times the king assumed a similar responsibility for the property of his incompetent subjects, among them those who were mentally ill. The purpose of this form of guardianship was to conserve the property for the estate's heirs, dependents, and creditors, and to make sure that the care of the incompetent subject did not burden the public coffers (2).

Contemporary Western law has extended the concept of guardianship to other decisions concerning personal affairs, in addition to or independently of decisions about property. Guardianship of person is intended to protect the well-being of an individual who is deemed incompetent to make decisions about his or her own life. A court-appointed guardian of the person has traditionally been charged with decision making in all areas of the ward's life, including place of residence, management of finances, and medical treatment. In recent years the concept of limited guardianship has evolved in the courts, based on a recognition that incompetence may be specific rather than global. Thus, an individual may be deemed incompetent only with respect to a particular area of decision making, in which case a guardian is appointed to make those decisions but not others. For example, concluding that a severely anorectic patient is incompetent to make decisions about feeding herself but is otherwise competent, a court might appoint a guardian to make decisions about food on the patient's behalf. The virtue of limited guardianship is that it preserves a greater measure of autonomy than general guardianship, providing protection that is limited to the vulnerable area of decision making. This approach also reduces the guardian's burden by limiting the scope of vicarious decision making.

Until recent decades, patients who were committed to psychiatric hospitals lost most of their rights as citizens. They were presumed to be incompetent by virtue of their mental illness, and treatment decisions were routinely made by the hospital clinicians. The 1960s saw a movement to restore the civil rights of patients, including the right to autonomy over one's own body. This led to case law establishing the psychiatric inpatient's right to refuse treatment, except under narrowly prescribed circumstances. In addition, psychiatric inpatients were no longer assumed to be inherently incompetent. Out of these legal and social trends has grown a system of vicarious decision making that struggles both to protect the rights of psychiatric patients and to ensure that they receive the best possible care.

Most states now have separate hearings to determine whether an individual should be involuntarily hospitalized and whether that individual is competent to make decisions about the treatment he or she receives, if hospitalized. The patient is presumed to be competent, without evidence to the contrary. Moreover, many states require an evaluation of competence for every person admitted to a psychiatric hospital. If a patient is found to be incompetent, the hospital must petition the local court for guardianship. The guardian appointed by the court assumes responsibility for deciding, on the patient's behalf, whether to accept or refuse treatment.

The growing emphasis on the right to refuse treatment, the presumption of competence, and statutes requiring routine screening for competence have combined to strain the system of vicarious decision making as it operates today. Ironically, guardianship has come full circle as an economic phenomenon. Initially intended to preserve the wealth of persons who could not manage their own financial affairs, guardianship is now frequently invoked on behalf of the many indigent patients in public institutions who have no family available to serve as guardian and no money of their own to pay for the services of a professional guardian (see Chapter 5). In terms of numbers as well as costs, the need has overwhelmed the supply. Even more important, the use of guardianship in case law over the past two decades has overburdened a system still struggling to resolve the tensions among social, ethical, and legal values.

CONCEPTS OF VICARIOUS DECISION MAKING

The law offers two main standards of vicarious decision making: best interests and substituted judgment.

Best Interests

The best interests standard instructs the vicarious decision maker to choose the course of action that best fosters the ward's well-being. Using this standard, for example, a guardian who must decide whether to accept or refuse a particular medical treatment on behalf of an incompetent patient frames the decision by asking whether the proposed treatment is in that person's best medical interests.

Best interests is philosophically akin to the parens patriae standard for civil commitment (see Chapter 5). Both reflect a paternalistic social policy: the state (through the law, a judge, or a guardian) has an obligation to take care of those who cannot care for themselves. The guardian, then, decides what the best interests of the ward are and makes a decision that promotes those interests, much as the parent makes decisions for the child according to what the parent considers to be the child's best interests.

Despite its good intentions, the best interests standard poses several problems. It calls for a determination of the ward's best interests yet offers no guidance in identifying those interests. Without explicit guidance—or perhaps even with it, to the extent that no decision is ever entirely devoid of subjective content—the vicarious decision is bound to be influenced by unconscious processes of perception and decision making, such as projection (the guardian identifies his or her own interests as those of the ward) and attribution (the guardian attributes his/her own personal goals to the ward). Thus, even though it strives for an objective approach to vicarious decision making, the best interests standard fosters a subjective assessment of the ward's needs. Moreover, the standard does little to retain a balance between civil rights and social protection. A decision based on best interests comes down squarely on the side of protection, as opposed to autonomy; the model is inescapably paternalistic.

Substituted Judgment

Substituted judgment provides more explicit guidance, instructing the guardian to make the decision that the now-incompetent ward would make if he or she were competent. Using substituted judgment, the guardian attempts to approach the decision from the ward's perspective (or, more precisely, the guardian's interpretation of the ward's perspective). Thus, whereas a guardian using the best interests standard would frame the decision as follows: "I choose X because I believe that it is best for the ward," a guardian using substituted judgment would say, "If the ward were competent, I believe he or she would choose X." In practice, however, this formulation is usually expressed in a subtly different form: "I choose X because, if I were the ward, that would be my choice."

In 19th century English law substituted judgment was used to justify authorization of a gift from the estate of an incompetent person to someone who was not a dependent of that person (i.e., a gift made on behalf of the ward in the absence of any legal obligation for the ward to support the recipient of the gift). The standard has been used more recently to make decisions about accepting medical treatment for patients considered incompetent to make those decisions themselves. Interestingly, however, this use of substituted judgment flourished first in judicial decisions about *stopping* (or withholding) treatment that would prolong the lives of critically ill patients.

In the Matter of Karen Quinlan was the first case in which the standard of substituted judgment was used to make a treatment decision for an incompetent patient (3). Karen Quinlan was a comatose patient who was not expected to regain consciousness. Her father petitioned a New Jersey court to appoint him guardian of his daughter so that he could discontinue the mechanical respiration that presumably kept her alive but in a vegetative state. The court granted the father's petition, explaining that Ms. Quinlan's constitutional right to privacy gave her the right to refuse artificial life support. "The only practical way to prevent destruction of the right is to permit the guardian and family of Karen to render their best judgment . . . as to whether she would exercise it in these circumstances" (4).

The court's reliance on substituted judgment in the *Quinlan* decision was influential in *Superintendent of Belchertown State School v Saikewicz*, a Massachusetts case that also centered on the question of prolonging the life of an incompetent patient (5). In this case, however, the patient had never been competent and was not being kept alive by artificial means. Joseph Saikewicz was a severely retarded man living in a state institution who had contracted acute myeloblastic monocytic leukemia, an incurable and rapidly fatal disease. His physicians asked the court to consider withholding chemotherapy, the usual treatment for this disease. The guardian ad litem, or "next friend" (see the discussion later in this chapter) who was appointed to represent the interests of the patient concurred with the physicians, citing the following reasons for withholding treatment. First, the disease was not curable, and the chemotherapy might or might not be effective in achieving a short remission. Second, the treatment would entail painful side effects. Third, Saikewicz's age (67 years) was a complicating factor, since patients over the age of 60 do not tolerate the treatment as well as younger patients and are not as likely to have a remission. Finally, Saikewicz, who had an IQ of 10 and a mental age of approximately two and a half years, would not be able to comprehend the treatment or its side effects, nor would he be able to cooperate during administration of the chemotherapy.

After considering the risks and benefits on each side (giving or withholding treatment), as well as the probability of remission, the Massachusetts Supreme Court decided to withhold chemotherapy. In arriving at this decision, the court used the substituted judgment standard as it had been applied by the New Jersey Supreme Court in the *Quinlan* ruling.

In its decision the court stated that competent and incompetent patients have the same rights, including the right to refuse treatment. The only difference lies in how those rights are to be protected and exercised. Therefore, the central question is "how an incompetent person is to be afforded the status in law of a competent person with respect to such rights."

In the *Quinlan* case the court justified its ruling in part by stating that most people, under similar circumstances, would make the same choice (i.e., to discontinue life support). In the case of Saikewicz, however, the Massachusetts court rejected this reasoning:

> . . . we realize that an inquiry into what a majority of people would do in circumstances that truly were similar assumes an objective viewpoint not far removed from a "reasonable person" inquiry. While we recognize the value of this kind of indirect evidence, we should make it plain that the primary test is subjective in nature—that is, the goal is to determine with as much accuracy as possible the wants and needs of the individual involved. This may or may not conform to what is thought wise or prudent by most people.

In rejecting the "reasonable person" formulation, the court seemed to be insisting on a purely subjective basis for substituted judgment— that is, a judgment made entirely from the standpoint of the ward. This approach might prove quite useful for a substituted judgment made on behalf of an incompetent patient who was previously competent, particularly if the ward, when competent, had expressed his or her preferences on the issue under question. In the case of a patient who has never been competent to express such preferences, however, this pure form of substituted judgment would seem to require an act of divination.

Two New York court decisions acknowledged the limitations of the substituted judgment standard. In one case the New York Court of Appeals ruled that the life of Brother Joseph Fox should not be prolonged by artificial respiration (6). The court based its decision on substituted judgment but noted that this standard was applicable to the case only because Brother Fox, before becoming comatose, had stated a preference not to be kept alive by artificial means (4). The second case concerned John Storar, who, like Saikewicz, was mentally retarded and stricken with cancer (7). Here, however, the question was whether to continue treatment, whereas in *Saikewicz* it was whether to initiate (or withhold) treatment. The court decided that substituted judgment could not be used to guide a decision about treatment in this case, because Storar had never been competent to express his wishes in the matter. Ruling that treatment should be continued, the court observed:

> . . . it is unrealistic to attempt to determine whether he would want to continue potentially life-prolonging treatment if he were competent. As one of the experts testified at the hearing, that would be similar to asking whether "if it snowed all summer, would it then be winter?"

In another case of vicarious decision making on behalf of a ward who had never been competent, the Massachusetts Supreme Judicial Court examined the question of court-ordered sterilization for a mentally retarded woman (8). Although the majority opinion held that substituted judgment was a proper standard for making a decision on behalf of the ward, one judge voiced strong opposition:

> The court today has decided that the probate judge has the power to divine the wishes of a severely mentally retarded women [sic] who "currently functions at the level of a four-year-old" as to whether she should permit herself to be rendered forever incapable of conceiving and bearing a child. To say the least, this is an impossible task. . . . The very condition of incompetence makes the doctrine of substituted judgment a cruel charade.

To summarize, both best interests and substituted judgment are, at best, imperfect standards for vicarious decision making. Best interests favors protection of the ward at the cost of autonomy and is thus inevitably paternalistic. A vicarious decision based on the best interests standard is not truly vicarious, since it represents the guardian's perceptions, values, and judgments, not those of the ward. Yet this standard does ensure that the ward's needs (at least as identified by the guardian) will be met. Substituted judgment, in contrast, favors autonomy over protection and instructs the guardian to set aside his or her own preferences in favor of those that the ward has expressed or might be expected to express. This standard poses particular problems in cases where the ward has never been competent, has never expressed preferences, or has expressed preferences distorted by illness. Although ostensibly more explicit than best interests in the guidance it provides, substituted judgment may thus be little more than a guessing game. These, then, are the conceptual difficulties that the two standards for vicarious decision making present. The next section explores the practical difficulties of applying these standards to actual cases of guardianship.

VICARIOUS DECISION MAKING IN PRACTICE

When concepts of vicarious decision making are translated into practice, two questions persist: who decides, and how is the decision made?

Who Decides?

Traditionally, physicians made treatment decisions on behalf of their incompetent patients. Such decisions were made according to the physician's assessment of the patient's best medical interests. The advent of informed consent principles, stressing patient-centered decision making, made it necessary to identify a third party who would preserve the incompetent patient's right to accept or refuse treatment by acting as a substitute decision maker. Guardianship provides the legal framework for appointing such vicarious decision makers.

Finding candidates for guardianship is often a problem, however. As noted earlier, the need for guardians has outstripped the pool of potential candidates, as a result of requirements concerning informed consent, patients' rights, and competence screening on admission. In many cases, no family members are available or willing to assume the responsibility for making treatment decisions on behalf of an incompetent patient (9). For example, Joseph Saikewicz had two sisters, but neither wished to be appointed her brother's legal guardian in order to make the decision whether or not to initiate treatment—indeed, as noted in the written opinion, neither sister wanted to be involved with him at all.

In the absence of a family member, the court may appoint a professional guardian (generally, an attorney) to represent the patient's interests. However, many of the patients in need of professional guardianship are indigent and cannot pay for these services. In the past, when guardianship was only occasionally sought for indigent patients, attorneys provided their services pro bono. Now that the demand for professional guardians has grown, attorneys are understandably less willing to donate their time and services.

Local jurisdictions have expressed different views on the question of who should make substituted judgments. In *Quinlan* the New Jersey court decided that the guardian, family, physicians, and hospital ethics committee were the appropriate parties to the vicarious decision concerning withdrawal of life support. In *Saikewicz*, however, the Massachusetts court stated that substituted judgments concerning matters of life and death should rest with the judiciary, because such decisions ". . . require the process of detached but passionate investigation and decision that forms the ideal on which the judicial branch of government was created. Achieving this ideal is our responsibility. . . ."

In another substituted judgment case the court reiterated this view. *In the Matter of Guardianship of Richard Roe III* concerned a 21-year-old schizophrenic man with a history of violent behavior who refused antipsychotic treatment (10). The court approved his father's petition for guardianship but ruled that any substituted judgment about treatment should be the province of the judiciary:

Decisions such as the one the guardian wishes to make in this case [consent to antipsychotic medication] pose exceedingly difficult problems for even the most capable, detached, and diligent decision maker. We intend no criticism of the guardian when we say that few parents could make this substituted judgment determination—by its nature a self-centered determination in which the decision maker is called upon to ignore all but the implementation of the values and preferences of the ward—when the ward, in his present condition, is living at home with other children. . . . Those characteristics laudable in a parent might often be a substantial handicap to a guardian faced with such a decision but who might in all other circumstances be an excellent guardian. . . . We are convinced that in this case, as in other cases, the regularity of the procedure— guaranteed by a judicial determination—will ensure that objectivity which other processes might lack.

In *Roe* and *Saikewicz* the court's insistence on judicial substituted judgment seems paradoxical. At least theoretically, substituted judgment rests on the principle of mirrored subjectivity: the vicarious decision should reflect the subjective preference of that individual (when competent) on whose behalf the decision is being made. Common sense suggests that a judge is far less likely to be attuned to the implicit wishes of an incompetent patient than family members or others who know the person well. Yet in both cases the court states that the appropriate decision maker is the judiciary, because only the judicial process can ensure the objectivity necessary to arrive at such a decision. Thus, the court appears to be saying that only a "detached," objective party can make a truly subjective (in the sense of substituted) judgment. How the judiciary, or any other party, could maintain the simultaneous distance and proximity necessary to meet this challenge remains to be seen.

Several more radical solutions to the problem of who decides have been proposed. Noting that treatment refusal is often an element of psychiatric disorders and that treatment responses are predictable, Stone has suggested that psychiatrists once again be given the authority to make treatment decisions without obtaining substituted consent (cited in Ref. 9). This authority would be limited to routine treatment conforming to standards established by the psychiatric community. Others have suggested that independent human rights committees provide substituted consent, but with the stipulation that they not be allowed to override a patient's refusal of treatment, regardless of whether that patient is competent or incompetent (9). A third proposal is a "living will" in which a psychiatric patient, while competent, can give anticipatory consent to later treatment, even later involuntary treatment, for any acute episodes of illness that might occur in the future (9).

In Utah the courts have attempted to resolve the problem of who decides by making competence to consent to treatment one of the criteria for involuntary commitment, thus linking treatment with commitment (11, 12). A judicial determination that a patient meets the criteria for commitment (including incompetence) paves the way for the hospital physicians to make treatment decisions on the basis of medical criteria. Thus, the courts decide at the entrance to the hospital, and the physicians decide within. The loophole in this approach is that a patient who is considered dangerous or desperately in need of treatment—yet competent—may not be committable, to the possible detriment of both the individual and society.

In spite of these and other possibilities, most jurisdictions rely on guardians or the judiciary itself to make vicarious decisions on behalf of incompetent psychiatric patients.

How Is the Decision Made?

The process of making a substituted judgment has three theoretical components: knowledge, empathy, and prediction (13). First, the decision maker draws on a knowledge of the ward and the sorts of decisions that person has made in the past. Second, the decision maker empathically intuits the ward's attitude toward the question at hand. Finally, on the basis of the ward's past decisions and general attitudes, the decision maker predicts the ward's preferences under the current circumstances.

In the case of a patient who has previously stated a preference while competent, the decision maker's task seems sufficiently straightforward. But what if the patient never expressed a preference while competent (as is usually the case) or, like Joseph Saikewicz, was never competent? In either case, substituted judgment, when put into practice, actually gives the vicarious decision maker substantial latitude in arriving at a decision. With this kind of discretion, the decision maker's preferences or biases are bound to influence the final decision.

Another problem with substituted judgment is its underlying assumptions that competent people make decisions on purely rational grounds and that their patterns of decision making are consistent. In fact, decision making is often inconsistent and ambivalent, reflecting irrational as well as rational intentions (13). Consider the following set of hypothetical examples.

Mr. A is a competent patient who seeks professional help for severe depression. His therapist recommends hospital treatment, and Mr. A agrees to this on the condition that he not be given any drug treatment. He explains that most of the members of his family are addicted to various drugs and that he himself was addicted to a variety of prescription drugs until the previous year. Since then, he has refrained from taking any medications, even aspirin. His therapist reassures him that no drugs will be given without his permission.

While in the hospital, Mr. A becomes psychotic and suicidal but refuses antipsychotic medications, claiming that the staff is trying to get him hooked on drugs again. As a result of his psychosis, he is considered incompetent, and a guardian is appointed by the court to make a substituted judgment concerning treatment.

Should the guardian decide to refuse or accept treatment on Mr. A's behalf? Guided by the substituted judgment standard, the guardian might decide to refuse treatment, in line with the patient's abhorrence of drugs and expressed wish to avoid them. On the other hand, the guardian might accept treatment, interpreting Mr. A's initial decision to seek help, his subsequent agreement to hospitalization, and even his previous refusal of drugs as reflections of a fundamental desire to be healthy. According to this line of reasoning, if Mr. A were competent, he would consent to nonaddicting antipsychotic medication, understanding that it would restore his mental health without posing the danger of addiction. The point here is that either decision—refusal or acceptance of antipsychotic medication on Mr. A's behalf—could be supported by the tenets of substituted judgment.

The second example is Ms. B, a 70-year-old woman who places great value on her autonomy and independence. Ms. B becomes psychotic and incompetent, but she refuses hospitalization or treatment of any kind. She is admitted as an involuntary patient, and her niece is appointed guardian to make decisions on Ms. B's behalf.

What should the niece do? She might decide to honor her aunt's expressed wish to be discharged without treatment, reasoning that involuntary treatment violates Ms. B's autonomy, which has always been so important in her aunt's life. On the other hand, she might decide that illness has obscured any hope of immediate autonomy for her aunt, and that the only hope for her eventual autonomy lies in her acceptance of antipsychotic medication. Once treated, Ms. B will again be able to make her own decisions and live her life as she wishes.

The third example concerns Mr. C, a patient with a long history of a cyclic affective disorder. Until recently, Mr. C's illness was relatively mild and well controlled with a mood stabilizer, lithium. Six months ago, however, he suffered an acute manic episode that required hospitalization and treatment with the antipsychotic haloperidol, in addition to lithium. Mr. C recovered quickly with this regimen and was soon able to return to lithium alone. When he was discharged, Mr. C said that he would follow any lithium regimen that his psychiatrist prescribed but that he would not take haloperidol again—"It dopes me up so much, I can't function." Now he is experiencing an even more severe manic episode, which the lithium alone cannot counteract. He is hospitalized and deemed incompetent by the court, which appoints a guardian to make a treatment decision on Mr. C's behalf.

The guardian could appropriately take any of three approaches in making a substituted judgment. Following the central tenet of the standard, the guardian might decide that since Mr. C, while competent, stated that he would not take haloperidol on any future occasions, treatment should be refused on his behalf. Alternatively, the guardian might question whether Mr. C intended to refuse haloperidol in particular or all neuroleptic drugs, including haloperidol. If his refusal is interpreted as specific rather than generic, the guardian might decide that substituted judgment would justify use of a different drug in the same pharmacologic family. Finally, the guardian might decide that even though Mr. C refused haloperidol while previously competent, the unexpected severity of the current episode of illness warrants overriding that refusal. According to this line of reasoning, if the patient, while competent, had foreseen the new and exceptional circumstances (i.e., a much more debilitating manic episode than any previously experienced), he would have agreed to the use of haloperidol.

As a fourth example, consider Ms. D, who has a lifelong history of self-destructive behavior and seeks professional help in changing this pattern. She becomes psychotic and incompetent, is hospitalized, and refuses all treatment, saying she just wants to be left alone. A guardian is appointed to make treatment decisions on her behalf.

The dilemma here is similar to that presented in the case of Mr. A. Should the guardian decide to refuse treatment of any kind, which would be consistent with Ms. D's clear preference over many years for actions that others (and perhaps even Ms. D) consider self-destructive? Or should the guardian accept treatment on the patient's behalf, in line with her earlier decision to seek professional help in changing her self-destructive behavior? Faced with this choice, many people would be inclined to adopt the second line of reasoning, but how sure could they be that the choice was not motivated, in some small measure at least, by a subjective judgment about Ms. D's best interests?

Finally, consider Mr. E, who has been diagnosed as having paranoid schizophrenia. He is admitted to the hospital during an acute psychotic episode but refuses antipsychotic treatment, claiming that his physician intends to kill him with the drugs. Mr. E is deemed incompetent by the court, as a consequence of his psychosis, and a guardian is appointed to make the treatment decision.

The problems encountered in using substituted judgment are reflected most dramatically in the case of Mr. E (13). The guardian must determine what the patient would decide if he were competent to do so himself. When applied to these circumstances—psychotic illness leading to incompetence and treatment refusal—substituted judgment poses a paradoxical question that is logically impossible to answer: If Mr. E were free of his illness, would he agree to receive treatment for it?

All these examples concern patients who have previously been competent, but what about the patient who has never been competent? How does one determine what that person would want? Here, as in the case of Ms. D, it seems unlikely that one could arrive at a "pure" substituted judgment, that is, a decision based entirely on a prediction of the ward's preferences, uncontaminated by the guardian's perception of the ward's best interests.

Although hypothetical, these examples are not unusual in actual clinical practice. They highlight the practical limitations of substituted judgment as a standard of vicarious decision making. Because of the ambiguity and inconsistency of human behavior, the decision maker must exercise considerable discretion in choosing an interpretation of past behavior that forms the basis for a substituted judgment. In many cases the distinctions between best interests and substituted judgment are blurred as a result. Thus, the individual choice that substituted judgment is designed to promote may reflect the subjective concerns of the vicarious decision maker at least as much as those of the incompetent patient.

The theory of substituted judgment does appear to be socially valuable in certain circumstances. For patients who have previously been competent and have expressed a clear preference on the issue in question, substituted judgment offers reasonable guidance in making a vicarious decision. If the patient's preferences are ambiguous, inconsistent, or unknown, however, or if the patient has never been competent to express a preference, an explicit use of the best interests standard may avoid the dilemmas illustrated by our examples. Although substituted judgment is intended to preserve individual autonomy, in many cases that end may be better served by overriding a refusal of treatment in the interest of restoring competence as soon as possible, so that patients can make subsequent decisions for themselves.

THE CLINICIAN'S DILEMMA

Vicarious treatment decisions are commonly made on behalf of minors, mentally retarded individuals, comatose patients, and psychiatric patients. Several features of psychiatric illness distinguish the last group from the other three. First, the illness tends to be periodic, and incompetence occurs intermittently in association with acute clinical episodes; that is, the incompetence is a product of the illness rather than of, say, age (minors) or level of consciousness (comatose patients). Second, the psychiatric patient, unlike the mentally retarded or comatose individual, can generally offer an opinion about treatment, although it may or may not be a rational opinion. Third, refusal of treatment typically reflects a denial of illness that is part of the disease itself, as empirical evidence indicates (14, 15). Finally, whereas incompetence itself is not a treatable condition in minors, mentally retarded persons, or irreversibly comatose patients, it is often treatable in psychiatric patients. (9).

These four characteristics frame the ethical dilemma that clinicians face in dealing with the issues of treatment refusal by psychiatric patients and substituted consent.

A closer look at the case of Mr. E will illuminate this dilemma. Suppose the guardian makes a substituted judgment to refuse antipsychotic treatment. Mr. E's physician, Dr. R, continues to believe that the treatment in question is the key to restoring Mr. E's mental and physical health. What is Dr. R's ethical obligation to her patient? Should she accept the guardian's decision and take no further action or look for other ways to obtain consent to treatment? An argument could be made for either side.

Dr. R has offered treatment, and a court-appointed guardian has declined that offer on Mr. E's behalf. Certainly, Dr. R is under no legal obligation to seek a reversal of this decision. If she is satisfied that the decision has been properly made, even though it conflicts with her medical opinion, she may feel that her ethical obligations to the patient have been met and that she has done all she can. Mr. E's right to refuse treatment has been preserved (and exercised) by the process of guardianship.

On the other hand, if Dr. R believes that her obligation is to provide the best possible care with all the resources that she has available, then she may well feel ethically bound to renew her efforts to obtain informed consent to treatment for Mr. E. She might, for instance, request that the court appoint another guardian, if she believes that the current guardian has not performed his role adequately. An alternative course of action would be to request that the court override the guardian's decision because it does not serve Mr. E's best interests (9).

If these approaches fail, Dr. R might file one or more appeals. The problem, of course, is that the quest could continue indefinitely, requiring considerable time and money. Mr. E's treatment is in limbo, as the hospital staff await a final decision, and Dr. R is spending more and more time in legal rather than clinical pursuits.

Another problem with this course of action is that it is inconsistent with the idea of a substituted judgment. The physician, in thus pursuing all possible avenues to treatment, is not seeking a judgment about treatment so much as an agreement to it.

Thus, Dr. R is left with a disturbing question on either side of the dilemma. By accepting a substituted judgment that leaves Mr. E untreated, is she in effect abandoning her patient? By rejecting that judgment, is Dr. R saying that her own opinion about what is best for Mr. E is the only valid one (9)?

VICARIOUS DECISION MAKING AND THE QUALITY OF CARE: A COLLABORATIVE APPROACH

As we pointed out at the beginning of this chapter, the problem of how to decide for others strikes at the heart of the conflict between autonomy and protection. When a patient is deemed incompetent to provide informed consent to treatment, a substitute decision must be made on behalf of that patient. How can we ensure that the vicarious decision will represent the patient's best interests? Those interests encompass both legal rights and clinical needs. Thus, procedures for vicarious decision making that bring to bear the clinical as well as the legal perspective will best serve the interests of the patient.

When the question of a patient's competence to accept or refuse treatment comes before a court, a guardian ad litem, or "next friend," is often appointed to help resolve the issue. By statute, courts can appoint a guardian ad litem to "become interested in any property, real or personal, or in the enforcement of any legal rights" (16).

Functions of the Guardian Ad Litem

The guardian ad litem may be asked to assume various roles in the case at hand. For example, the court may appoint a guardian ad litem to represent the special interests of the patient in the case or to participate in certain aspects of the vicarious decision making on the patient's behalf. The guardian ad litem may also be asked to submit a report to the court that outlines the important issues of the case: the condition of the patient, the nature of the hospital setting, the treatment plan and its rationale, the risks and benefits of the proposed treatment (as well as the risks and benefits of no treatment), and other pertinent medical considerations. Depending on the issues at stake, the guardian ad litem is sometimes instructed to combine these roles, serving as legal advocate, fact finder, and court investigator. In fact, the guardian ad litem has played a pivotal part in the evolution of certain cases of important litigation through several levels of appeal (2).

Legal and Psychiatric Perspectives

The proper role of the guardian ad litem has been subject to different interpretations. Baron has argued that the guardian ad litem should assume an adversarial role, advocating whatever position is opposed to that of the petitioner or moving party (17). An adversarial role, Baron reasons, is important to "insure that all viewpoints and alternatives will be aggressively pursued" (quoted in Ref. 16). As legal advocate, the guardian ad litem helps preserve due process of law and safeguards the legal interests of the patient. Attorneys, of course, are well-suited to this role of legal advocacy and protection of rights.

In cases of questionable competence and treatment refusal, however, the patient's interests encompass clinical needs, in addition to legal rights. A purely adversarial role for the guardian ad litem will help protect the rights but not necessarily meet the needs of the patient under these circumstances (e.g., the need for treatment). It is here that the perspectives of law and medicine may diverge.

For the attorney intent on protecting the patient's legal rights and avoiding losses, the risks of a proposed treatment may eclipse its benefits (or the corresponding risks of nontreatment). Some court decisions reflect this legal perception, citing at length the risks of treatment but giving little space to the potential benefits (10).

A psychiatrist, on the other hand, is accustomed to balancing risks and benefits in making treatment decisions—for example, weighing the possible side effects of neuroleptic medications against the benefits of diminished psychosis. By making probabilistic estimates of the benefits as well as the risks of treating and not treating, the clinician chooses the course of action that he or she believes will best meet the patient's clinical needs.

A COLLABORATIVE APPROACH TO VICARIOUS DECISION MAKING

Legal and medical aims need not be mutually exclusive. The guardian ad litem's dual role as legal advocate and independent investigator suggests a framework for a collaboration between attorney and psychiatrist that will safeguard the patient's interests, both legal and clinical.

Three cases offer a precedent for incorporating medical and legal perspectives on treatment decisions. Two U.S. Supreme Court decisions have held that significant discretion should be accorded to medical judgment in areas of decision making such as the treatment of mental illness or mental retardation (18, 19). How this discretion can be exercised in the context of judicial protection of a patient's right to adequate treatment is addressed by a New Jersey case, *Rennie v Klein* (20).

The original *Rennie* case concluded that under certain circumstances, if a patient of questionable competence refused medication while in a New Jersey state hospital, an independent psychiatrist should be consulted to evaluate the proposed treatment plan and report to the court. The report would address the risks and benefits of the treatment in question, as well as those of available alternatives. The outside psychiatrist in effect was called upon to play a multifaceted role that combined some of the features of a guardian ad litem, special consultant, supervisor, and mediator (since part of the process involved the participation of patient advocates).

Unlike some related cases (e.g., *Mills v Rogers* [21]), *Rennie* left the decision making within the medical profession but required a second opinion in the form of an independent evaluation of the proposed treatment plan. An interesting and no doubt unintentional result of this ruling was that patients in New Jersey state hospitals who accepted their medication were simply left with the standard treatment, whereas patients who refused medication had the benefit of a second opinion. Paradoxically, the quality of care was more likely to be ensured by refusing treatment than by accepting it (12)!

In most jurisdictions, of course, the mere refusal of treatment does not guarantee the kind of review that will give reasonable assurance of good treatment. However, the *Rennie* paradox provides a valuable lesson. It suggests that a legal procedure focused exclusively on the patient's competence to give or withhold consent to treatment ignores the equally important question of the adequacy of the treatment being offered—a question attorneys are not trained to address. In the first place, a patient who refuses treatment may recognize, consciously or unconsciously, that it is not helpful. Thus, the quality of the treatment is relevant to the determination of the patient's competence to make treatment decisions. Furthermore, in the case of a patient considered incompetent to give informed consent, the vicarious decision maker (whether guardian or judge) would not want to accept inadequate care on the patient's behalf.

The *Rennie* decision suggests a way out of this dilemma by requiring that an outside psychiatrist (one with special expertise in psychopharmacology) participate in the judicial procedure for resolving the problem of treatment refusal by an incompetent patient. Modeled after an established medical tradition, this second (independent) opinion provides a clinical basis for the judicial determination and at the same time ensures a high standard of care for the patient, as the following case demonstrates.

A 25-year-old man with a diagnosis of paranoid schizophrenia had been an inpatient of a state hospital since the age of 15, when his parents first admitted him. When the patient began to refuse medication, the hospital staff went to court to request the appointment of a guardian ad litem. The attorney who assumed this role concluded that he could not adequately address the legal issues without some clinical understanding of the patient's diagnosis and competence, as well as the quality of care he was receiving. With the court's permission the attorney therefore consulted a psychiatrist outside the hospital. In effect, the psychiatrist functioned as co-guardian ad litem, reporting on the clinical issues in the case.

The psychiatrist submitted a report to the court in which he evaluated the patient's diagnosis, competence, and treatment. He concluded, first, that the patient had chronic undifferentiated schizophrenia (rather than paranoid schizophrenia); second, that the patient was psychotic and incompetent to give informed consent to treatment; and, third, that the proposed treatment plan fell below the standard of good care.

The psychiatrist pointed out in his report that the hospital staff had not documented either their treatment plan or the risks and benefits of the medications they had been giving the patient. Members of the staff had reportedly observed signs of tardive dyskinesia in the patient but had not documented them or reassessed the benefits of the medication in light of this complication of treatment. In addition, no effort had been made to determine whether lower doses of medication would be equally effective. In reviewing the patient's chart, the psychiatrist noted that in previous years the patient had done well on a much lower dosage (22).

Thus, an independent medical review, together with a review of the patient's legal status, resulted in a clarification of the diagnosis and a revision of the treatment plan. Without the psychiatrist's participation, the diagnostic and therapeutic errors would probably have gone unnoticed and therefore uncorrected.

This case illustrates the value of a collaboration between attorney and psychiatrist in cases of treatment refusal that come before the courts. Working together as co-guardians ad litem, they can inform the judiciary about the critical legal and clinical issues presented by a particular case, including the quality of the treatment in question. Underlying any collaboration of this sort is the principle that a patient's competence to accept or refuse treatment cannot be assessed meaningfully without considering the quality of that treatment, which in turn cannot be addressed without clinical participation.

REFERENCES

1. Stone A. Personal communication.
2. Gutheil TG, Appelbaum PS. Clinical handbook of psychiatry and the law. New York: McGraw-Hill, 1980, Chapter 5.
3. *In the Matter of Karen Quinlan*, 70 NJ 10, 35 A2d 647 (1976).
4. Gutheil TG, Appelbaum PS. Substituted judgment; best interests in disguise. Hastings Center Report June 1983; 13(3):8–11.
5. *Superintendent of Belchertown State School v Saikewicz*, 373 Mass 728, 320 NE2d 471 (1977).
6. *Eichner v Dillon*, 52 NY2d 363, 420 NE2d 64 (NY 1981).
7. *In the Matter of Storar*, 52 NY2d 363, 420 NE2d 64 (NY 1981).
8. *In the Matter of Moe*, 385 Mass 555 (1982).
9. Gutheil TG, Appelbaum PS. Substituted judgment and the physician's ethical dilemma: with special reference to the problem of the psychiatric patient. J Clin Psychiatry 1980; 41:303–305.
10. *In the Matter of Guardianship of Richard Roe III*, 421 NE2d 40 (Mass 1981).
11. *A.E. and R.R. v Mitchell*, F Supp (D Utah 1980).
12. Gutheil TG. The right to refuse treatment. In: Grinspoon L, ed. Psychiatry '82: the American Psychiatric Annual Review. Washington, D.C.: American Psychiatric Press, 1982.
13. Gutheil TG, Appelbaum PS. The substituted judgment approach: its difficulties and paradoxes in mental health settings. Law Med Health Care 1985; 13:61–64.
14. Appelbaum PS, Gutheil TG. Drug refusal: a study of psychiatric inpatients. Am J Psychiatry 1980; 137(3):340–346.
15. Appelbaum PS, Gutheil TG. "Rotting with their rights on": constitutional theory and clinical reality in drug refusal by psychiatric patients. Bull Am Acad Psychiatry Law 1979; 7(3):306–315.
16. Mental disabilities: the legal response. Boston: MCLE-NEILI, Inc., 1979.
17. Baron WR. Guardians in Saikewicz-type case. Am J Law Med 1981; 4:111.
18. *Parham v J.R.*, 442 US 584 (1979).
19. *Romeo v Youngberg*, 102 SCt 2442 (1982).
20. *Rennie v Klein*, 462 F Supp 1131 (D NJ 1978).
21. *Mills v Rogers*, 478 F Supp 1342 (D Mass 1979), *aff'd in part*, 634 F2d 650 (1st Cir 1980), *cert. granted*, 49 USL W 3779 (1981).
22. Gutheil TG, Bursztajn H, Kaplan AN, Brodsky A. Participation in competency assessment and treatment decisions: the role of a psychiatrist-attorney team. Ment Phys Disabil Law Rptr 1987; 11:446–449.

chapter 8.
AFFECTIVE DISORDERS, COMPETENCE, AND DECISION MAKING

Most discussions of competence emphasize its cognitive elements and propose cognitively based criteria for its assessment (1, 2). It is our thesis in this chapter that affective states and disorders, as well as cognition, can influence competence in identifiable ways. We suggest that an affective disorder such as mania or depression may alter the meaning and weight that a patient gives to the risks and benefits of a proposed treatment and, specifically, that an important defect in competence may be the inability to appreciate the benefits of treatment, coupled with a disproportionate sensitivity to the risks.

The clinical relevance of this issue can be seen in the introductory case. In deciding whether or not to hospitalize Ms. Adams, Dr. Newell assessed her competence to weigh the risks and benefits of giving or withholding information about her condition, that is, about her suicidal intent. Had Ms. Adams been floridly psychotic or had she manifested a thought disorder, her competence would obviously have been in question, since any interference with thought, reasoning, and orientation to reality would clearly have impaired her decision-making capacity. Yet, although she manifested none of these profound disorders, was there perhaps an impairment, at a more subtle level, from the depression itself? This question and its exploration serve as the central issue of this chapter.

LEGAL CONCEPTS OF COMPETENCE

Earlier sections of this book have stressed the importance of competence—that capacity to weigh and assess the information required for decision making. Strictly in terms of the legal requirements, competence is a determination made only by the court (competence in law). In both civil and criminal assessments of competence, however, psychiatric perspectives play a central role. If a patient is found to be "incompetent in fact" (i.e., by preliminary clinical assessment), a psychiatrist may be asked to deliver an opinion to the court, which then "tests" this opinion through judicial validation. Surprisingly enough, despite the legal importance of the competence determination—which actually authenticates a person's status as a decision-making adult—the law does not offer precise standards for assessing competence in relation to a number of particular acts, tasks, and choices. While the criteria for competence to stand trial or to make a will, for example, are relatively explicit (3), the criteria for competence to consent to medical treatment are ambiguous and inconsistent.

Legal criteria for competence, moreover, although ostensibly based on the specific language of statutes or opinions, are tied in practice to operational terms. The Uniform Probate Code defines incompetence as follows: "A mentally incompetent person is one who is so affected mentally as to be deprived of sane and normal action, or who lacks sufficient capacity to understand in a reasonable manner the nature and effect of the act he is performing" (3). It is left to clinical and legal experts to develop pragmatic definitions for "sane," "normal," and "sufficient capacity"; these varying functional definitions become the criteria for determining competence to accept or refuse treatment.

One notable consistency among the various definitions of competence in all its different forms has been a reliance on cognitive criteria. Thus, for example, the most influential case on competence to stand trial—*Dusky v U.S.* (4)—requires a "rational as well as a factual understanding" of the trial issues. The individual must "know," "understand," or "be aware of" certain facts and relationships that emphasize rational, logical thinking. More important, the existing definitions of competence tend to focus on cognitive processes as the sole factors constituting competence. The role of affective processes has been scanted.

Under certain circumstances, cognition and affect are at odds in the clinical assessment of a patient; clinicians may struggle with this issue. When such cases are brought before the courts, the legal system also struggles with the issues in a way that highlights the confusion that can result from this tension between the cognitive and affective dimensions of competence.

A legal case that dramatizes these issues is *Rumbaugh v Procunier* (5). Charles Rumbaugh was about to be executed on a sentence for murder and had declined to exercise his rights to repeat appeals of his case. The question was whether he possessed the requisite mental competence to waive these rights. Because of its interest and relevance for our thesis, this case will be discussed in some detail.

Charles Rumbaugh was first convicted of capital murder and sentenced to death by a Texas state court on 4/4/75. The conviction was reversed on appeal. . . . At the trial Rumbaugh was again convicted of capital murder and sentenced to death. The second conviction was affirmed on direct appeal [citation omitted]. Following affirmance of his second conviction, Rumbaugh asked his court-appointed counsel to take no further steps to attack his conviction and sentence. . . . [He] wrote the state trial judge requesting that his execution be set without further delay. (5)

Before the date of the execution came due, Mr. Rumbaugh's parents petitioned the court for a stay of execution and applied for a "habeas release," a procedure that permits a rehearing based on the defendant's possible incompetence. Eventually, the district court ordered Charles Rumbaugh transferred to the U.S. Medical Center in Springfield, MO, to be examined for the specific purpose of determining his mental competence to waive further review of his conviction and sentence.

Following Mr. Rumbaugh's examination by a team of mental health professionals, a hearing was held, and a number of individuals gave testimony. The main psychiatric examiner, a Dr. Logan, was asked to explain his diagnosis and prognosis. Dr. Logan testified later, the prisoner himself took the stand and attempted to explain the situation to the court:

Well, I don't feel I'm depressed right now. . . . And it really doesn't matter to me what this court decides today because I've already decided to take matters into my own hands. So it doesn't make any difference. . . . I've already picked my own executioner and I'll just make them kill me. . . . If they don't want to take me down there and execute me, I'll make them shoot me. . . . I think I'll make them shoot me right now. (5)

At this point, the prisoner pulled out a homemade, prison-style knife and advanced on a U.S. deputy marshal, screaming, "Shoot!" For want of any alternative measure, the deputy marshal was indeed forced to shoot the prisoner. He was taken by ambulance to the hospital, and the hearing went on:

Dr. Logan, who had witnessed the entire episode, was recalled to the stand and testified that the bizarre occurrence did not shake his opinion but reinforced his conclusions that Rumbaugh was acting knowingly and intentionally with full knowledge and appreciation of the situation in which he found himself. (5)

The hearing by the district court at this point came to the conclusion that Mr. Rumbaugh was mentally competent to forgo future proceedings. His parents again appealed this finding. After a series of legal maneuverings, the case was brought to the Court of Appeals of the 5th

Circuit, resulting in the case opinion now being discussed. The standard used to determine competence had been enunciated in a local case:

Whether he was the capacity to appreciate his position and make a rational choice with respect to continuing or abandoning further litigation or on the other hand whether he is suffering from a mental disease, disorder or defect which may substantially affect his capacity in the premises. (5)

The standard was broken down into a series of three questions given in the opinion:

1. Is the person suffering from a mental disease or defect?
2. If the person is suffering from a mental disease or defect, does that disease or defect prevent him from understanding his legal position and the options available to him?
3. If the person is suffering from a mental disease or defect which does not prevent him from understanding his legal position and the options available to him, does that disease or defect nevertheless prevent him from making a rational choice among his options? (5)

In the Rumbaugh case the medical testimony essentially pointed out that the patient had a cognitive grasp of the situation but that his depression—an affective state—significantly clouded his decision-making capacity, so that he was essentially trying to get the court to help him commit suicide. The opinion of the Court of Appeals reflects its struggle to grasp the tension between cognition and affect as they influence competence.

A statement from Dr. Logan's testimony is relevant here:

This examiner feels that Mr. Rumbaugh is currently profoundly depressed. Mr. Rumbaugh, despite his depression, does have the capacity to appreciate his position. His choice regarding continuing to decline further litigation is rational in light of his past experience and presuming one can rationally make a decision to die. It must be emphasized, however, the extent of Rumbaugh's depression does substantially affect his capacity in the premises. Mr. Rumbaugh's perception of his current situation as hopeless, although realistic in light of his past experience, is a reflection of this depression. (5)

The court, in remarking on this testimony, indicated that the other examining physician had given a report that "reflected a similar apparent anomaly." "Anomaly" is the first of nine terms in the opinion that suggest the court's struggle with the concept of a person who is cognitively competent but affectively incompetent. At other places in the opinion, the court referred to a "seemingly self-contradictory response," "conflict—or apparent conflict," "dilemma," "ambiguities," "enigmatic conclusion," "apparently inconsistent conclusion," and "enigma of psychology." At one point the court described its own struggle as an attempt to "bridge the synapses"!

Dr. Logan, under lengthy and detailed cross-examination, attempted to draw a parallel with terminally ill patients. He pointed out that they may be very depressed but have unimpaired cognitive abilities and a clear and rational understanding of their situation. But when such patients decline further treatment and essentially choose to die, their depression, though "realistic," does influence their decision. Asked why Mr. Rumbaugh's depression constituted a "coercive force," Dr. Logan responded:

> It affects him to the extent that, were his depression not present . . . or he not so hopeless about his position, he might be better able mentally to cope with spending an additional eight years on death row . . . and continue with appeals. But his mental condition is not that it would permit him to do so. (5)

Despite Dr. Logan's remarkably precise depiction of Mr. Rumbaugh's divided mental and emotional states, the court found for the majority that:

> Charles Rumbaugh is able to feed relevant facts into a rational decision-making process and come to a reasonable decision . . . that Rumbaugh's assessment of his legal and medical situation and the options available to him are reasonable. In other words, Rumbaugh's disease influences his decision because it is the source of mental pain which contributes to his invitation of death. (5)

In sum, the court found the patient competent to forgo further legal proceedings.

The dissent in this case, filed by Circuit Judge Goldberg, is a persuasive and eloquent document in its own right, but one that we will employ here only to examine further the struggle of the legal system to make sense of the tension between cognitive and affective dimensions of competence.

> The structure of the . . . standard suggests "rational choice" comprises two elements; first, the notion that a person choose means that relate logically to ends. If a person's ability to reason logically is seriously impaired, he is incapable of rational choice. Second, rational choice requires that the ends of his actions are his ends. That is, rational choice embraces "autonomous" choice. If a

person takes logical steps toward a goal that is substantially the product of a mental illness, the decision in a fundamental sense is not his: he is incompetent. . . . A person [under the standard] either is capable of rational choice or has a mental disease that "substantially affects his capacity in the premises" but he cannot have both conditions. If [the standard] were read to require only an inquiry into a person's ability to reason logically, without an inquiry into the person's autonomy, then both conditions would be possible. Yet a person can be both logical and have a mental disease that "substantially affects his capacity in the premises", i.e., that affects what a person in an ultimate sense desires. Indeed, this is precisely the situation in the present case, where the doctors testified that, although Rumbaugh is capable of logical thought, his present condition substantially affects his capacity in the premises. (5)

Note that the dissenting justice is not merely suggesting that affect, as well as cognition, may impair competence. Beyond that, he points out that an affective disorder (in this case, depression) may interfere with "autonomy," which might perhaps be better understood here as a sense of the personal relevance of the alleged objective facts and choices confronting the decision maker. He suggests that "[b]y equating 'rational' with 'logical,' the court . . . disregarded substantial uncontroverted testimony that Rumbaugh's state of depression diminishes his capacity for free autonomous choice." This element will become particularly important later in this chapter when we review different models of competence.

The dissent also underscores a point that contradicts the majority opinion:

Rumbaugh's decision to abandon appeal was an effort to secure the state's assistance in committing suicide . . . and the decision to commit suicide was a direct product of severe depression. (5)

Like the courts, clinicians often grapple with the cognitive and affective dimensions of competence, particularly competence to consent to treatment, as other chapters have addressed. Clinical authorities in this area generally agree that competence to consent to treatment rests on the ability to assimilate information related to the risks and benefits of a proposed treatment plan, to consider the risks and benefits of alternative treatments, and to weigh the risks and benefits of no treatment at all. What is noteworthy in these determinations is that they involve the dynamic processes of assimilating, considering, and weighing, as well as substantive content (the actual risks and benefits). The question is: Can these dynamic processes be understood in strictly cognitive terms, as is usually assumed in legal discussions, or must their affective components also be considered? We believe they must.

CLINICAL MODELS OF COMPETENCE ASSESSMENT

Roth et al. have provided a very thoughtful and provocative review of the various criteria, or tests, that have been proposed for assessing competence to make treatment decisions (1). They suggest that such tests can be divided into five categories. The first, evidencing a choice, they describe as the most respectful of the patient's autonomy. These tests merely require that the patient be able to evidence an actual preference. This would exclude the mute or silent patient, unable to express even bare assent or refusal.

The second category includes tests that examine the patient's ability to reach the "reasonable," "right," or "responsible" decision. These tests emphasize the outcome of the decision rather than either the fact of the decision, as in the first category, or how it has been reached. Roth et al. caution that this category of tests may be biased in favor of the decision to accept treatment, since it is usually recommended in a reasonable or plausible context, and since those assessing reasonableness are usually those recommending treatment.

Richard Bonnie, a legal scholar at the University of Virginia, has suggested that it would be defensible to have a lower standard of competence for making a so-called reasonable or responsible choice than for rejecting such a choice (6). This asymmetry, according to Bonnie, would both protect the patient's fundamental "competent" autonomy and indicate that a patient "swimming upstream against consensus," as it were, might appropriately be held to a higher standard of competence to make that decision. For example, a patient with a treatable illness who decides to die instead of accepting treatment should—perhaps on grounds of fairness, respect for persons, and social policy—have to pass a stricter test of competence to make this decision than that for consent to the treatment recommendation.

Tests in the third category require that the patient's choice be based on "rational" reasons. Among other questions, these tests ask whether the patient's decision may be related in some way to the presence of a mental illness. They focus on the quality of the patient's thinking and reasoning processes as these may influence a particular decision. Delusional thinking or thinking based on psychotic distortions of the reality about treatment would fail this type of test. Note that, because it pays attention to dynamic clinical processes, such a test would find favor with clinicians; however, in the legal context, it would not fare so well because of the difficulty in distinguishing rational from irrational reasons. Other difficulties might include the subjective judgment of what counts as rational reasons; the interweaving of reasons in this context with individual values, as well as conflicts; and the fact that many decisions, in ordinary life among ordinary people, might well not pass the test of rationality.

The fourth category of tests addresses the person's ability to understand the substantive issues concerning the decision: the risks and benefits of the proposed treatment, alternative treatments, and no treatment. Roth et al. note that this type of test is most consistent with the law of informed consent. Unwise choices would theoretically be permitted, since the test focuses on the patient's ability to understand the information needed to make a treatment decision, whether or not the patient makes the decision that the clinician believes is correct:

> What matters in this test is that the patient is able to comprehend the elements that are presumed by law to be a part of the treatment decision making. How the patient weighs these elements, values, and then puts them together to reach a decision is not important. (1)

Roth et al. offer a caution that is particularly relevant to our discussion in this chapter:

> Some of the questions raised by this test of competence are, what is to be done if the patient can understand the risks but not the benefits or vice versa? Alternatively what if the patient views the risks as the benefits? (1)

They give an example of a very depressed patient who expressed the hope that she would be the 1 patient in 3000 likely to die from electroconvulsive therapy.

The fifth category of competence tests examines "actual understanding." These tests delineate a potentially "high level of competence, one that might be difficult to achieve." The authors appropriately caution: "What constitutes adequate understanding is vague, and sufficient understanding may be attributable in whole or in part to physician behavior as well as to the patient's behavior or character" (p. 282). They go on to discuss the risk-benefit analysis as it might affect competence testing and conclude, somewhat ruefully. "The search for a single test of competency is a search for a Holy Grail" (p. 283).

Note that all these categories of competence tests look to largely cognitive capacities. Although some may touch indirectly on affective elements, all the tests appear to have a cognitive basis.

Appelbaum and Roth, extending this discussion, have outlined ways in which a number of clinical dimensions, in addition to cognition, might bear on a person's competence (7). The authors point out that the clinician must consider the following factors in his or her assessment: 1) psychodynamic elements of the patient's personality, 2) the accuracy of the historical information conveyed by the patient, 3) the accuracy and completeness of the information given to the patient, 4) the stability of the patient's mental status over time, and 5) the effect of the setting in which consent is obtained.

In discussing the psychodynamic factors, the authors note:

The legal model of informed consent seems to anticipate that the average decision maker will attend to the information that is presented and will then rationally evaluate his or her alternatives on the basis of the medically relevant risks and benefits. Clinicians, however, are aware that decisions are rarely made in such an affective vacuum. Seemingly neutral words of the informed consent form or doctor/patient consent interview can, in fact, be highly charged for the patient. (7)

The authors draw an interesting parallel between a simple cognitive grasp of the issues and the M'Naghten test for criminal responsibility, which is based on a "knowledge of right and wrong." They point out that in many jurisdictions the law has evolved toward the notion of an "appreciation of the wrongfulness of [one's] conduct," a phrase in which "appreciation" is intended to be broader than "knowledge," speaking to both emotional factors and a sense that the consequences of potentially criminal actions are personally relevant. In another article these authors and their colleagues conclude:

Similarly, to evaluate [the patient described in an example] as having the capacity to make treatment decisions can be seen to give undue weight to a single area of mental functioning, that of cognitive understanding. For intellectual understanding of the risks, benefits and alternatives to the proposed treatment, however thorough, cannot have meant the same thing to her as it would have to a person who believes that this information was directly relevant to him or her. Cognitive understanding appears to be an insufficient measure of the individual's capacity for interpreting his or her situation. (8)

Members of the Program in Psychiatry and the Law at the Massachusetts Mental Health Center have developed a competence schema designed to call attention to certain realities of clinical functioning often misunderstood or insufficiently acknowledged in the theoretical literature on competence determination. Like previous models, this one is based on substantive elements of the treatment decision, four in number: 1) the facts pertaining to the decision at hand; 2) the values that characterize the patient's system of belief, that is, the importance that he or she assigns to life, health, autonomy, freedom from pain, bodily integrity, liberty, etc. 3) the probabilities relating to the decision (e.g., probabilities of success or failure and of side effects); and 4) the relationships involved in the decision—usually, the relationship between the patient who is to make the decision about a medical procedure and the clinician who recommends it, although at times the pivotal relationships are those among family members.

This last point in particular is often scanted in theoretical discussions of competence. Yet our clinical experience makes it clear that a patient's competence can be so powerfully affected by the quality of the doctor-patient relationship as to be almost wholly contingent upon it. A patient may thus be competent with one therapist but not with another because of differences in the two relationships. (In an analogous way, it is occasionally the case that a patient is competent to stand trial when working with one attorney but incompetent when working with another.) An implication of this point is that competence does not "reside" in the patient alone but to some extent represents a dyadic phenomenon. Like psychotherapy, then, competence assessment is a process shaped by the relationship between therapist and patient.

We propose that each of the four elements of decision making—facts, values, probabilities, and relationships—is influenced by the cognitive and affective dimensions of a person's makeup, both as strengths and as possible impairments. By viewing competence in these bimodal terms (cognitive and affective), we advance our thesis: that competence is as often influenced by subjective emotional processes as it is by those of objective, logical, or rational thought.

In the remainder of this chapter we will examine mania and depression in an attempt to illuminate the ways in which these affective disorders may impair competence in the clinical and legal settings.

MANIA AND COMPETENCE: A CASE EXAMPLE

Mr. M, a 30-year-old man with an eight-year history of bipolar illness, was admitted from the court on charges of creating a public disturbance. Mental status examination revealed rapid press of speech, flight of ideas, persecutory and grandiose delusions, and very irritable mood; previous psychological testing had revealed an IQ of 120. The patient's lithium level on admission was 0.1 ng/ml (a sub-therapeutic level, suggesting the patient had not followed his prescribed dosage). The purpose of this admission—the fifth in this hospital in two years—was to evaluate Mr. M's competence to stand trial, each previous admission having occurred under similar circumstances.

Prior to these admissions, Mr. M had been hospitalized twice elsewhere for manic behavior, which had responded well to lithium carbonate when maintained at adequate blood levels. Upon his first admission to this hospital, he had refused combined neuroleptic and lithium treatment, stating that the neuroleptic affected his tongue but noting that he would take lithium alone, since it had been helpful in the past. On that and three subsequent admissions he took lithium, with or without a neuroleptic. On each occasion, in two or three weeks he was able to return to his apartment and resume his job at an accounting firm.

During the hospital stay under discussion, Mr. M was repeatedly offered lithium, and he refused it each time. In discussing his reasons, he described accurately the uncomfortable side effects and possible renal damage. He also denied that lithium could possibly help him, saying, "Lithium is for manic depression and I'm not manic." He also stated repeatedly that, although he had been manic in the past, lithium had never been helpful.

On the advice of a consultant, guardianship for consent to medication was sought. Due to the scheduling of the court, however, a hearing was not obtained for 40 days, during which time Mr. M's symptoms remained unchanged. At the hearing, the consultant stated that the patient's amnesia or denial of established prior benefit indicated an inability to weigh the possible risks and benefits of the treatment—how can one weigh an element of the decision (i.e., a benefit), if one does not even recognize it? The judge accepted this reasoning and guardianship was granted.

Eventually, when informed that guardianship had been granted, the patient began taking lithium voluntarily. Within two weeks his manic symptoms had begun to abate, and one week later he was discharged to outpatient follow-up. Six months after discharge, still on lithium, Mr. M was working as an administrative assistant and living independently.

Several features of this case are noteworthy. The patient had an above-average IQ and, when not suffering from an acute episode of mental illness, performed well at his work. When these abilities are viewed together with Mr. M's clear articulation of the negative effects of medication, it appears unlikely that a lack of cognitive ability was involved in his incapacity to recognize the previously experienced, documented benefits of lithium. He aptly demonstrated an ability to recognize the risks of treatment but consistently denied the history of positive effects, despite earlier requests for this medication because of its beneficial effect.

This case demonstrates with particular clarity two important factors pertaining to the determination of competence: first, that variations in the clinical state of a patient with an affective disorder may alter competence even when some cognitive capacities are preserved; and second, that competence to make a treatment decision requires that both risks and benefits be considered during the decision-making process.

The case further dramatizes how, in actual clinical situations, cognition and affect are closely tied to one another; they are distinguishable yet interactive. Manic denial is, strictly speaking, a defensive cognition—a by-product of manic euphoria: "Nothing is wrong or could be wrong with me, hence no benefits could flow from treatment." Yet such denial is intimately related to, even springs from, a mood state, yielding a specific synergistic response. The expected outcome of nontreatment—"I'll be just great"—is predicted subjectively, not rationally, and the notion of a desirable benefit finds no place in the patient's world view.

In his discussion of the competence criteria reviewed by Roth et al., Friedman offers a convincing argument for the "rational reasons" or "recognizable reasons" criterion as best fulfilling the purposes of a test of competence (9). By this criterion one is competent to give or withhold consent to treatment if one can give recognizable reasons (i.e., acceptable relevant premises and related conclusions) for the choice one makes. This test gives proper attention to the process (rather than merely the result) of decision making. It also respects personal freedom and individual variation, provided they are interpreted in the context of a person's demonstrated capacity or incapacity to order his or her life satisfactorily.

Friedman cites two examples of failure to provide recognizable reasons: false premises and non sequitur conclusions. Non sequiturs are more common in cognitive disturbances, while false premises may be associated more frequently with affective disorders. In the case of Mr. M, the false premise is the view that nothing is wrong, which is rooted in the manic feeling of self-sufficiency and invulnerability. To need anything (such as the benefit of a treatment) is to be less than perfect—a position inconsistent with the manic state. The false premise that nothing is wrong thus leads to denial of the possibility that a proposed treatment could offer any benefit. An inability to acknowledge a benefit, in turn, vitiates the patient's capacity to make a decision that is based on a risk-benefit analysis, which is the essence of discussions of consent and competence in regard to proposed medical treatments.

DEPRESSION AND COMPETENCE: THEORETICAL ISSUES

> Mr. D was a 50-year-old man who had been recommended for electroconvulsive therapy (ECT) for depression. He appeared able to grasp cognitively the fact that ECT had a 90 percent success rate; he was also able to recite back the relevant side effects, thereby ostensibly demonstrating his competence to comprehend the facts of the treatment. In his depressed state, however, he arrived at conclusions regarding these facts that were distorted by his illness. He assumed he was doomed to be in the 10 percent failure group—a view reflecting his depressive pessimism. He further expected that the side effects were absolutely certain to occur in his case because "that's just what I deserve"—a view reflecting the guilty feelings so common in depression. Such reasoning would suggest that this patient was not competent to weigh the risks and benefits of treatment, since his affective state altered his ability to assimilate operationally and realistically the probabilities involved in the decision. (9)

This case provides another example of Friedman's false premises as a predominant form of incompetent reasoning (9). In this case, the false premise is the patient's conviction that his depression will never abate and that he is incurable. Recall that in the previous case feelings of grandiosity and self-sufficiency led the patient to deny any benefit of treatment, thus impairing his ability to weigh the risks and benefits in order to make a competent decision about treatment. Here, somewhat like the schizophrenic patients described by Soskis (10)—who recalled very well all the side effects of treatment but not as well the expected benefits—Mr. D is particularly sensitive to the risks of treatment and is convinced of a bad outcome. This depressive reasoning impairs his competence in making a treatment decision.

An important contribution to the question of affective factors influencing competence was provided by Beck in a study of great relevance to our investigations here (11). For the sake of clarity, a few prefatory words about Beck are required. Responding to what he called a relative lack of emphasis on the thought processes in depression (11), Beck studied these processes in depressed patients and found a number of manifestations of disordered thinking. To differentiate his findings from older formulations of depression, Beck used the term "cognition" to denote "a specific thought, such as an interpretation, a self-command or a self-criticism." Thus, Beck's idiosyncratic definition differs from that implicitly employed by legal authorities, for whom the term "cognition" connotes the entire process of logical or rational manipulation of information—not, as Beck defines it, single specific thoughts, most often self-evaluative and self-reflective, that pervade the patient's entire life experience. To avert possible confusion, note that Beck is describing the role of an affective state (depression) in shaping a person's thoughts; thus, although he uses the word "cognition" to refer to these thoughts, he is still proposing a model based on affect.

Beck has claimed that specific cognitions (thoughts) are associated with the affect of depression: the depressed person thinks in idiosyncratic and predominantly negative terms about the self, the environment, and the future (11). Among the objects of such thinking are one's own moods (part of the self), the physician (part of the environment), and the predicted course of illness in response to treatment (part of the future).

Table 8.1 lists 10 specific manifestations of disordered thinking that Beck observed in depressed patients. While they all represent the depressive end of the spectrum of major affective disorders, one might well expect to see some counterparts on the manic end as well. Next to each manifestation listed, we provide a clinical example of how it might strongly influence the patient's decision-making process and thus, in essence, bias the choices regarding treatment. The table illustrates that any one or more of the 10 aspects of affectively disordered thinking may impede the patient's ability to weigh the risks and benefits of treatment and, thus, to make a competent decision in this area.

For our purposes here, it is useful to view these manifestations of disordered thought as associated with decision making in the depressed state. Whether the factors that Beck describes actually cause depression or, as some of his critics would suggest, whether they are merely epiphenomena and symptoms of depression remains unclear. Our analysis is essentially neutral with respect to this debate, since we rely only on translations of Beck's phenomenology into terms relevant to "decision-making disorders."

This model might be interpreted to suggest that competence in patients with major affective disorders is mediated only through the specific cognitions described. We propose that this perspective may eventually prove too limited. Empirical investigation is needed to establish the extent of selective perceptions and causal reasoning, as well as to define the exact mechanism by which competence is impaired. This question cannot be definitively answered at this point.

Table 8.1.
Beck's Manifestations of Depressive Cognition in Clinical Situations[a]

Depressive Cognition	Clinical Instance
1. All-or-nothing thinking	Medication that does not bring full relief is thought to be worthless.
2. Overgeneralization	Medication is rejected on the basis of one side effect.
3. Mental filter	View of treatment or prognosis is darkened by one negative detail.
4. Disqualifying the positive	Beneficial effects of medication are not considered.
5. Jumping to conclusions	A merely possible side effect is viewed as certainty.
6. Catastrophization and minimization	Severity of side effects is overestimated and the value of positive effects is underestimated.
7. Emotional reasoning	Negative emotions such as hopelessness are assumed to reflect the state of reality.
8. "Should" statements	Treatment is seen as interfering with deserved punishment: "I should suffer."
9. Labeling and mis-labeling	One brands oneself as a failure and rejects disconfirmation.
10. Personalization	One blames oneself for illness or holds oneself fully responsible for success of treatment.

[a]Adapted from: Beck AT. Depression: Causes and treatment. Philadelphia: University of Pennsylvania Press, 1967.

In any case, an additional contribution by Beck can here serve the function of dovetailing the clinical realities of affective disorders with the existing legal criteria for competence. Beck identified four nonratiocinative characteristics of depressive cognition: automatic quality, involuntarity, plausibility, and perseveration (11). These characteristics result in what he calls "idiosyncratic thoughts," which in turn may influence decision making. Since they are directly relevant to legal interpretations of the existing criteria for competence, these characteristics can be used heuristically to clarify the relation between affectively disordered decision making and legal competence determinations. Some illustrations may be in order.

Beck's "automatic thoughts" are those that occur "without any apparent antecedent reflection or reasoning." Clearly, the individual whose decision making is thus "automatic" is not acting in the reasoned manner envisioned by the formulators of competence criteria.

In Beck's formulation, "involuntary thoughts" cannot be prevented, even though the patient may realize that they are involuntary and resolve not to have them; such thoughts "pre-empt a more rational process." The affectively disturbed patient's awareness of the facts or personally preferred choices would not prevent penetration of idiosyncratic thoughts into the decision-making process. The manner in which such a process might intrude on the initial weighing of risks and benefits is probably self-evident, provided that patients can report adequately on their own thought processes.

In regard to plausibility, Beck found that depressed patients accept uncritically thoughts that are consonant with their mood disturbance, without regard for their world view or goals and beliefs before they became depressed. Affectively disordered patients thus may include in an otherwise intact decision-making process either information or a belief that—although untrue—they accept uncritically. The thoroughgoing pessimism of the man who expected only negative results from ECT is one example of this type of idiosyncratic thought and its interference with competent decision making. In that case, the man did not understand that his certainty about a bleak future was the product of his illness rather than reality. A patient in this situation might well be able to identify the risks of treatment but would bring to that identification a depression-born certainty of their occurrence, rendering the treatment decision unrealistic and hence incompetent.

Finally, in regard to perseveration, Beck found that:

> Despite the multiplicity and complexity of life situations, the depressed patient was prone to interpret a wide range of experiences in terms of a few stereotyped ideas. The role of this mental functioning in contaminating decision making is self-evident. (11)

One point remains unaddressed: the problem of translating the foregoing clinical material into a legal context. From a practical viewpoint, it is true in competence assessment as it is in many other areas of medicine that classic cases are readily recognizable. The unmistakable form of a syndrome poses no challenge to the diagnostician. Similarly, the patient who is floridly psychotic, demented, or otherwise grossly incompetent poses little challenge for either the clinician or the court.

However, it is not uncommon to encounter instances in which a patient's capacity to make treatment decisions is impaired in a very subtle degree, so that the impairment may be missed by the assessing clinician or, even if detected, may be rejected by the court that later rules on the matter. As the foregoing discussion suggests, a number of these cases involve affective impairment of competence. Either the clinician or the court may be inexperienced with these matters of subtle incompetence. Our experience has taught that the capacity to articulate coherent sentences, containing plausibly valid facts, by itself may appear to offer a significant argument for a patient's competence. That is, articulateness may be confused with a full-fledged decision-making capacity (12).

This confusion is directly relevant to the denying manic or hypomanic patient and the pessimistically depressed patient, as above described. In each case the illness often leaves the patient's intellect, articulateness, and coherence of thought unscathed while striking at the fundamental capacity to make decisions in ways that this chapter in part illustrates.

Thus, the manic patient who can explain the risks of a proposed treatment, while denying or ignoring the benefits, might well pass for competent in the courtroom. By their very nature, courts tend to be risk-aversive (since, throughout case law, individuals litigate harms— that is, the consequences of risks—and no one litigates benefits). From the court's perspective, a patient who can articulate the risks of treatment might seem to be properly focused on the more significant side of the equation and thus appear to be competent, unless the patient's denial of benefits is detected and pointed out to the court, as it was in the case of Mr. M. The ability to communicate such information to courts is a skill clinicians would do well to learn.

CONCLUSION

We hypothesize, on the basis of both Beck's theory and the observations reported here, that individuals with major affective disorders may be predisposed to minimize or deny the benefits of treatment and perhaps to overemphasize the risks. The ability of such patients to comprehend and cite explicit negative effects of medication, on the one hand, demonstrates the retention of at least some cognitive capacity, although their certainty of a bad outcome clouds the realism of this assessment. Denial of the therapeutic benefits of the same medication (even previously experienced benefits, as in the case of Mr. M), on the other hand, is also a function of the affective disturbance. Such an imbalance may lead to decision making that is itself imbalanced to the degree that it is incompetent.

We hope that empirical work will shed more light on the role of affect in impairing competence. More practically, since clinicians play an important part in determining competence to make treatment decisions, it is essential that they become familiar with the ways in which affective states can impair competence. These issues can then be clearly presented to courts involved in competence assessment (12), thus sparing patients the negative consequences of being deemed competent to refuse treatment, their true incompetence going unrecognized.

REFERENCES

1. Roth LH, Meisel A, Lidz CW. Tests of competency with the consent to treatment. Am J Psychiatry 1977;134:279–284.
2. Grisso T. Evaluating competencies: forensic assessments and instruments. New York: Plenum, 1986.
3. Gutheil TG, Appelbaum PS. Clinical handbook of psychiatry and the law. New York: McGraw-Hill, 1982.
4. *Dusky v U.S.* 362 US 402 (1960).
5. *Rumbaugh v Procunier* (83-1161 U.S. Court of Appeals, 5th Cir, Feb. 20, 1985).
6. Bonnie R. Personal communication, 1984.
7. Appelbaum PS, Roth LH. Clinical issues in the assessment of competency. Am J Psychiatry 1981;138:1462–1467.
8. Roth LH, Appelbaum PS, Sallee R, et al. The dilemma of denial in the assessment of competency to refuse treatment. Am J Psychiatry 1982;139:910–913.
9. Freidman B. Competence, marginal and otherwise: concepts and ethics. Intl J Law Psychiatry 1981;4:53–72.
10. Soskis DA. Schizophrenic and medical inpatients as informed drug consumers. Arch Gen Psychiatry 1978;35:645–647.
11. Beck AT. Depression: Causes and treatment. Philadelphia: University of Pennsylvania Press, 1967.
12. Gutheil TG, Bursztajn HJ. Clinicians guidelines for assessing and presenting subtle forms of patient incompetence in legal settings. Am J Psychiatry 1986;143:1020–1023.

chapter 9.
DECISION MAKING: THE LEGAL PERSPECTIVE

Attorneys, like physicians and other clinicians, make decisions affected by a wide range of data and subject to a broad spectrum of both subtle and overt influences. But clinicians often view the behavior of attorneys—indeed, the legal process itself—with a mixture of perplexity and outrage. Not surprisingly, our strongest reactions are usually reserved for opposing legal counsel; attorneys may be beasts of a different species, but we tend to regard our own legal representative as being at least partially domesticated, if not fully understandable.

The reactions of clinicians to attorneys do not arise solely from the stresses of being involved in litigation, however. The entire legal system is alien and mysterious, as well as aggravating, to most non-attorneys. It is our goal in this chapter to reduce some of the mystery by discussing the similar dilemmas that clinicians and attorneys face, as well as the differences between the two groups; by looking at the relationship between attorneys and their clients; and by exploring the process that attorneys engage in when deciding whether to accept a given case.

CLINICIANS AND ATTORNEYS: SOME ETHICAL COMPARISONS

Most clinicians are willing to subscribe to the position that they, and their work, are fundamentally different from that of attorneys. Hundert has described the differing ethical theories upon which the legal system and the clinical (medical) systems are based (1). He notes that law is grounded in deontological theory: there are certain rules that govern behavior and designate whether a given action is a virtue or vice; an ethical person embraces the former and eschews the latter. The end result of such behavior is largely immaterial; so long as the action itself is in accordance with the prescribed behavior, it is moral. Medicine, in contrast, and clinical practice in general are grounded in teleology. A type of utilitarianism, teleological theory dictates that moral behavior is that which helps to achieve the best end for the most individuals. A person behaves ethically if his or her actions help to further this goal.

Distinguishing between law and medicine on this basis helps shed light on the difficulties that lawyers and clinicians have in understanding one another. Yet this distinction misrepresents the ethical lives of both most attorneys and most clinicians. Clinical practice is not so firmly rooted in teleology that we disregard rules of procedure and fairness in making our decisions. And lawyers, while working within a system based upon procedure and fairness, do not ignore teleological issues. Indeed, Fuller (2) has suggested that the morality of law is composed of two separate duties, the morality of duty (deontological) and the morality of aspiration (teleological). He explains that latter by noting that the law has an obligation to help each individual reach his or her highest level of attainment—a goal strikingly familiar to clinicians.

Both authors of this chapter have practiced within the legal and clinical systems, and both have had the experience of hearing those who practice within each of these systems berate the members of the other. In this chapter we hope to correct some of this misunderstanding. And at the risk of being branded as apologists for the legal profession, we will argue against the position taken by most clinicians that we (the clinicians) are moral and they (the attorneys) are immoral or, at best, amoral. The difficulties that each has with the other stem primarily from frustration in balancing the moral priorities of the two systems; and this balancing, in turn, reflects the larger requirement of society to balance the needs and rights of the individual against the needs and rights of the whole.

For the purpose of this discussion, let us identify two ethical principles underlying clinical practice: beneficence and respect for autonomy (3, 4). The principle of beneficence requires clinicians to use their skills to provide maximum benefits to the patient and to prevent harm and the potential for harm. The principle of autonomy requires us to view our patients, and others, as free beings with a right to be self-governing in all matters, including the choice of medical treatment. It is characteristic of ethical analysis that these pillars of ethics should so readily and frequently conflict. Indeed, it is the nature of moral reasoning that there is often more than one moral answer; the ultimate decision is reached by balancing moral priorities. As Hundert has pointed out, for a situation to merit the denotation, "ethical dilemma," it must have no clear right answer (5).

Our introductory case demonstrates nicely how Dr. Newell and his supervisor are caught in an ethical bind. Their decision-making process is the subject of a large portion of this volume, and we will not repeat that analysis here. What should be noted is the shifting nature of their decision-making process as the case progresses. For example, Dr. Newell initially approaches the problem from the standpoint of the patient's beneficence: What are Ms. Adams' problems and what can be done to relieve them? He starts by examining the risk factors and concludes that Ms. Adams will be best served by hospitalization. The suggestion of voluntary hospitalization, grounded in the principle of beneficence, falters, however, when Ms. Adams exercises her autonomy and refuses.

Dr. Newell is now faced with an ethical dilemma. If he strongly favors hospitalization, does he have an obligation to persuade her, as Callahan (6) would suggest, or is he required to yield to her refusal? In thinking about this dilemma, he weighs various clinical and nonclinical factors: the courts are too crowded to handle another commitment, the institution will get a bad reputation if the commitment is not upheld, patients can sue for false imprisonment, patients kill themselves in the hospital anyway, and is it fair to hospitalize her for the physician's peace of mind? After consideration of all these and the countervailing factors, Dr. Newell decides that the conservative approach—hospitalization—would be the safest, even though he does not believe the patient is committable. He then looks to his supervisor, presenting the case to her in a fashion that is by necessity biased, and transmits his own ambivalence about the situation. They reach agreement that she will not be hospitalized.

Dr. Newell's decision-making process is familiar to anyone who has worked in psychiatric emergency rooms and has been faced with patients who play out their ambivalence toward life through others, giving out one message and then another. It is a clinical and moral roller coaster ride, with beneficence, autonomy, fairness, the law, the duty to follow procedures, and our own sense of responsibility providing the twists and turns. Distinctions between deontology and teleology become increasingly blurred in the process, as their relative merits are balanced. Dr. Newell has the opportunity to make a choice to resolve this dilemma, a choice based upon a weighing of a variety of factors: beneficence, respect for autonomy, a sense of fairness to self and patient, a need to avoid potential malpractice liability. Some of these may be regarded as "moral" and others as "nonmoral."[a] Dr. Newell defers this balancing by looking to his supervisor for her input. The result is a decision at odds with both his initial and final conclusions as to what is best for the patient: hospitalization, a choice based in good faith.

---

[a]For the purpose of this chapter, we refer to moral principles in the narrow sense, equating them with questions of values.

Few of us would condemn Dr. Newell as being immoral because he avoided making a decision based solely on moral values; he simply chose a path that would allow him to share the burden of his decision with others and to base it on a full range of considerations (including his own uncertainty) rather than on moral values alone. This is a choice which many of us make routinely in our lives and our practices. Such choices are often guided by the particular function we each play in the decision-making process. Dr. Newell in this case was the resident on call. We can imagine him a few years hence, serving as director of an inpatient unit, with a duty of beneficence to individual patients, as well as to the unit as a whole and to the larger institution. In that role, he will often be forced to balance the needs of the patient against the needs of the unit. Fear of loss of credibility in the commitment process will be joined with fears of loss of credibility with utilization reviewers; the patient's right to confidentiality may be sacrificed in an effort to gain insurer approval for a longer length of stay, and so on. Each of these encounters may require that Dr. Newell identify and resolve a moral dilemma—which will allow avoidance of the moral conflict. It is not uncommon for clinicians and health care administrators to seek such a procedural or systemic solution by turning to the law.

In the paragraphs above, we have seen how clinicians can differ not only among themselves, but within themselves, on how they balance moral priorities. The fact that individual clinicians may or may not reach a "correct" decision does not define him or her as moral or immoral; the question is whether or not moral principles play a role in the decision-making process. Using this standard, we can agree that, while he may not have done so in a deliberate fashion, Dr. Newell acted in a manner consistent with what we would view as moral behavior. What, then, of the claim that clinicians are good (moral) and attorneys are evil (immoral)? The answer lies in an examination of the structure of the legal system, the duties attorneys owe to their clients, the manner in which attorneys relate to their clients, and the efforts they make to discharge their duties.

THE ADVERSARIAL SYSTEM

The clinician encountering the legal system finds a very different world from that of clinical practice. In clinical care, particularly mental health care, ambiguity tends to be the rule rather than the exception. The internist may be called to treat a fever of unknown origin or an infection from an unknown source. The neurologist is asked to treat headaches symptomatically when no physiological cause can be found. The psychiatrist caring for a manic patient with psychotic symptoms may deliberate over a diagnosis of bipolar disorder versus schizoaffective disorder, yet the treatment initially is the same. Moreover, the psychotherapist not only tolerates ambiguity but uses it as a tool. In each of these cases, truth appears to be measured against an absolute standard, based upon empirical observations and consensus within the scientific community. It is the result that is the judge in medicine; truth is determined by the response to treatment or at autopsy. So long as there is relief of suffering and no undue harm to the patient, the clinical behavior is moral.

The adversarial system of the law is quite different. Its search for truth is procedural, rather than empirical, based upon the notion that each party to a dispute should argue the case from that party's perspective and present what evidence it has, with truth determined by a neutral trier of fact according to a groundwork of rules. The law is primarily deontological—its "rightness" depends upon the extent to which proper procedures are followed in reaching the result, not whether the result provides the most good for the most people. Let us use an example from mental health practice to compare the two systems.

Suppose a clinical syndrome involving flashbacks, nightmares, anxiety, and self-destructive impulses is identified. Patients seem to benefit from treatment with benzodiazepines and supportive psycho-therapy. Various theories are developed regarding the causes of this disorder: infection, early physical trauma, radiation from a new brand of toaster, and unresolved Oedipal conflicts are all postulated as causes. Each school of thought has its devoted members, although most clinicians remain open to any possibilities and use whatever aspects of each approach seem most helpful. Eventually, after much research, an identifiable cause may be found. In the meantime, however, treatment will continue as before in an effort to reduce the symptoms. Suppose further that a patient, Mr. D, suffers from this syndrome and claims that it developed shortly after he purchased a toaster for home use. He and his attorney decide to file suit against the toaster manufacturer, seeking to recover monetary damages for the harm allegedly caused to him by the toaster.

In the adversarial process, representatives from each of the schools of thought regarding causes of the syndrome might be called as expert witnesses. Mr. D would ask that the expert on "toaster exposure syndrome" testify, while the defense would call those who believe that infection, early trauma, or unresolved Oedipal impulses cause the symptoms in question. The empirical process is displaced by the adversarial process. At the end of the trial (assuming there is no settlement) a nonclinician or group of nonclinicians (judge or jury) will decide whether or not toasters cause the syndrome. This is a decision that the scientific community may accept or reject, but the ultimate conclusions of the scientific community will be irrelevant to this proceeding.

These are clearly two very different means of approaching conflict resolution and truth finding. The law requires that a decision be made; the accuracy and acceptability of the result are determined by the extent to which the decision making *process* is followed. There are good reasons for this. The legal system was developed to move conflict resolution from the battlefield and street to a more civilized arena. It was designed to avoid prolongation of conflict and to provide a set of rules by which conflicts could be contained and resolved, and innocence or guilt determined, so that society could then move on to other, more productive activities. The premise is that if each side has an opportunity to present its version of events, and the opportunity to question the other side's version, the fact finder (judge or jury) will be afforded the best opportunity to determine the "truth." Thus, trial by jury is considered to be an improvement over trial by ordeal (fire, dunking stool, the rack), because it is more rationally designed to establish truth, as well as more socially efficient than warfare.

THE ATTORNEY-CLIENT RELATIONSHIP

The proposition that clinicians have certain duties toward their patients has been discussed extensively in early chapters. These duties are established by custom, codes of professional ethics, and statute. They are examined, refined, and sometimes created by judges and juries faced with the question of whether an individual practitioner has failed to fulfill his or her responsibility to a given patient.

Attorneys have similar duties toward their clients, established in a similar manner, and these duties have also come under the scrutiny of the adversarial system as the number of legal malpractice cases has increased. Among the duties considered foremost for attorneys is the fiduciary duty, which requires the attorney to exercise professional judgment solely in the best interest of the client. This should sound familiar; it is analogous to the medical ethic of beneficence, which is sometimes referred to as the clinician's fiduciary duty to the patient. Other duties include representing clients "zealously within the bounds of the law"; maintaining confidentiality of all information revealed in the context of the attorney-client relationship, whether or not it is related to the task at hand; and avoiding conflicts of interest (7).

Just as the clinician gets into an ethical bind in trying to carry out simultaneously the duties to respect the often conflicting values of autonomy, beneficence, and fairness, so does the attorney get caught between the duty to serve the best interests of the client and the other duties noted. As in medicine, the question arises as to who defines "best interest." While informed consent is hardly a mainstay of modern legal practice, it is the client who must make the decision to continue a contract dispute or to settle it, to plead guilty or to exercise the right to a jury trial. Nevertheless, the attorney's influence, like that of doctors of old, is extremely powerful, and legal paternalism is quite common. The constraint on the attorney, more so than on physicians, lies in the initial contract for services. While many potential clients approach an attorney with no idea of their ultimate goal, many others have their goals firmly in mind and are looking only for someone who can help them maneuver around the legal obstacles. It was for these clients that the old maxim was coined: The lawyer's job isn't to tell clients what they can't do; it's to tell them how they can do what they want to do. The ethical dilemmas created by this situation are numerous, just as they are for the physician approached by a patient with set ideas about acceptable treatment options.

The introductory case in this volume provides an example of these legal dilemmas. Mr. Adams approaches his old friend Mr. Jameson, unsure of whether or not he wants to file a lawsuit. Mr. Jameson listens to the story and responds in a manner reminiscent of a clinician engaging in an informed consent dialogue with a patient. He defines the problem; outlines the risks, costs, and benefits of pursuing litigation; suggests alternatives; and gives Mr. Adams a chance to ask questions. While he leaves the decision up to Mr. Adams, he gives his professional opinion on the issue as an objective party, not an advocate. He leaves himself free either to act on his old friend's behalf or to turn down the case if Mr. Adams decides to proceed against his advice. Mr. Adams leaves the office angry at the suggestion that he find some other means of resolving his emotional reaction to the suicide, but he has gathered some important information. He has learned about those elements of the situation that make it look like a "bad case" and diminish its desirability for litigation.

Mr. Jameson's ethical dilemma results from his conflicting duties to Mr. Adams. His professional duty is to listen, diagnose his friend's problem, and render an honest, objective opinion as to the possibility of a lawsuit and the likelihood of its success. As a counselor, a consultant, this is his job. But what if Mr. Adams decides that the benefits of a suit outweigh the risks and asks Mr. Jameson to file suit on his behalf? Does he refer the case to someone else because he disagrees with the client's risk-benefit analysis, or does he allow the client to make the decision and accept the case because everyone is entitled to pursue his/her remedies for legitimate complaints in court? This is the familiar conflict among beneficence, autonomy, and justice. Strict adherence to deontological theory, which we later see practiced by the senior partner in the second law firm, would seem to require that Mr. Jameson accept the case. Yet we see Mr. Jameson placed in a position where he struggles with the balance, just as many a clinician has struggled in a variety of settings.

Unlike Mr. Jameson, Mr. Lyons is forced to face these issues more directly. As the reader will recall from the case example, Mr. Lyons is an associate (a junior attorney) at the law firm Mr. Adams next consults. Mr. Lyons hears a slightly different version of Mr. Adams's relationship with his wife, her treatment, and her suicide: the difficulties in the relationship are minimized, Mr. Adams' desire to help his wife is maximized, and his exclusion from her treatment is emphasized. Finally, Mr. Adams presents his motives as altruistic in nature: he is willing to pursue the suit, in spite of the emotional burden of proceeding, "if it will help save someone else's life." The case is presented not only as one with merit, but as one in which recovery for the plaintiff would represent justice.

Following the detailed explanation of the contingency fee arrangement and some additional questioning, Mr. Lyons begins the critical process of reviewing the facts of the case to determine its merits. His conclusion is that, while it appears that some mistakes were made, there "wasn't obvious malpractice." He remains doubtful about the merits of the case after it is reviewed by two other psychiatrists. One of these apparently is a well-known plaintiff's expert, who clearly lacks objectivity and renders an opinion of malpractice in this case as he does in most others. The other expert, Dr. Flaherty, delineates both sides of the argument but points out that there is little evidence of malpractice.

The discussion between Mr. Lyons and his senior partner focuses on the decision whether or not to take the case; this specific issue will be discussed in the next section. But the discussion is also about whether or not Mr. Lyons, as an attorney, can fulfill his obligations to his client, Mr. Adams, to the best of his ability and within the confines of his professional and personal ethics. Foremost among his concerns is whether or not justice will be served by litigating this case; or to put it somewhat literally, whether he will truly serve his calling as an attorney by lending his intellect and skills to an end he considers potentially unjust. This is a difficult struggle for any attorney, but especially so for the young attorney whose livelihood is so dependent upon the approval of his senior colleagues. Like Dr. Newell, Mr. Lyons must examine a variety of factors before making a decision whether or not to recommend that Mr. Adams pursue the case, analogous to Dr. Newell's decision whether or not to pursue commitment. Like Dr.

Newell, Mr. Lyons avoids facing the ethical dilemma squarely by deferring to the judgment of his senior partner and yielding to pragmatic considerations related to his own career progress.

The senior partner, on the other hand, cites the importance of procedures and role fulfillment in the legal process. He points out that it is not for the advocates to decide what outcome is just, but to advocate, based upon their good-faith belief that there is a cause of action. The relative merits of the case are not to be decided by the attorneys but by the trier of fact. The analogous dilemma for the clinician would be posed by the question of whether to commit a patient who only marginally meets commitment criteria but whose best interest is served by hospitalization. There, hospitalization is in service of the primary goal of beneficence; here, litigation is in service of the primary goal of allowing all individuals an opportunity to pursue their remedies at law. This partner would argue, we think, that the ability to separate one's personal views about the merits of a case from one's professional position is what makes one a professional: objectivity, not personal belief, is the desideratum. Otherwise, only those who personally believed that it was proper behavior to rob banks could represent a bank robber and still be deemed "moral" under our standards. This is reflected in the ethical directive which requires attorneys to accept "unpopular" cases (8). Society would be poorly served if we had bank robbers representing bank robbers; instead, we value having those who believe in the constitutional mandates of the criminal justice system defend those accused of crime, even if they disapprove of their clients' behavior. Similarly, the physician who believes that a certain treatment is in the best interest of the patient may have to choose to transfer the care of that patient to another physician if the patient disagrees with the treatment or to modify the treatment plan to what the patient decides is in his or her own best interests; that is, individuals vary too widely in their personal preferences for society to provide a physician who will match the preferences of each individual.

Should Mr. Lyons and his senior partner have given greater consideration to Mr. Adams' deeper motives for filing suit and their psychological ramifications? To the extent that a client should be made aware of the costs (financial and emotional) of bringing suit, it is important for an attorney to attend to this issue. On the other hand, the nature of the adversarial system is such that prolonged inquiry beyond that necessary to ascertain that there is a reasonable basis for the claim would be inappropriate. The good-enough therapist inquires further; the good-enough attorney need go no further than Mr. Lyons did. Some attorneys do pursue these issues—indeed, those who are most successful are likely to probe a client's motives as a means of ascertaining the strength of his or her conviction and willingness to pursue the case to completion.

For the relationship between attorney and client to succeed, there must be some unity of purpose and collaboration; in short, there must be an "advocacy alliance" similar to the therapeutic alliance mentioned earlier. Such alliances are based in part upon mutual trust. The client must be able to trust that the attorney is adhering to his or her professional duties: acting in the client's best interests, pursuing matters zealously, and sharing information. The attorney must be satisfied that the client is sharing information fully, that the information is accurate, and that the goals expressed are indeed those that the client holds. In other words, there is a need for absolute honesty between attorney and client. Recognition of the need for such a degree of honesty is demonstrated by the strict application of rules of confidentiality and privilege to attorney-client communications.

Beyond this issue of honesty, however, little attention is paid to the quality of the attorney-client relationship. Unlike the clinician-patient relationship, which is often a major focus of the work of therapy, the majority of the work in the legal relationship is done by the attorney alone in the library, the office, or the courtroom. Attorneys are rigorously trained in the various stages of the litigation process: examination and cross-examination of witnesses in and out of the courtroom, jury selection, courtroom demeanor, opening and closing arguments, and the myriad subtleties of evidentiary rules and practice. When we understand that attorneys are primarily invested in the *process* of litigation, the rationale for the preferential focus on these areas, with relative disregard for the attorney-client relationship, is clear. What also become clear are some of the reasons that clinicians and attorneys experience mutual frustration when confronted with the need to understand the other's mode of practice: each is convinced that the other's system is fixated on the wrong things and therefore misses the point. In fact, the two systems attempt to deal with many of the same questions—truth and reality, accountability and responsibility— and each is greatly concerned with the integrity of the process in which those issues are raised, examined and resolved. While the nature of the relationship between attorney and client is thought to be of relatively little importance in the overall scheme of the legal process, it is worth speculating about the effect that improved attorney-client interactions might have on the outcome of litigation.

Elsewhere in this volume, the notion of sharing uncertainty with patients has been discussed. Uncertainty in the legal process is externalized; it is attributed to the nature of the adversarial process and left to that process for resolution. As Sarat and Felstiner (9) point out, lawyers frequently emphasize to their clients the discretionary power of judges, suggesting that in divorce proceedings, at least, the legal process is only a limited form of justice. The legal process does not so much share uncertainty as externalize it, which perhaps accounts for the fact that the parties to litigation often feel dissatisfied with the outcome, even if they "win." The level of dissatisfaction is clearly even greater in the case of a "loss."

In summary, the relationships between clinician and patient and attorney and client differ in certain ways that reflect the different clinical and adversarial systems in which these relationships occur. But there are also some basic similarities, especially the duties to act in the best interests of the patient/client, to respect individual autonomy, and to promote justice.

THE DECISION TO TAKE A CASE

A variety of forces are at work as the potential plaintiff and his or her attorney ponder the issue of whether or not to pursue litigation. Several of these issues have been mentioned: the risks, costs, and benefits of litigation; the potential plaintiff's need to resolve feelings of guilt, anger, and loss; and the attorney's occasional belief that the potential client would be better served by pursuing some route other than litigation.

Dollars and Cents Issues

Law is a profession; it is a money-making occupation as well. One of the primary considerations in deciding to take a case is whether it is going to help pay the firm's bills. These include salaries for attorneys and support staff, as well as overhead expenses. Defense counsel in personal injury cases are paid on an hourly basis. Conversely, as pointed out in our sample case, the plaintiff's attorney is paid on a contingency fee basis. That is, if the plaintiff wins, the attorney's expenses are subtracted from the total award (expenses are often added onto the judgment), and the attorney receives approximately 30% of the remaining amount. Under this system, the attorney, after assessing a case and deciding that it has some potential for success, assumes the risks of that case. If the plaintiff loses, the attorney receives nothing and, in most cases, absorbs the expenses incurred during preparation of the case, including expert witness fees and the costs of obtaining deposition transcripts and medical records. The plaintiff has no direct financial costs, although the indirect costs of lost time from work and emotional stress are often considerable.

The contingency system has several potential effects. First, it encourages attorneys to take only those cases that are likely to be won. However, it may also lead an attorney to take a case with a low likelihood of a win but a high likelihood of a settlement in jurisdictions where juries are known to award large judgments. When a defendant clinician and his or her attorney are aware of the tendency of juries to make large awards, they will be more likely to settle a case that they could lose; they (or at least the defendant's insurer) will be moved to make the cautious decision.

The plaintiff's attorney will be moved to assess his or her risk based on the same information. In addition to being winnable, a case must be worth winning. This assessment requires the attorney to estimate the economic damages as well as the potential pain and suffering.

It is difficult, of course, to attach a dollar amount to pain and suffering. Estimates have been attempted, but the ultimate determination still rests on the emotional reaction of the jurors to the facts of the case and to the plaintiff and defendant. It is for this reason that legislative efforts at tort reform often attempt to put a dollar limit on awards for pain and suffering.

The financial component of the judgment (economic damages) consists of medical expenses, lost value of future earnings, and lost value of household services. The overall amount of damages in a wrongful death case may be decreased by the saved "consumption costs" (e.g., what the decedent would have consumed in terms of food, clothing, rent, and other services had she lived a normal life expectancy).

If the plaintiff prevails, the amount awarded is not simply the sum of pain and suffering, medical expenses, and lost future earnings. Money paid today is worth more than money paid out over time, because some portion of the amount paid today can be invested to generate more income. In order to avoid an overpayment to the plaintiffs, the "present value" is calculated. It is that amount that is awarded to the prevailing plaintiff (10).

In making these calculations, some attorneys rely upon educated guesses to decide whether the amount is high enough to make their efforts worthwhile. For those who seek a more detailed and accurate estimate, as well as a stronger basis for settlement negotiations, the services of expert witness economists and actuaries are available. These individuals can then be called to testify on damage issues at trial. At the early stages, which we are discussing here, attorneys generally use their own estimates, hand calculations, or a computer program which can provide a more accurate estimate of potential damages.

Thus, for the attorney deciding whether to take a malpractice case, a major consideration is the amount of money that the client may stand to be awarded (economic damages and pain and suffering). In assessing the potential damages, the attorney makes sure that the plaintiff is going to gain more than the emotional satisfaction that he assumes, initially, may come from dragging a clinician through the courts, and that the attorney is going to be compensated for his or her efforts. The emotional satisfaction derived by plaintiffs, win or lose, is usually uncertain, but the cost of the attorneys' time is a given.

Nonfinancial Matters

The plaintiff is likely to incur other costs if litigation is pursued. At some level, the filing of a malpractice action is an act of hostility and aggression. Thus, once filed, the plaintiff must have made a decision that the clinical relationship with the defendant is expendable—few such relationships survive legal action. Yet the decision to pursue litigation also means that the plaintiff will now have an adversarial relationship with the defendant—one that may continue for years. Like divorce proceedings, the malpractice suit does not signal the letting go of a relationship but, just the opposite, the establishment of a long-term but adversarial relationship.

The stress of litigation is substantial, for both plaintiffs and defendants. The plaintiff in a wrongful death case involving suicide, for example, can expect to be asked about personal interactions with the decedent, sexual matters, domestic disputes, extramarital affairs, and his or her personal psychiatric history. The plaintiff who sues seeking swift vengeance faces, in reality, a complicated, prolonged process fraught with delays, which may go on for years. Such stress—itself a "cost"—may negate any financial gains to be realized. The impact of litigation on the defendant clinician may be substantial (11, 12).

The attorney also faces a number of nonfinancial issues. Certainly, he or she must strike a balance between taking only those cases that are "sure winners" and also taking those that may yield a large settlement but have a low probability of succeeding. Holding out for the former would not be financially viable for the majority of personal injury attorneys; becoming involved in too many of the latter would result in too many financial losses. Failure to strike a balance may lead to the demise of the practice. But it is also important to the attorney's self-confidence and professional reputation that he or she have a good track record. Attorneys, like clinicians, like to be successful at what they do. This provides a basic motivation to select cases that are winners and allows for some degree of satisfaction even if the judgment is not large.

A different mixture of motives may influence the plaintiff's decision to sue. While the prospect of a substantial bottom-line recovery is of obvious importance, the final decision may be fueled by emotions other than simple greed. Anger at a physician for failing to share information or apologize for a mishap, or general bad relationships between doctor and patient or patient's family, may inspire the plaintiff to seek vengeance. Other emotions, such as guilt, may allow the plaintiff to displace his or her affect to the potential defendant. The plaintiff may feel, at least in the initial stages of a lawsuit, that he or she will gain more psychologically than financially from suing.

Earlier, we raised the question as to whether or not Mr. Lyons and his partner should have given consideration to Mr. Adams' deeper motives for pursuing litigation. Some might argue that a "good" attorney will seek to uncover the underlying motives of a potential client and turn down those cases in which psychological conflicts or other unconscious forces are pushing the client to sue. Such a position ignores several facts that go to the heart of what it means to practice a profession. First, *all* suits have a psychological dimension. In addition, attorneys, like clinicians, practice their profession as a form of livelihood. The economic considerations involved in offering legal (or clinical) services are intertwined with ethical obligations that can be seen as requiring actions that might be deemed unethical by those outside the profession. For example, attorneys take on an obligation of supporting and participating in the legal system, a system that embodies as a fundamental principle the notion of access for all. The premises of the adversarial system are that there are issues about which reasonable people may differ, and trial by jury is the fairest way of arriving at the "truth." Truth is to be determined in a rational manner, with procedure and fairness showing the way to accuracy. The fact that the plaintiff may have psychological conflicts and may have based the decision to sue on feelings rather than on conclusive proof may be fair game for the defense, but these conditions do not bar entry into the legal arena.

Most attorneys, like Mr. Jameson, will make some assessment of the extent to which the decision to sue is emotionally driven and try to dissuade the potential plaintiff from embarking on a course of litigation that will have little chance of satisfying this drive. The existence of such motivation alone does not count against the decision; indeed, in combination with a favorable loss profile, it may help sustain the resolve to see a difficult case through to a successful finish. As Mr. Jameson suggests, however, it may also be a warning signal that a potential plaintiff is in the "wrong court" to effect a resolution of his or her conflicts.

Over the preceding pages we have drawn attention to some of the similarities between clinicians and attorneys. Each of these professions has a very different focus on its work. This difference in focus accounts for some of the mutual discomfort and distrust which attorneys and clinicians feel for each other. Both seek the "truth" in some form but the processes through which they attempt to reach it are quite different. The therapeutic process, when successful, shares uncertainty and makes it possible to own and therefore to bear it. The legal process, when successful, displaces the uncertainty onto the adversarial system and strives to eliminate it entirely, thus allowing clients to disown it, that is, to avoid uncertainty and to tolerate the adversarial role in which they find themselves. The ongoing discomfort between clinicians and attorneys may well arise, at least in part, from this fundamental difference in tolerance for ambiguity and the manner in which it is handled. Clinicians will always question the ethics of attorneys, so long as the latter's adversarial approach of ignoring the uncertainties of one's position is viewed as a moral flaw rather than as an essential component of the adversarial process.

REFERENCES

1. Hundert EM. Competing medical and legal ethical values. In: Ethical practice in psychiatry and the law. Rosner R, Weinstock R, eds. New York: Plenum, 1990: 54–57.
2. Fuller LL. The morality of law. 2nd ed. New Haven: Yale University Press, 1969.
3. Beauchamp T, McCullough LB. Medical ethics: the moral responsibility of physicians. Englewood Cliffs, NJ: Prentice-Hall, 1984.
4. Beauchamp T, Childress JF. Principles of biomedical ethics. New York: Oxford University Press, 1989.
5. Hundert EM. Competing medical and legal ethical values. In: Ethical practice in psychiatry and the law. Rosner R, Weinstock R, eds. New York: Plenum, 1990: 53.
6. Callahan D. Minimalist ethics. Hastings Cent Rep 1981;11:19–25.
7. See, for example, Massachusetts Supreme Judicial Court Rule 3:07 Canons of Ethics: Disciplinary Rules Canon No. 7.
8. See, for example, Massachusetts Supreme Judicial Court Rule 3:07 Canons of Ethics: Disciplinary Rules Canon No. 2.
9. Sarat A, Felstiner WLF. Legal realism in lawyer-client communications. American Bar Foundation Working Paper No. 8723.
10. Shapiro AC. Moderate corporate finance. New York: McMallon, 1990, Ch. 2.
11. Charles SC, Wilbert JR, Kennedy EC. Physicians' self-reports of reactions to malpractice litigation. Am J Psychiatry 1984;141:563–565.
12. Charles SC, Warnecke RB, Wilbert JR. Stress among sued and nonsued physicians. Psychosomatics 1987;28:462–468.

SECTION IV. THE PROBLEM OF LIABILITY

chapter 10.
SUICIDE, MAGICAL THINKING, AND LIABILITY

A great clinician once referred to suicide as the final outcome of a "web of cause and chance," but such clarity is rare (1). A suicide leaves in its wake unanswered questions that reverberate through the lives of those who survive the victim. After the suicide of a patient, both family and psychiatrist are forced to reexamine their relationship with that person, their interactions at the time of the suicide, and their feelings about the victim. The way we think about suicide greatly affects how we think about malpractice litigation in its wake. To examine this complex subject, we will first look at the case that began this book.

FIXING THE BLAME FOR SUICIDE

A striking similarity in the responses of those who were involved in the immediate circumstances surrounding the death of Ms. Adams is that they all sought to fix the blame for her suicide. First, recall that in the note she left, she said, "I cannot live without my husband. Now that he has walked out on me, I cannot go on. Please do not blame the doctors. They have done the best they could." In this note Ms. Adams puts the blame squarely on her husband and absolves her physicians. Yet is not this explicit absolution, like the very fact of the suicide, itself an indirect form of indictment? The patient whom the doctors so evidently failed to help now exonerates them.

Dr. Newell expresses several different emotions in reaction to the news of the suicide. First, he is shocked, then angry. He admits to frustration with Mr. Adams, but stops short of blaming him explicitly for his wife's death. The resident fears that if he attends the funeral, the patient's family will "attack me, murder me, eat me alive." He blames himself for his patient's suicide and believes that others will do the same.

Mr. Adams blames himself for his wife's suicide and is also blamed by her family. A television advertisement suggests a way to shift this heavy burden of blame to the doctors. When he meets with a plaintiff's attorney, the process of fixing blame moves to a legal setting.

What we see, then, in the aftermath of a suicide, is a series of efforts to find a scapegoat, a single person at fault. Historically, the suicidal victim was "blamed" for his or her own death, at least in the eyes of the law. Until the 1940s, physicians were not found liable for malpractice in relation to the suicide of a patient, since the suicide itself was perceived as an intervening cause between the doctor's alleged negligence and the harm. As society's view of responsibility for suicide changed, and as case law evolved, legal fault-finding—blaming someone besides the dead person—became possible. Despite the existential paradox that the patient is both agent and victim of the suicidal act, a malpractice suit in the wake of suicide seeks to fix blame on other parties. Strange as the concept may seem to clinicians, a malpractice suit alleges that the physician's negligence directly caused the patient's death.

In psychodynamic terms, the struggle to come to grips with suicide by fixing blame—whether that struggle is undertaken by survivors, scholars, or jurors—can be regarded as a form of "magical thinking," magical in the sense that it bears the stamp of childhood reasoning or of the unconscious. We propose that in the determination of responsibility (and, hence, in the courtroom, medical negligence) for suicide, magical thinking has several distinctive characteristics. First, it leaves no room for uncertainty, chance, or change, holding that the suicide was absolutely foreseeable and predictable. Second, magical reasoning uses "20-20 hindsight" rather than the kind of retrospective foresight that is necessary to reconstruct the conditions under which the clinical evaluation of suicidality took place. Third, magical thinking assumes that each suicide has a single determinative cause. Fourth, this type of reasoning portrays the physician as the only active agent, leading to the assumption that the means of death is exclusively controlled by the physician. Finally, magical thinking tends to assign disproportionate weight to the specific means of death (e.g., pills) as a factor in determining whether the suicide could have been foreseen or prevented. Our experience suggests that one or more aspects of this primitive reasoning may dominate clinical and legal decision making in connection with suicide.

RISK FACTORS AND THE PROBLEM OF PREDICTION

The literature on suicide demonstrates the difficulty of pinpointing single causes. Suicide is the culmination of a multifactorial process, and our efforts to explain it, both in the psychiatrist's office and in the courtroom, must be based on multicausal reasoning rather than unicausal or otherwise magical thinking (2–7).

Understanding this process is important because of the significant impact of suicide on society. In 1981, the number of reported suicides in the United States was 26,832, although the actual total may have been two to three times as high, since many deaths by suicide are attributed to other causes (8). Suicide is one of the top 10 causes of death nationwide. Some 42% of those who commit suicide have made one or more previous attempts, and 10% of those who have made attempts ultimately succeed (8).

Studies suggest that a host of demographic and clinical factors may be associated with a risk of suicide. While the list is extremely long, some commonly attributed risks include (9–13):

Personal Characteristics:
    Age (elderly)
    Sex (male)
    Marital status (single, divorced, or widowed)

Psychodynamic Characteristics:
    Depression
    Pain
    Hopelessness/helplessness
    Alienation
    Anxiety
    Anger
    Expressed suicidality

Life Situation:
    Physical illness
    Mental illness
    Drug abuse/alcoholism
    Recent changes in patient's life
    Social isolation

History:
    Previous attempt
    Family history of suicide or psychosis
    Physical complaints
    History of violence

Studies of depressed populations provide two important statistics. First, over 15% of depressed patients eventually commit suicide. Second, more than 70% of those who commit suicide were previously diagnosed as having some type of depression (8).

With over 15 risk factors for suicide, the psychiatrist evaluating a patient cannot give too much weight to any one, lest the true complexity of the patient's situation be overlooked. By the same token, after a suicide, it is almost inevitable that one or more risk factors can be identified as having played an important part in the circumstances leading up to the death. Consider the dilemma in the case of depression. If one in seven depressed people commits suicide, the fact that someone is depressed might argue for hospitalization, since most suicide victims were, indeed, depressed before they died. Yet the same data indicate reciprocally that most depressed persons do not commit suicide, and no one should be needlessly hospitalized.

Suicide prediction and prevention, then, depend on balancing a series of variables to arrive at the best possible clinical assessment. This assessment must not be based primarily on statistics but on clinical evaluative skills (14). Knowledge of the risk factors should inform a clinical decision, but simply knowing the numbers is not sufficient (15). Thus, a clinical evaluation that includes both a consideration of actuarial risk factors and an appreciation of the individuality of each person remains the only solution to these uncertainties.

The problem of prediction is further complicated by the fact that long-term risk factors may be independent of short-term factors affecting an individual patient. Many dynamic factors influence the decision to take one's own life, including revenge, punishment, riddance, and feelings of hopelessness (16). Identifying these factors in a patient's subconscious during an evaluation for potential suicidality may be highly problematic.

One of the most important studies of suicide prediction, and one of the few prospective ones, was conducted by Pokorny (9) who suggests that the task may ultimately be impossible. Following almost 5000 patients prospectively, Pokorny found that he was unable to predict on the basis of risk factors which subjects would take their own lives. (He considered the following risk factors: previous attempt, affective disorder, marital status, expressed suicidality, schizophrenia, current social involvement, and history of violence.) While some risk factors showed significant correlations with eventual suicide, none were predictive (i.e., none could select an actual suicide prior to the event). For all risk factors there were many false negatives (i.e., many patients who did kill themselves were missed) and many false positives (i.e., many nonsuicidal patients were identified as being at high risk).

Other studies, although more optimistic about the possibility of predicting suicide, suggest factors to consider that are different from the classic long-term risks. The three major risk factors cited in a recent work by Fawcett (17) are: anxiety (panic disorder, severe anxiety, or alcohol-related anxiety), hopelessness and/or loss of interest and pleasure, and past suicidal behavior or ideation. A study by Kaplan (11) suggests that the most reliable predictor for suicide is the seriousness of past attempts. In a 10-year prospective study by Beck et al. (13), hopelessness was the most important factor for long-term risk but was surprisingly less important as a sign of immediate risk.

Many malpractice cases involve suicide by hospitalized patients, and studies of this population present an even more complicated picture. For example, hospitalized patients who attempt suicide frequently have a history of drug and alcohol abuse, they tend to have a psychiatric illness with a distinct onset, they have specific and violent plans for suicide, they tend to be depressed, and they rarely overdose (18). Overall, male psychiatric inpatients are 5 times as likely to kill themselves as men in the general population, while for females the rate is 10 times as high, despite the common factor of hospitalization (19). One inference that might be drawn from these data is that the ability to kill oneself transcends anyone's ability to prevent it.

The clinician must consider two additional factors in evaluating the risk of suicide. The first is the relation between the location and means of suicide. The most common means of suicide in the community is a gun; in a general hospital, leaping from a window; and in a psychiatric hospital, hanging (20). The explanation offered for this variation is the availability of the means to a lethal end in each setting. Thus, the method chosen for suicide may be less a product of attachment to a particular agent than attachment to the plan to kill oneself, using whatever means is at hand.

The second factor to consider is the lethality of previous attempts. Drug overdose is the least reliable method of self-harm. Guns are the most reliable. However, the same research indicates that essentially all attempts, regardless of method, are planned; suicide is rarely an entirely impulsive act (21).

We are left with an extremely complicated picture in trying to predict and prevent suicide. The known risk factors, the patient's current and long-term mental status, the availability of a method as well as its lethality—all complicate what may well be a life-and-death clinical judgment. To grope through this maze with some hope of developing a reasonable plan for prevention requires a multicausal analysis. Ideally, decision making should be systematic yet flexible, entailing a process that cannot easily be swayed by a single "magical" aspect.

Having considered the causes and prediction of suicide, we turn now to its aftermath: How does magical thinking enter into the judgments about a physician's liability for the suicide of a patient?

EMPIRICAL STUDIES OF DECISION MAKING IN SUICIDE LIABILITY

The Program in Psychiatry and the Law at the Massachusetts Mental Health Center has examined both legal and clinical decision making in the wake of suicide.

The Courts and Magical Thinking

In a study of court decisions involving suicide and liability we sought to answer one of the questions posed earlier in our definition of magical

thinking: Does the court, in its hindsight analysis, focus disproportion-
ately on the means of suicide at the expense of a comprehensive (and
hence, multicausal) vision of the event? Specifically, if a patient
committed suicide by overdosing on pills prescribed by his or her
psychiatrist, did this element affect the way the judges thought about
the suicide, in spite of other factors involved?

We analyzed 57 cases, principally at the appellate level, from several
states. In each case a claim of wrongful death or negligence had been
brought against a psychiatrist, a hospital, or both for the injury or
death of a patient by suicide. We divided the cases into two groups,
according to whether or not the court found liability, and compared
them with respect to the judicial reasoning used to arrive at the
decision. In 25 cases the court found negligence; in 32 cases it found no
negligence. (This proportion—44% for the plaintiff—approaches the
actual average outcome in suicide litigation.)

Only cases decided in or after 1940 were included. A preliminary
analysis of earlier cases seemed to indicate a formulaic approach to
judicial reasoning, in part because, as noted above, before the 1940s
the law held that suicide was to be considered an independent
intervening cause (22).

We analyzed several factors in each case, including the method used
for suicide, whether the written opinion contained a discussion of the
method, and whether the opinion referred to a psychiatric assessment
of suicide risk.

A review of the cases revealed a correlation between the factors
emphasized in the judicial opinion and the ultimate findings of the
court. With marked consistency, when a court's ultimate decision was
to find negligence, the written opinion emphasized the *method* of the
suicide as the *cause*. In these cases the judicial reasoning in the opinion
reflected a hindsight connection between the availability of a specific
method and the resulting suicide. The court appeared to assume that
removal of the specific means (identified, of course, only by hindsight
knowledge of the patient's injury or death) could have prevented the
suicide.

In cases where the court found no negligence, the method was not
emphasized in the court's written opinion. Instead, the court tended to
cite the method as one of several factors to be weighed in arriving at the
decision not to impose liability. In this group of cases the judicial
reasoning centered on the assessment of suicide risk performed by the
psychiatrist and tended to defer to that prospective evaluation, even
though it was ultimately proved wrong in hindsight—that is, by
subsequent events.

To summarize, in the group of cases that resulted in a finding of negligence, the judicial opinion showed elements of magical thinking. In contrast, opinions in the no negligence group of cases acknowledged the more realistic multifactorial nature of suicide assessment and prediction. The opinions that follow exemplify the different modes of judicial reasoning employed in the two groups of cases.

In *Abille v United States* (23) the court found a Veterans Administration hospital negligent for the death of a patient who had jumped from a window of the hospital. The psychiatrist had classified the patient in such a way as to permit him full access to the hospital grounds. The court reasoned that "the death caused by Abille's jump from a window could have been prevented had Abille been reclassified and . . . not permitted to go out unescorted." The court did not consider whether the patient was at risk of suicide or whether he was psychiatrically assessed as suicidal. Instead, the court reasoned narrowly that Abille's suicide could have been prevented by preventing his access to windows, even though no clinical data suggested that windows were a risk factor for this patient.

In *Dinnerstein v United States* (24) another Veterans Administration hospital was found negligent in the death of a patient who had also jumped to his death, in this case from a seventh story hospital window. Here the court reasoned, "As [Dinnerstein] was assigned to a ward on the seventh floor, measures should have been taken to see that he could not jump from a window. His own denial upon admission and even Dr. Guttlieb's belief that he was not immediately suicidal, cannot excuse the complete absence of precautions [leaving the patient unsupervised in his hospital room] to insure the safety of a patient with a suicidal gesture in his past [and] a long history of psychiatric treatment. . . ." Of course, a large number of patients in Veterans Administration hospitals have made at least one "suicide gesture" in the past and a large number have long histories of suicidality. Moreover, no attempt is made to address the risks and benefits of leaving a patient undisturbed as well as unsupervised.

The trial court's reasoning in *Hirsh v State of New York* (25) typifies the oversimplification inherent in magical thinking. Here, a state hospital was found negligent in the death of a 38-year-old patient, diagnosed as manic-depressive, depressed type, who took an overdose of Seconal. The patient, who was noted to be suicidal at the time of admission, had made two recent suicide attempts (by hanging and overdose) at another hospital. The source of the Seconal was never identified.

Although the trial court's finding of negligence was reversed on appeal, its reasoning exemplifies a common form of thinking about suicide. The trial court held that "the State violated simple rules which should have been followed so that [the patient] *could not have taken* his own life." The "simple rules" entailed inspecting the patient's person and bed for any unauthorized medications:

> The decedent would have committed suicide only in either of two ways. Either he had the Seconal in his clothing, in which case the hospital should have found and removed it, or he procured it in the hospital from the pharmacy or storeroom or from a person in the hospital. In either of these cases, the State would have been negligent . . .

This statement demonstrates several elements of magical thinking—hindsight certainty, unicausal reasoning, confusion of past action with inevitable future action, and a disproportionate emphasis on method. The multiplicity of possible paths to suicide is reduced to the single fact of the patient's access to the means actually used to kill himself. So seductive is the hindsight knowledge of how the patient died that the court simply ignores the possibility that this patient, an obviously determined man, could have used a window, his shirt, his shoelace, or some other method to die, if the drugs had been unavailable. Yet the court states, without any support, that Seconal was the only possible instrument.

Although the patient admittedly was, and was known to be, at high risk for suicide, the trial court did not consider whether the staff could realistically have taken precautions that would have been certain to prevent him (and, simultaneously, all other suicidal patients in their care) from gaining access to this or any other means of suicide. The appellate court, which reversed the judgment and dismissed the claim of negligence, did consider these very questions:

> The State could not have provided an employee to watch every move made by this unfortunate man during 24 hours of the day. We are not persuaded that it is evidence of negligence that he was not repeatedly wakened and his bed searched during the night. If institutions for the mentally ill are required to take all of the precautions contended for in this case, and are to be held liable for such delicate mistakes in judgment, patients would be kept in strait jackets or some other form of strict confinement which would hardly be conducive to recovery. . . . An ingenious patient harboring a steady purpose to take his own life cannot always be thwarted.

This realistic assessment, in contrast to the more magical view of the lower court, reflects the appellate court's awareness of clinical uncertainty, the need to balance risks and benefits when making decisions about clinical management, and the problem of resource allocation. Moreover, the court implies that the patient's actions must be seen as an independent factor contributing to his death.

The opinion in *White v United States* (26) typifies the judicial reasoning employed in cases where no negligence was found. A 36-year-old mentally incompetent patient with a diagnosis of paranoid schizophrenia, White escaped from a Veterans Administration hospital while on full privileges and committed suicide by standing in front of a train. He had been living on an open ward with free access to the hospital grounds.

Over the previous 11 years the patient had experienced numerous exacerbations of his psychiatric illness and had required hospitalization on four occasions. Each admission was precipitated by a psychotic episode in which the patient was hostile, profane, and hyperactive. With medication he would improve, showing some insight into his illness and becoming more calm and cooperative. The suicide occurred during one of these periods of remission. The patient had expressed concern that his condition was deteriorating. He was, however, evaluated as not being at increased risk for suicide and was kept on full privileges, but with an increase in his medication.

The suit against the hospital charged that failure to withdraw the patient's privileges after he gave warning of a "change in condition" constituted negligence. In rejecting this claim the court reasoned as follows. First, the court acknowledged clinical uncertainty, stating, "The practice of medicine—and especially psychiatry—is not an exact science."

Second, it explicitly made and then rejected the argument from hindsight: "In hindsight it was apparent that the evaluation made by the physicians was erroneous. There is no 'crystal ball' or x-ray capable of determining what may be in the mind of a normal person, to say nothing of one who is mentally ill."

Third, the court allowed for multiple causation (e.g., taking into account the effect on the patient of a recent discussion with his wife about divorce as well as his concerns about deterioration).

Fourth, the patient's previous suicide attempts were interpreted as evidence not merely of the forseeability or predictability of future suicide attempts but of the patient's enduring determination and capacity to take his own life. The court noted, "Every living person is a suicide risk. If the person is sufficiently determined, he is bound to succeed." (Elsewhere in the opinion the court stated that a psychiatrist is not "responsible for every movement of the patient," thus accepting the premise that psychiatric patients are active and independent agents, with some responsibility for their own actions.)

Fifth, and most important, the court weighed the risks of treatment against the benefits, recognizing that: "a therapy program entails risks to the patient and to society as a whole, but it involves a balancing of interests which is most important in the psychiatric field. A psychiatrist is not a warranter of the patient's care." In sum, the court expressed a judicial policy that liability is not to be imposed by the hindsight acknowledgment of an erroneous psychiatric judgment.

This court found persuasive the judicial reasoning in a previous case, *Baker v United States* (27):

> [C]alculated risks of necessity must be taken if the modern and enlightened treatment of the mentally ill is to be pursued intelligently and rationally. Neither the doctors nor hospitals are insurers of the patient's health and safety. They can only be required to use that degree of knowledge, skill, care and attention exercised by others in like circumstances.

These examples demonstrate two different types of judicial reasoning about suicide and liability: multicausal and unicausal (or multifactorial and magical). While either type of reasoning could theoretically result in a finding of negligence or no negligence, unicausal reasoning (the "if only . . . then" formulation that typifies magical thinking) is characteristic of opinions in cases where the court finds negligence. Even judges are in danger of oversimplifying a case by searching for a single explanation of the suicide rather than a more complex understanding of the person who has died and the multiple forces that propelled him or her along the course ending in suicide. When the victim of a suicide is seen in many dimensions rather than one, the court can appropriately evaluate the adequacy of the clinician's prospective assessment of suicide risk, as well as the process of weighing the risks and benefits of possible courses of action.

Clinicians and Magical Thinking

Of course, the courtroom is not the only place where this dichotomous thinking about suicide occurs. As we noted in the case of Ms. Adams, Dr. Newell's initial response to her suicide was to seek someone (including himself) to blame. Indeed, as hospital experience reveals, when a patient dies, many are quick to point fingers (28). The Program in Psychiatry and the Law sought to discover whether mental health professionals are susceptible to magical thinking in assessing patients for suicide risk and whether certain elements in a clinical case might promote a more complex consideration of that risk.

To explore these questions we presented the following vignette to a group of 367 mental health professionals from various disciplines:

Mr. H is a 24-year-old male who has been seen by Dr. K for six months. He began therapy after his wife and child died in an auto accident. He was being treated for both depression and anxiety with appropriate medications. On the day in question, he came to his psychiatrist's office complaining of worsening depression and thoughts of killing himself. While he continued to be depressed and anxious, there was no evidence of psychosis. He had no previous history of suicide gestures or attempts. His psychiatrist was not able to discover a precipitant to his worsening condition. The patient denied having a suicidal plan.

At this point, the vignette diverged with respect to four dichotomous variables, yielding 16 different stories. First, half the vignettes stated that Dr. K felt he could *trust* the patient, and the other half stated that he did not feel he could trust the patient. Second, the doctor *admitted* the patient to a hospital in some versions and sent him home in others. Third, the patient killed himself either by leaping from a *window* (in the hospital) or *overdosing* (at home). Finally, the suicide of the patient was *revealed* in some versions but not in others before the respondent was asked to predict the probability of suicide. The respondent was thus either in the hindsight (court's) or foresight (treating psychiatrist's) position. (See Appendix 10.1 for the questionnaire and complete set of vignette variables.)

We then asked each respondent a series of questions concerning the case, including 1) the probability of the suicide, 2) whether it was foreseeable, and 3) whether the psychiatrist was liable for the patient's suicide. The statistically significant results indicated not only that magical thinking is as prevalent among mental health professionals as among judges but also that certain factors in the presentation promote more well-rounded and complex reasoning.

We found that from the hindsight position (i.e., the respondent knew the suicide had occurred before answering the questions), the decision to send the patient home was associated with a higher estimated probability of suicide than it was in the foresight position (i.e., where the respondent did not know the outcome). This finding reveals clearly the hindsight bias: the tendency to overestimate the probability of suicide when one knows it has occurred. In addition, specific factors (in this case, the decision to send the patient home) were singled out in retrospect as increasing the likelihood of death (even though before the suicide they were not perceived the same way). Thus, the hindsight knowledge of suicide triggered both a higher prediction of the probability of the (known) outcome and the search for a single cause.

Hindsight respondents seemed to attach special importance to the method of suicide. When asked whether they thought the suicide was planned, a majority of respondents believed that an overdose was planned but that a leap from a window was not. Although this distinction has a certain commonsense logic, it may not agree with clinical experience. Studies (20, 21) indicate that few suicides are impulsive, and there is no evidence to suggest that leaping from a window is a more impulsive act than overdosing. The latent assumption in court may be that if a patient who went home and overdosed had a plan, it could have been detected; failure to detect the plan may be negligence.

On the other hand, we found that in almost all versions of the case, if the psychiatrist trusted the patient, then the estimated probability of suicide was sharply reduced. In addition, respondents felt that an eventual finding of malpractice was less likely if the psychiatrist trusted the patient. One interpretation is that our respondents viewed the doctor's trust of the patient as a clinical judgment of the patient's suicidality. Alternatively, they may have seen the psychiatrist's trust as a stand-in for the patient's trustworthiness, although this personal characteristic of a patient is hardly a proven protection against suicide. Either way, reliance on trust probably reflects the prevalent belief among mental health professionals that the relationship between the clinician and the patient is itself important in predicting and, perhaps, decreasing the risk of suicide.

The test vignette was constructed as a case that did not actually demonstrate clear negligence. We infer that the respondents' views stem from factors other than the strict legal grounds for malpractice. The tendency to single out the psychiatrist's trust in the patient is a striking example of this and a kind of magical thinking. It appears that the respondents used the variable of the doctor's trust to gauge the risk of suicide rather than the far more complicated process of formulating a clinical judgment of that risk. The belief that the psychiatrist's feelings about the patient affect the probability of his or her suicide may well be a wishful defense against the difficulty of this task of suicide assessment.

The earlier discussion of legal cases and magical thinking seems to reflect this difficulty. When the court put itself in the foresight position and considered the clinical evaluation of suicidality from the perspective of the treating psychiatrist, a finding of malpractice was much less likely. From a purely retrospective stance, however, single factors, whether they be method or trust, replace a much wider view of the causes of a suicide (29, 30).

SUICIDALITY AND MAGICAL THINKING: IMPLICATIONS FOR PRACTICE

(Adapted from Bursztajn et al.; Magical Thinking, Suicide and Malpractice Litigation (31).)

The special meaning that a family member, clinician, or court ascribes to the manner or means of a patient's suicide may reflect the meaning that it had for the patient. In this sense, magical thinking may have an infectious quality, originating in the mind of a suicidal patient, carried out through the act of suicide, and transmitted to those who struggle to come to terms with that act.

Two cases are presented in this section. The first suggests the magical meanings that a suicidal patient may attach to prescribed medication. The second demonstrates a therapeutic response to magical thinking on the patient's part.

A borderline adolescent with juvenile onset diabetes took a massive overdose of her own injectable insulin and left the empty bottles—each with the prescribing psychiatrist's name on the label—in that psychiatrist's hospital mailbox. Subsequent litigation turned upon the issue of the patient's being responsible for keeping and managing her own insulin while being hospitalized for depression and impulsivity. Although she had made previous suicide attempts, some serious, she had not used this specific method before, nor had she given warning of an increase in her suicidal intent.

In this case the grounds for finding the physician negligent on the basis of the means chosen for suicide would probably be relatively weak, since the patient's autonomy in managing her own illness is clearly a strong desideratum. There remains, however, the troubling fact that the patient indeed chose the prescribed insulin to kill herself and placed the empty bottles in the psychiatrist's mailbox, a fairly transparent expression of hostility toward the physician. From certain factors of this case (such as the patient's hostility and a diagnosis of borderline personality disorder which is often characterized by impulsivity) we might infer that some patients, when suicidal, may be more at risk for using a physician-prescribed medication than another means.

What therapeutic measures can be taken to protect patients likely to act out in this way, without denying them the benefits of medications (or of taking responsibility for them)? At the same time, how can clinicians protect themselves against the subsequent retrospective imputation of blame—that is, liability—in the event of a patient's suicide? The following case exemplifies a comprehensive therapeutic approach in which the therapist openly anticipates the risk of the *patient's* engaging in magical thinking with respect to medication and explicitly assesses this risk along with the other risks and benefits.

A woman with a history of alcoholism, depression, and mood swings was admitted following a massive, self-administered overdose of insulin prescribed for her diabetic son. By the time of her psychiatric admission the patient no longer exhibited the vegetative symptoms of depression present prior to her suicide attempt. Instead, she became manic during her first two weeks in the hospital. During this period, the factors precipitating the insulin overdose were explored. Not diabetic herself, the patient had suffered the death of a brother from complications of diabetes two years earlier. At the same time, she felt her relationship with her son to be threatened by his impending marriage. By overdosing on her son's insulin, she unconsciously sought to reestablish a close connection with her deceased brother as well as with her son.

The risks and benefits of medication were discussed with the patient in the context of her recent reaction to loss. In her case, the usual risks of lithium were exacerbated by an additional risk— namely, that she might overdose, "magically" to join her dead brother, who had worked for a firm that made lithium. Since she was not depressed at the time, the risks of lithium were judged to outweigh the benefits. During the hospitalization, when the patient became manic, she agreed to a trial of the neuroleptic drug perphenazine, which has a lower likelihood of life-threatening complications in the event of an overdose (therapy/toxicity index of 100/1, as compared with 3/1 for lithium).

The patient's mania cleared within days. During the remaining four weeks of hospitalization, the effects of the drug were monitored and psychotherapy was started. At the time of discharge the risks and benefits of outpatient medications were reviewed with the patient. Lithium prophylaxis was contraindicated in part because the patient had become euthymic (that is, her mood was now at her normal base line). Also, she still had not completed the work of grieving. She was assessed as being at risk both for acting on the medication's magical association with her brother and for resuming alcohol use, and consequently becoming more impulsive. Therefore, with the patient's consent, lithium was not prescribed on discharge. The daily dosage of perphenazine was gradually tapered, and outpatient follow-up was arranged.

Six months later, as she experienced her grief more fully, she became depressed and started drinking again. Admitted at her own request, she became manic as she worked through her grief. After her condition had stabilized, she was judged competent to disclose her suicidality (if present) and to address the risks and benefits of lithium. After the magical associations of lithium were further clarified in psychotherapy, the patient and her physicians together decided that the risks of long-term use of perphenazine now outweighed the risk of an overdose of lithium. Two weeks after admission perphenazine was discontinued and lithium begun. A euthymic response was rapidly achieved. During the ensuing four weeks of therapy the competence assessment and risk-benefit discussions were repeated, and it was judged to be safe to discharge the patient on lithium. One year later the patient was functioning well and had continued outpatient therapy.

In this case, the patient's alcoholism, her prior use of insulin to establish a self-destructive bond with her brother and son, and her brother's involvement in the manufacture of lithium alerted her therapists to the heightened personal significance that lithium might have for her. The treaters could thus anticipate and perhaps avoid the potentially destructive consequences of such associations. The magical dimension of the drug may even have operated for the patient's benefit when used in this manner, since lithium produced euthymia with unusual speed.

For the clinician, there are both clinical and legal pitfalls in allowing precautions related to particular means of suicide to dominate the decision-making field. Excessive focus on the details regarding a particular means might obscure the broader need for a careful clinical assessment, followed by appropriate standard precautions against suicide, irrespective of particular means. For example, the practice of prescribing medications in small doses, currently favored by some clinicians, may or may not impress a judge or jury with the clinician's foresight. In either case, it is unlikely to deter patients intent on self-destruction (32), who can easily store up small doses until a lethal supply is at hand, obtain medications from another source, use medications intended for someone else, or resort to some other means of suicide. Again, suicide is almost always a planned rather than impulsive act. Adequate means for committing suicide are, after all, available even in the clothing worn to the physician's office. A naive reliance on limited dosages may reflect the clinician's magical belief in his or her ability to prevent suicide—a belief that certain patients may feel compelled to disprove (thus, ironically, increasing the risk as well as feeding the clinician's guilt about having "caused" a suicide).

The practice of prescribing medications in small doses may yet be therapeutic insofar as it communicates the physician's concern for the patient's well-being, but only in the context of an alliance between patient and therapist, and with the patient's active participation and consent. Otherwise, this approach may communicate distrust or infantilization and thus actually invite dangerous regression or acting out (32). When the clinician acts without communication, the patient is invited to do the same: the physician's "impulsivity" (i.e., action without discussion) may thus mirror and amplify the patient's impulsivity (suicide without warning). The result is that a unilateral caution becomes provocative rather than palliative.

The best precaution against magical thinking is a carefully documented risk-benefit analysis, actively shared with the patient through informed consent procedures (see Chapter 4) (33). "Risks" arising from the magical potency of medications can be explored by asking the patient directly about feelings of hopelessness and suicidal intent (34). When the patient's vision of an intolerable life situation is brought into the open, it can be examined critically rather than accepted fatalistically. Moreover, explicit engagement with the patient's suicidal ideation helps patient and therapist form an alliance based on safeguarding the patient's life.

Thus, when prescribing medication for a suicidal patient, the clinician should explicitly ask the patient to consider—along with the other risks of the medication—the risks of impulsivity and magical thinking. By treating these risks as though they were properties of the medication and by using similar counterprojective techniques (35), the clinician may encourage the patient to speak freely about uncomfortable emotions. For example, the clinician might say, "We've noticed that one side effect of this medicine is that it can tempt people to take too much and to harm themselves. You know, people have all kinds of ideas about pills. . . ." Particular care should govern such an exploration in cases where drugs have a special meaning, as in our earlier example.

These assessments may help provide the patient with a conceptual framework for acting more rationally; they may also provide the basis for a more rational, realistic outcome of any legal action that might ensue from a suicide. One malpractice case provides a judicial precedent in this regard. In the case of an outpatient who overdosed on a prescribed medication, the court reasoned that since the patient had been judged competent to live outside the hospital, the suicidal action itself was the proximate cause of the patient's death and the suicide was not a foreseeable consequence of the physician's prescription of the medication used (36). Such reasoning, rather than simply returning to a pre-1945 conceptualization of suicide, actually recasts the issue in terms of autonomy and protection, with the assumption that a competent patient is able to make autonomous decisions about his or her life, independently of a treating psychiatrist. If this precedent is widely followed, so that the standard of care for the suicidal patient includes assessment of competence or capacity to participate in treatment planning, the freedom of patients will be safeguarded, while clinicians will be freed (at least in a court of law) from "magical" expectations that they be omniscient and exercise total control of their patients' decisions.

TRANSCENDING MAGICAL THINKING

The more that patients are viewed as autonomous adults, both in the psychiatrist's office and in the courtroom, the less likely it is that magical thinking will influence our responses to suicide. As clinicians, we can transform the ways in which we communicate with our patients, by openly engaging in risk-benefit discussions and explicitly acknowledging clinical uncertainty (4). These steps not only promote a more realistic and healthy therapeutic alliance but may also serve to protect the clinician in court, if a suicide does occur.

REFERENCES

1. Havens LL. Personal communication, 1983.
2. Douglas M, Wildanasky A. Risk and culture. Berkeley, CA. Univ. of California Press, 1982.
3. Fischoff B, Lichtenstein S, Slovic P, et al. Acceptable risk. Cambridge, UK. Cambridge Univ. Press, 1981.
4. Bursztajn H, Feinbloom RI, Hamm RM, Brodsky A. Medical choices, medical chances: how patients, families and physicians can cope with uncertainty. New York: Delacorte/Lawrence, 1981.
5. Einhorn HJ, Hogarth RM. Judging probable cause. Psychol Bull 1986;99:1–19.
6. Einhorn HJ, Hogarth RM. Confidence in judgement: persistence of the illusion of validity. Psychol Rev 1978;85:395–476.
7. Einhorn HJ, Hogarth RM. Decision making: going forward in reverse. Harv Bus Rev Jan-Feb 1987:66–70.
8. Bursztajn H, Gutheil TG, Hamm RM, Brodsky A. Subjective data and suicide assessment in the light of recent legal developments. II. Clinical uses of legal standards in the interpretation of subjective data. Int J Psychiatry Law 1983;6:331–350.
9. Pokorny AD. Prediction of suicide in psychiatric patients. Arch Gen Psychiatry 1983;40:249–257.
10. Roy A. Risk factors for suicide in psychiatric patients. Arch Gen Psychiatry 1982;39:1089–1095.
11. Kaplan RD, Kottler DB, Frances AJ. Reliability and rationality in prediction of suicide. Hosp Community Psychiatry 1982;33(3):212–215.
12. Rich CL, Young D, Fowler RC. San Diego suicide study 1. Arch Gen Psychiatry 1986;43:577–600.
13. Beck AT, Steer RA, Kovacs M, et al. Hopelessness and eventual suicide: a 10-year prospective study of patients hospitalized with suicidal ideation. Am J Psychiatry 1985;142(5):559–564.
14. Murphy GE. On suicide prediction and prevention. Arch Gen Psychiatry 1983;40:343–344.

15. Schwartz DA, Flinn DE, Slawson PF. Treatment of the suicidal character. Am J Psychotherapy 1974;28:194–207.
16. Maltsberger JT, Buie DH. The devices of suicide: revenge, riddance and rebirth. Int Rev Psychoanal 1980;7:61–72.
17. Fawcett J. Clinical predictors of suicide in patients with major affective disorders: a controlled prospective study. Am J Psychiatry 1987;144:35–40.
18. Paykel ES, Halowell C, Dressler DM, et al. Treatment of suicide attempts. Arch Gen Psychiatry Hosp 1974;31:487–491.
19. Evenson RC, et al. Suicide rates among public mental health patients. Acta Psychiatr Scand 1982;66:254.
20. Rabiner CJ, Wegner JT, Kane JM. Suicide in a psychiatric hospital. Psychiatr Hosp. 1982;13(2):55.
21. Large AJ. Preventitive action. Wall St. Journal; Aug. 10, 1983.
22. Il ALR, 2d 757, Later case service at 601.
23. *Abille v United States,* 482 F Supp 703 (ND Cal 1980)
24. *Dinnerstein v United States,* 486 F2d 34 (CA2 Conn 1973)
25. *Hirsch v State of New York,* 1983 NYS 2d 175 (1959), 202 NYS 2d.
26. *White v United States,* 244 F Supp 127 (ED V 1965), 359 F2d 989 (CA4 VA 1966)
27. *Baker v United States,* 255 F Supp 129 (SD Iowa 1964) 343 F2d 222 (CA8 Iowa 1965)
28. Appelbaum PS. The expansion of liability for patients' violent acts. Hosp Community Psychiatry 1984;35(1):13–14.
29. Kong AK, et al. How medical professionals evaluate expressions of probability. N Engl J Med 1981;315(12):740–744.
30. Bursztajn H, Hamm RM, Gutheil TG, Brodsky A. The decision-analytic approach to medical malpractice laws. Med Decis Making 1984;4(4):401–414.
31. Bursztajn H, Gutheil TG, Brodsky A, Swagerty EL. "Magical thinking," suicide and malpractice litigation. Bull Am Acad Psychiatry Law 1988;16(4):369–377.
32. Gutheil TG, Appelbaum PS. Clinical handbook of psychiatry and the law. New York: McGraw-Hill, 1982.
33. Bursztajn H, Gutheil TG, Hamm RM, Brodsky A. Subjective data and suicide assessment in the light of recent legal developments. II. Clinical uses of legal standards in the interpretation of subjective data. Int J Psychiatry Law 1983;6:331–350.
34. Shein HM, Stone AA. Psychotherapy designed to protect and treat suicidal potential. Am J Psychiatry 1969;125:1247–1251.
35. Havens LL. Explorations in the uses of language in psychotherapy: counterprojective statements. Contemp Psychoanal 1980; 16:53–67.
36. *Speer v United States,* 512 F Supp 670 (ND Tex 1981).

Basic Vignette

Mr. H is a 24-year-old male who had been seen by Dr. K for six months. He had come into therapy after the death of his wife and child in an automobile accident. He was being treated for both depression and anxiety with appropriate medications. On the day in question he came to his psychiatrist's office complaining of worsening depression and thoughts of killing himself. While continuing to be depressed and anxious, there was no evidence of psychosis. He had no previous history of suicide gestures or attempts. His psychiatrist was not able to discover a precipitant to this worsening of his condition. Patient did not have a suicidal plan.

Mr. H agreed to a contract with Dr. K to call him or go to a hospital emergency room if he felt he could not contain his suicidal impulses. Dr. K increased his medications and gave him a week's supply. [*OR*: Dr. K felt he could not trust Mr. H to contact him. . . . He therefore admitted him to a psychiatric hospital]

Outcomes of case

1. Patient goes home and overdoses *or* shoots self.

2. Patient hospitalized and jumps out window.

Viewpoint of subject filling out questionnaire

1. Foresight (suicide not known in advance to subject)

2. Hindsight (suicide already known to subject)

Questions

1. As the evaluating psychiatrist assess the probability of suicide for this patient. Circle the number closest to your estimate.

No chance   Certainty
0   10   20   30   40   50   60   70   80   90   100

2. Was this suicide foreseeable? (Circle one)   yes   no

3. Is Dr. K liable for malpractice? (Circle one)   yes   no

4. In the two years following the patient's death, the following sums

have been discussed as the amount of the settlement that the psychiatrist's insurer might pay. Which would you consider just?

a) $0   b) $100,000   c) $500,000
d) $1,000,000   e) $2,000,000   f) $3,000,000

chapter 11.
FEAR OF MALPRACTICE LIABILITY AND ITS ROLE IN CLINICAL DECISION MAKING

As the number of malpractice suits against physicians escalates, the fear of being sued increases comparably, influencing medical decision making and often resulting in an approach known as defensive medicine. This chapter examines the phenomenon of defensive medical practice, its effects on decision making, and an alternative approach that offers better protection against litigation by fostering a collaborative rather than adversarial relationship between physician and patient.

THE MALPRACTICE LITIGATION CRISIS

Over the past 20 years, malpractice litigation has increased dramatically, affecting both the medical profession and the larger community. Despite the fact that litigation and claims appeared to peak around 1985 (1), the number of claims and suits could still be described as epidemic. This alarming increase has not only led to greater awareness of liability issues on the part of the public and the medical profession but has also triggered widespread (and not always realistic) fear.

Malpractice lawsuits have high visibility, particularly those resulting in large awards. To make matters worse, a lawsuit for a large amount of money constitutes front page news, whereas a physician's exoneration in a lawsuit is often a back page entry. This asymmetry persists despite the fact that, of the approximately 6% of malpractice cases that actually get to court, 80% are won by the defendant physician (2).

As noted elsewhere in this volume, claims of malpractice occur when "bad outcomes" are combined with "bad feelings." Litigation has become a common response to bad outcome. All doctors—even those who practice good medicine—are vulnerable to litigation. Although many physicians continue to believe that litigation is something that happens "to the others," most are keenly aware of the risks.

The popular press frequently trumpets issues central to the question. For example, an article (3) under the heading of "Medical Malpractice Upheaval in Florida" states: "Spiralling costs of medical malpractice lawsuits and the insurance to pay the awards have reached a breaking point in southern Florida. . . ."

What are the effects of this view of the medical profession as a "belegaled" sect (4, 5)? One of the major effects is a distinctly defensive approach to practice, with the patients seen as adversaries long before any hint of litigation supervenes. Frequent attention in the media to the issue of malpractice may increase the level of paranoia among practitioners, in which doctor-patient relationships become doctor-customer relations or—at worst—defendant-litigant relations; and medical services are viewed as some kind of product with concomitant warranties and guarantees. Defensive practice may also usurp the clinical judgment of practitioners, and doctors may lose enthusiasm for attending to the needs of patients because of a perceived loss of autonomous control over the interaction. Nationwide, physicians have left the high risk areas of practice (obstetrics, orthopedics, and emergency medicine) or have abandoned the field of medicine entirely (6–10). Emergency rooms are difficult to staff (11), and insurance companies are accused of profiteering.

In striking contrast, the American Trial Lawyers Association has reported that there is no crisis (12). The inference of this remarkable statement is that doctors are in no greater danger of being sued than anyone else in society and that complaints to the contrary are both unwarranted and self-serving. From the viewpoint of this association of plaintiff's attorneys, the notion of a "crisis" is a fantasy cooked up by physicians anxious to invoke various legal protections and to justify higher fees. Besides highlighting a source of significant disagreement between the medical and legal professions, this statement and public reaction to it account in part for the decline in the quality of the patient-practitioner relationship and for the increase in the practice of defensive medicine.

SOME DATA FROM THE MEDIA

Despite the ubiquity of the phrase "defensive medicine," few studies have demonstrated concrete signs of this approach to medical practice. For the most part, articles on the subject occur as reports on isolated and current malpractice predicaments. The *American Medical News* features almost weekly articles on malpractice litigation. A *short* sampling of information gleaned from articles on malpractice provides the following data:

–34% of physicians think the biggest problem in medicine is malpractice liability (13).
–Between 1976 and 1986 there has been a 100% increase in claims against psychiatrists (14).
–The victory in a lawsuit does not eliminate the detrimental psychological effects of litigation (15).

–A fear of litigation increases the cost of medical care (i.e., more tests) without observably better results (16).

–78% of M.D.s think fear of lawsuits leads to unnecessary testing (13).

–OB/GYNs face a 17% chance of lawsuits in a given year (11).

–95% of Florida's neurosurgeons have been sued (11).

–10% of medical fees received by New York physicians go toward liability policy payments (17).

–Defensive medicine adds $2 billion annually to medical costs in New York state (20).

–The public is more aware of malpractice and desires compensation (18, 19).

–Defensive medicine nationwide is costing an additional $15 billion annually (20), an amount translating to $1.19 per week for every American.

–Physicians in 42% of all lawsuits closed in 1984 had previously been sued (21).

Practitioners suffer from what Carol Turkington has termed "litigaphobia" (22), an exaggerated fear of lawsuit that cripples practice and does the patient a disservice. The legal system is viewed by physicians as a third party or interloper in the doctor-patient relationship. Current data leave it unclear whether the geographic patterns of litigation (higher by several orders of magnitude in some places) reflect the local distribution of physicians in particular specialties or the presence of a vigorous plaintiff's bar.

WHAT IS DEFENSIVE MEDICINE?

Defensive medicine is a practice of medicine centering, as its primary aim, around self-protection from liability in the event of a tragic outcome, rather than affording primacy to the patient's well-being; often it is portrayed as a mechanism to anticipate and forestall hindsight-based second-guessing of clinical decisions, e.g., whether or not to order a particular diagnostic test. Defensive medicine may alter the individual clinician's practice or the practice adopted by an entire institution.

Defensive medicine brings with it exponential increases in the costs associated with clinical practice. Practitioners, the public, and third party insurers all experience the same impact on the price of medical care in the form of additional testing (even unnecessary testing). More importantly, fear among health care practitioners and administrators has contributed to a different kind of cost expressed in the shut-down or unavailability of services in sectors of high-risk exposure. Yet, most problematic of all, the practice of defensive medicine compromises not only the cost but the *quality* of care given. In short, the fear of malpractice litigation has a tangible effect on the manner in which *all* clinical decisions are made, not just risky ones, but all varieties, from the mundane to the most profound.

Discussants of defensive medicine in the literature have tended to emphasize its harmful effects. For example, Simon defines the term as follows (23):

> ... defensive medicine refers to any act or omission by a psychiatrist that is performed not for the benefit of the patient but solely to avoid malpractice liability or to provide a good legal defense against a malpractice claim.

Although this definition refers specifically to psychiatrists, defensive medicine is practiced by physicians from every specialty, as well as by others involved in the health care industry, including allied health professionals and administrative policy makers. Furthermore, practices that are defensive in essence have been mandated in some circumstances by statute, judicial decree, or institutional regulations and policies.

A defensive stance undermines (sabotages) one of medicine's basic tasks: providing the best possible health care. We argue that a partial explanation of this failure involves the adverse affects for defensive practice on the therapeutic alliance between doctor and patient. The defensive clinician may become less empathic, more distant, in his or her stance toward the patient. Clinicians who practice defensively tend to seek data of an objective nature in preference to the sometimes more meaningful subjective data such as psychosocial information. To put it another way, an unintimidated clinician may seek to know the patient better as a person, whereas a fearful clinician is more likely to focus and act upon test results.

Proponents of defensive medical practice may point to one possible exception to an exclusively negative view: the notion of "defensive documentation." Physicians who defend against subsequent second-guessing in the courtroom by writing a great deal—although using up time that might otherwise be profitably put to other purposes—nevertheless may leave an improved record for future caretakers. Some clinicians claim, indeed, that by focusing their defensive posture only on documentation they can continue to look at the patient with less fearful and thus less adversarial eyes. We would challenge this view by noting that quantity is no substitute for quality. Careful documentation of the key points in evaluation and decision making offers much better liability protection than a record that bulges with indiscriminate details (but there is room for debate on this point).

Conversely, not all *thorough* medical practice is necessarily defensive: many other factors inspire thoroughness, including the quest for knowledge and improved data collection, the desire to fight disease, and the belief that doing everything possible is indeed best for the patient. Such practice may be distinguishable from defensive medicine primarily in the focus of the physician's concern on the patient's care and the resulting effect on the therapeutic alliance.

We would suggest that a good part of the blame for increased litigation may lie in the increasingly adversarial nature of the doctor-patient relationship even prior to the inherently adversarial nature of litigation proper. Defensive medicine, itself an adversarial model, may thus not only result from an increasingly litigious response to bad outcome but may actually cause such a response. An obvious remedy for this dilemma would be to improve the patient-practitioner alliance; however, in an atmosphere in which both parties are frankly suspicious of one another, it is difficult to build a mutually supportive relationship.

More than the pain, distress, and possible morbidity from unnecessary testing results from defensive practice. The deterioration of the therapeutic alliance conveys to the patient a strong sense of the practitioner's emotional detachment; the emphasis of the doctor-patient interaction shifts from concern for the well-being of the patient to concern with the legal vulnerability of the practitioner. Thus, in a bitter irony, defensive medicine exacerbates the very problem it is designed to solve: rather than protecting the practitioner from lawsuits it may create a climate of provocation in which lawsuits are even more likely to occur, due to the bad feelings engendered by the impaired therapeutic alliance.

The following example noted earlier may illustrate this point:

> A woman went to a gynecologist for a problem and a minor surgical procedure was recommended. At the beginning of the discussion of this procedure, the physician commented, "The law requires me to inform you of certain facts about this operation." And then, in a perceptible alteration of his normal patterns of speech, the gynecologist began to chant a litany of side effects, risks, morbidity, mortality, percentages, probabilities, etc. The patient later reported that after about ten seconds of listening to this, her mind shut down entirely. "This appears to be some sort of arcane ritual! The communication was not directed to me for any benefit of mine whatsoever."

Studies of informed consent interactions uniformly reveal how little medical information is retained and how rapidly recall of that small amount decays. Indeed, one can readily predict that, in this instance, the patient would have had almost no recall after a few minutes of *any* of the substantive material "shared" with her. But this regrettable result did not occur because of the physician's problems in explaining the procedure, or because of the patient's incapacity to understand it. Instead, the mechanistic, purely "pro forma" presentation of information—in sharp contrast to information shared as part of an open and honest dialogue between physician and patient—ironically defeated its own purpose in conveying information to the patient that might be used constructively in the process of making a decision about treatment. A legalistically designed attempt to give all possible information to the patient resulted in no useful information being communicated at all.

A primitive form of defensive medicine was referred to in the old sociomedical literature as the "hanging of crepe" (24). The allusion here is to the hanging of crepe on the front door or gateposts to signify the imminent or recent death of a family member. Less metaphorically, however, this term was designed to reflect a carefully crafted pessimism, employed by the old country doctors as a strategy to protect one's reputation. The physician would paint the picture as looking as grim, dark, and hopeless, so that a bad outcome would be taken as a matter of course and a good outcome would represent a miracle of the doctor's healing power. This technique dated clearly from the pre-litigation era and—although representing a primitive form of defensive medicine—is really aimed more at reputation than at litigation. However, crepe hanging contains some elements of our current, more complex notion, the sharing of uncertainty. We now recommend that one not present either a magically optimistic or a "crepe-hung" pessimistic view of an uncertain situation, but merely a willingness to confront that uncertainty.

CAUSES OF THE FEAR OF MALPRACTICE LIABILITY

Social Factors

We turn now from the issue of defensive practice to a related and even more widespread phenomenon, that is, fear of liability. We will examine social, legal, and medical factors that lead to such fear.

First, like other widespread phenomena, the medical malpractice crisis does not occur in a social vacuum: indeed, we live in a litigious climate where everyone seems to be suing everyone else on very little provocation. School districts and municipalities experience difficulties in obtaining liability insurance for otherwise ordinary services such as playgrounds, child care, and the organization of athletic activities. Ice skating rinks and bowling alleys have had to close because of the cost of liability insurance premiums. In some instances, without any signs of an increase in actual claims, premiums may suddenly double, triple, or quadruple.

A second social force leading to fear may be the perception that the medical profession requires outside scrutiny and regulation. In this context, public awareness of malpractice suits creates a self-fulfilling prophecy: the more the public becomes aware that the medical profession is vulnerable to litigation, the more likely the number of suits is to increase. From this viewpoint, a judicial ruling by the legal system is increasingly seen as an important mechanism for regulating the medical profession.

Another social factor relevant here is the rise of consumerism. While one might envision the informed consumer as the ideal person with whom to hold an informed consent dialogue, promoting openness in the relationship and thus staving off litigation, the rise of consumerism has at times resulted in an adversarial stance: the consumer is inclined to struggle with and resist the no-longer-authoritarian physician. As a result, the enlightened consumer is seen all too often by the physician as a problem rather than as a particularly good ally.

An additional dimension of the problem has to do with the social aspects of medical practice itself, in the form of entitlement and elitism. Medical training is long, expensive, and usually quite grueling. This apprenticeship is commonly compared to college fraternity hazing. Those who survive the "ordeal" often feel that they belong to a distinct class, separate and different from lay persons, and that their labors have justified a kind of entitlement. Such entitlement and the heavy weight placed on the practitioners' judgment may prove alienating to patients and to the public, as well as fostering a climate of counter-entitlement on the patient's side. That is, patients may feel entitled to a perfect result.

Legal Factors

It is impossible to open many magazines today without seeing large ads in a type face suitable for announcing the arrival of World War III:

INJURED?
YOU MAY HAVE A CASE!
GIVE US A CALL AT OUR TOLL FREE NUMBER
FOR A CONSULTATION WITHOUT COST OR OBLIGATION
AS TO WHETHER YOU ARE ENTITLED TO COLLECT!

Such advertisements support a common mechanistic model of malpractice: if there is injury, then there *must* have been negligence.

This notion, of course, is subscribed to enthusiastically by many plaintiffs' attorneys.

The manner in which malpractice cases are decided hinges on the concept of compensation for the victim of a bad outcome. Indeed, the simple fact that the doctor has a large malpractice insurance policy reinforces the inference in the public mind that more than adequate resources are available to pay the deserved compensation and that, psychologically, it is not really the doctor who is paying—a distortion that allows patients not to feel conflict in relation to their "biting the hand that tried (and failed) to cure them." Many inappropriate and disproportionate jury awards appear to be based on such reasoning.

Finally, the intrusion of legal mediation between doctor and patient has clouded the question of practitioner responsibility. While many attorneys may maintain that the threat of malpractice litigation is a stimulus, by representing a perceived threat of punishment, to sound medical care, experience suggests that the intrusion of legal concepts into medical practice may paralyze flexible and patient-centered decision making to the point where it may actually be harmful to the patient. For example, needless involuntary hospitalization springing from defensive practice is costly and may be harmful to the patient.

Medical Factors

Why does medical malpractice insurance compensate individuals in the present system? In theory, such insurance is designed to protect against the risk of negligence by providing an opportunity for fair compensation when injuries occur as a result of that negligence. One of the most significant limitations of the insurance model based on fault (negligence) is that litigation in malpractice may stem in part from magical fantasies of restoring of the status quo: the fantasy, for example, that the patient who has had an amputation will somehow "get the leg back." These and related intrapsychic factors may not be satisfied by a malpractice award, which can, after all, provide only money for the perceived injury, not restoration of the limb.

Another dimension of the problem is the third party payment system, which places both the physician and the patient in somewhat remote positions in regard to the actual transfer of money or services. The patient, all too often, does not experience him or herself as actually paying for the doctor's time: "the insurance will take care of it." A side effect of this phenomenon is that physicians may order many additional tests, including unnecessary ones, to assuage their fears of medical malpractice liability, yet may act as though no additional costs supervened.

FEAR OF MALPRACTICE LIABILITY AND CLINICAL DECISION MAKING

Some fears can be healthy and can lead to adaptive responses. Let us explore the implications of the fear of being sued for malpractice as it bears on clinical work, addressing both positive and negative effects.

Benefits

We would argue that the primary benefit that may derive from the fear of malpractice liability—but only when this fear is constructively and not defensively used—is strengthened therapeutic alliance between clinician and patient. Once clinicians openly acknowledge their own fears of liability, they may then choose to address these concerns by putting their energies into building mutually supportive relationships with their patients. This is the response most likely to offer protection against a suit, since it establishes good feeling between the two parties and creates an alliance capable of withstanding a bad outcome. A strong alliance serves as an anticipatory antidote to bad feelings concurring with a bad outcome.

The therapeutic alliance promotes these "good feelings" by establishing as a shared goal the well-being of the patient. Instead of being pitted against each other as adversaries, clinician and patient can work together against the common enemy of disease.

A healthy alliance not only creates good feelings but can also contribute to the likelihood of good outcomes, further decreasing the chances of litigation. Patients who mistrust their physicians may fail to take medications properly, or sabotage their care in other ways. They are also likely to feel helpless and out of control, a condition leading to increased stress and to potential deterioration of their actual medical status.

Physicians can engage in a number of specific behaviors that will strengthen their relationships with patients. By sharing the uncertainty inherent in many medical situations, physicians remove themselves from the pedestal of infallibility upon which they are frequently placed and assume a more collaborative stance. In addition, patients who understand the inevitable uncertainties of their treatment are better able to give truly informed consent and to have reasonable expectations about their future health. Thus, those bad outcomes that do occur may already have been anticipated, lessening their negative impact by allowing the patient opportunities to prepare both psychologically and otherwise. Anticipation specifically prevents surprise, one of the most powerful "bad feelings" leading to litigation.

Failure to provide adequate follow-up care, which has long been a weakness of some physicians, can obviously have negative results, ranging from continued or exacerbated health problems to a feeling on the part of the patient that the physician is not interested in his or her health. Those physicians who make themselves available for follow-up can positively influence patient feelings and outcome, thus decreasing their chances of being sued for malpractice. Clinicians have a special duty to follow up the tragic outcomes that are inevitable in medical practice. Lawsuits are particularly likely to result from cases of irreparable physical impairment or death. To militate against such suits, physicians must remain available to patients and their families, to provide continuing care and support following such a tragedy as occurred in the case example in Chapter 1. The patient (or family) who believes that the practitioner's primary concern is (or was) the patient's well-being is more likely to perceive the practitioner as having done his or her best.

Fear of malpractice can also lead positively to an appropriate use of supervisors and consultants. Decisions made by a treatment team obviously have the potential to reach a better outcome, two heads being better than one. In addition, the support of other physicians can serve to mitigate liability in the case of a lawsuit.

Finally, under appropriate circumstances, fear of liability may lead to improved training, as long as that training does *not* result in either instruction or modeling by faculty of excessive defensiveness in the ordering of tests and use of protective procedures. Ideally, training should focus on the importance of building a therapeutic alliance with the patient and of viewing informed consent as a process in which patient and physician engage in an open dialogue, rather than as merely a signature on a form.

Adverse Effects

Perhaps the most far-reaching negative result of fear of malpractice liability is an alteration in the clinician's stance toward the patient, as addressed earlier. The focus of clinical practice may shift from the patient's well-being to legal self-protection. Thus, the physician views the patient as a legal case posing a certain risk, rather than as a suffering person in need of care. The physician-patient relationship may be so transformed as to undermine the alliance entirely, so that the two parties assume adversarial roles, each trying to protect himself or herself from the other.

One of the best-known problems arising from defensive medicine is the increased use of needless tests or overly conservative hospitalization. In their efforts to protect themselves from lawsuits, physicians often shift their focus from the patient to the data. The desire for certainty in making a diagnosis is understandable; however, there is a point at which the danger and cost of additional tests come to outweigh the benefits. *All* tests involve some degree of risk, and for some procedures that risk is substantial. Thus, the marginal value of further information may not be worth the increased risk to the patient's well-being.

Furthermore, it is simply impossible to eliminate all uncertainty, regardless of the number of tests given; often it is unclear whether or not additional tests will be helpful. Physicians and patients both need to understand these limits, to acknowledge that judgment calls are required in medicine as in other professions, and to share—and thus, to tolerate better—the uncertainty from this limitation. Patients who are misled into believing that tests can provide absolute accuracy about their health may be more likely to sue if these tests later fail than those patients who understand the inherent limits of testing and diagnosis.

In psychiatry a defensive response might include a needlessly low threshold for involuntary hospitalization, where the patient's liberty and autonomy are, in essence, sacrificed in favor of conservative practice for the sake of self-protection.

An extreme example of defensive medicine is abandonment. In this case the physician decides that the risk of a lawsuit in treating a particular patient is too great and responds by terminating the relationship entirely: "dumping" or "turfing" the patient. The bad feelings that such behavior is likely to engender on the part of the patient may be very strong, and thus the risk of a lawsuit may increase dramatically in such situations.

An Empirical Study

The literature as a whole has not addressed the ramifications of fear of malpractice liability in clinical decision making. While we do not have data from the front lines of practice, we did conduct a pilot study to examine these effects. Specifically, we wanted to test the hypothesis that the fear of being sued for malpractice changes the way clinicians deal with patients. In other words, we studied how physicians cope with anxiety and responsibility in cases where malpractice liability is an issue.

Methods

We developed questionnaires for administration to clinicians in these areas of practice: surgery, medicine, and psychiatry. For each area, a hypothetical clinical vignette was presented, involving a diagnostic dilemma and a potential tragic outcome. Surgeons were told about abdominal pain and asked about a surgical emergency. Internists were told about angina and asked about myocardial infarction. Psychiatrists were told about a depressed patient and asked about suicide (see Appendix 11.1). Half of the vignettes noted that the patient in question was currently suing a previous clinician. In the other half, there was no mention of a suit. A series of questions followed the vignettes:

–What further information would you require to make clinical decisions?
–Which tests would you order?
–What consultations would you request?
–Would you admit the patient to the hospital for inpatient assessment and treatment?
–What estimate would you make about the probability of a tragic outcome?
–Would you continue to provide care for the patient?

The questionnaires were administered in two settings: to a group of family practice residents in Idaho and to a variety of clinicians at Beth Israel Hospital in Boston, Massachusetts, including residents and faculty in the departments of surgery, medicine, and psychiatry.

We predicted that those clinicians who were informed that the patient in question was suing another physician would order more tests, request more consultations, and be more willing to hospitalize and less willing to follow patients themselves than clinicians who were not told about a suit.

Findings

Respondents requested more information in almost all cases, regardless of whether or not they were told about a suit. However, the type of data requested varied in significant ways. The group of clinicians who were not told about a suit tended to request more information of a *psychosocial* nature, whereas those who were told about a suit asked for more *objective* data, requested more consultations, and were more likely to recommend admission. In addition, the clinicians who knew about the suit were most likely to predict a tragic outcome. The two groups of respondents did not differ appreciably in terms of the number of laboratory tests they would order or whether they would continue to provide care for the patient.

Discussion of Study

We hypothesized that the incidental mention of a suit in a patient's presentation would increase the perception of a liability threat and that some signs of defensive practice would be evident in response to that threat. While this proved true, the differences between the two groups of respondents were not as dramatic as we had expected. It may be that clinicians have already been fully sensitized to the threat of malpractice litigation by previous experience and by exposure to the professional literature and to the media, and were further alerted by the sparse clinical data in the vignettes. Practice patterns and clinical decision making may, therefore, have already been influenced significantly, perhaps even maximally. Therefore, clinical judgment may not be subject to provocation by selected information in the hypothetical case.

Nevertheless, more consultations were requested by respondents informed of a suit. This may reflect a greater wish to share responsibility for the patient care or even an attempt to avoid responsibility and increase self-protection. Respondents told of a suit also were more likely to recommend for admission, perhaps reflecting the desire to cover all bases and to share, or avoid, responsibility. In addition, estimates of the probability of a tragic outcome were higher in this group, confirming a finding described elsewhere (see Chapter 10): clinicians tend to overestimate the likelihood of tragedy in the face of uncertainty, here generated by the threat of suit. One might worry that this tendency decreases investment in the patient or in the success of treatment.

The question about remaining the provider of care yielded interesting findings: clinicians who knew of a suit were not unwilling to remain providers of care. Numbers of years in practice and status as a trainee appeared to be significant factors: almost all residents were willing to provide continued care, whereas faculty often were not. This finding may reflect changes in training programs and personal ideals.

In our study, clinicians were asked to make decisions on the basis of incomplete data. They responded by requesting more data, a reflection of clinical curiosity, the wish to obtain maximum information before making a decision, and a desire to see the "full picture" to decrease uncertainty. The focus of curiosity shifted, however, with the knowledge that the patient was suing another physician, from psychosocial information to objective data. This finding highlights a subtle but dangerous form of defensive practice: by relying on "scientific" data, the clinician retreats to a "legal" distance, perhaps (at an extreme) losing interest in the patient as a person and, thus, abdicating a clinical position in favor of a legal one.

THE FUTURE: WHAT MIGHT BE DONE TO MITIGATE THE EFFECTS OF THE FEAR OF MALPRACTICE

As medicine becomes more complex, as diagnoses become both more arcane and obscure, the average patient will face an increasingly difficult process of decision making. Even with expert systems and computer-aided diagnostic procedures the core decisions will be made in a familiar arena—the doctor-patient relationship. Clinicians must be taught that good practice is the best antidote to malpractice accusations. Explicit information about the physician-patient relationship, the therapeutic alliance, and informed consent must become part of standard curricula and clinical instruction. The patient's experience of illness and similar factors must also become part of the doctor's fundamental training. By diminishing the fear of liability, this instructional process will mitigate the destructive effects of fear on the physician-patient relationship.

Public education, too, can play an important role, if carefully addressed to the limits of certainty, of collaborative decision making, and the function of informed consent as a dialogue about uncertain outcomes. Such steps may improve the patient's end of the alliance, with salutary results as above.

Role playing and hypothetical scenarios, such as those used in our study, might increase physicians' empathy and perspective taking, which may in turn foster alliance building. While the essential part of the alliance does not necessarily derive from the doctor's experiencing what the patient is experiencing, attempts at altering the doctor's role may be of some value.

An important consideration is the lack of alternatives for patients who wish to object to the care they receive or its outcome. Litigation is certainly one way to be heard. But alternative channels might be provided to draw off the bad feelings in ways that satisfy patients and influence physicians but avoid litigation. Such alternatives may shift the focus away from purely monetary damages and offer pathways for the expression of legitimate feelings and concerns. Additional advantages may accrue from no-fault insurance of victim-compensation models, which might clarify issues or injury and cost in ways that avoid disproportionate jury awards. Whether the public will support such changes remains to be seen.

REFERENCES

1. Hilliard J. Personal communication regarding Joint Underwriters Assn., 1988 data.
2. Estimated Data.
3. Ingwerson M. Medical malpractice upheaval in Florida. Christian Science Monitor Jul. 7, 1987;3.
4. "Belegalment" still hounds U.S. psychiatry. Psychiatric News Dec 5, 1986;12.
5. Rappeport JR. Epilogue: we are belegaled. Simon R I, ed. Clinical psychiatry and the law. Washington, D.C.: American Psychiatric Press, Inc., 1987:467–468.
6. Family M.D. gives up deliveries. American Medical News Aug 15, 1986;2.
7. Rate hike may force OB's from state. American Medical News Jul 18, 1986;3.
8. Ga. ob-gyns refuse to treat lawyers who've filed suits. American Medical News June 13, 1986;4.
9. Rowan CT. Malpractice-suit madness. American Medical News June 13, 1986;4.

10. Texas liability survey shows physicians limiting practices, adding tests and procedures. American Medical News Jan 9, 1987;12.

11. Patients, M.D.s relate effects of liability situation. American Medical News May 23, 1986;27.

12. Taylor S. Jr. Lawyers deny crisis in medical malpractice insurance. New York Times Mar 7, 1985;A16.

13. Public has changed its thinking on malpractice crisis, survey results show. Psychiatric News Jan 2, 1987;29.

14. "Belegalment" still hounds U.S. psychiatry. Psychiatric News Dec 5, 1986;13.

15. Wassersug JD. Tips on facing malpractice suit. American Medical News Aug 22/29, 1986;17.

16. Owens, A. Will defensive medicine really protect you? Medical Economics Apr 18, 1988;88–100.

17. Liability policies cost N.Y. doctors 10% of their fees. Hospital Tribune Mar 12, 1986; 15.

18. Hearings held on Hatch's malpractice reform bill. Psychiatric News Oct 3, 1986;XXI (19):1. quoting Senator Orrin Hatch (R - Utah): ". . . the general public expects 'immediate medical miracles' and demands 'compensation for anything less.' "

19. Glass J. Malpractice as an M.D.-attorney sees it. Hospital Tribune Mar 12, 1986;15, quoting Dr. Harvey Wachsman: "The public is far more aware today than years ago and wants compensation if mistreated."

20. Alarm over malpractice. Time Jan 28, 1985;75.

21. Malpractice: hospitals likely focus of govt. action. Clinical Psychiatry News, July, 1987;6.

22. Turkington C. Litigaphobia: practitioners' exaggerated fear of lawsuits cripples them and does patients a disservice. The American Psychological Association Monitor Nov, 1986;17, (11).

23. Simon RI. Clinical psychiatry and the law. Washington, D.C.: American Psychiatric Press, Inc., 1987:29.

24. Siegler M. Pascal's wager and the hanging of crepe. N Engl J Med Oct 13, 1975;293 (17):853–857.

Case 1B (Psychiatric)

A 40-year-old married white female has symptoms of anergia, anhedonia, hopelessness, sleeplessness, and a 15-pound weight loss over the past three months. The patient has no previous psychiatric hospitalizations. Physical examination is within normal limits. Although she denies any suicide attempts, she states that over the past two weeks she has felt the impulse to jump off the bridge over which she drives home from work. On formal mental status examination her speech is somewhat slow and she has the feeling that people are talking behind her back. There is no evidence of frank delusions and she denies hallucinations. She does complain of bifrontal headaches of increasing severity. On further history it is revealed that six months ago the patient had minor cosmetic surgery performed. She is currently suing the plastic surgeon for malpractice.

Questions

1. What other information do you feel is needed with this patient? __

2. Circle any of the following laboratory studies that you would order:

   a. Chest x-ray

   b. CBC—differential

   c. ECG

   d. SMAC 25

   e. EEG

   f. DST suppression

   g. CT scan

   h. Other _____

3. Would you admit the patient to the hospital?   Yes   No

   If so, estimate length of stay __ ____ days

4. Circle any of the following medications that you would prescribe:

   a. Antidepressants (e.g., imipramine)

b. Neuroleptics (e.g., haloperidol)

c. Both antidepressants and neuroleptics

5. Circle any consultation that you would ask for:

a. Neurologist

b. Internist

c. Psychiatrist

d. A second opinion

6. Estimate the probability that the patient would respond positively to the following medications within the next three weeks:

a. Antidepressants _____%

b. Neuroleptics _____%

c. Both antidepressants and neuroleptics _____%

7. Estimate the probability that the patient will attempt suicide within the next two weeks _____%

8. Would you remain as the primary provider of care for this patient? Yes No

chapter 12.

COMMUNICATIONS IN PSYCHIATRIC PRACTICE: DECISION MAKING AND THE USE OF THE TELEPHONE

The telephone is a form of technology that affects every area of life in the United States, including health care. Indeed, the telephone has become so embedded in our daily lives that we hardly think of it as technology any more; it has taken its place in the natural order of contemporary reality.

Introduced in 1876, the telephone revolutionized medical practice by providing a communication link between doctor and patient that was not restricted to the physical boundaries of the hospital (1). In recent years, beeper paging systems and telephone answering devices have augmented the opportunities for doctor-patient communication by eliminating many of the limits imposed by time as well as space.

Communications technology has proved to be enormously valuable for treatment and consultation, especially in emergency situations. In making it possible to practice medicine at a distance, however, the telephone and its more recent companions pose certain dangers, since they alter not only the physical location of the physician in relation to the patient but also that which the physician actually sees and hears of the patient. Willett (2) points out that the use of the telephone in medical practice brings with it a special potential for malpractice liability:

> Those instances where physicians have treated a disembodied voice they couldn't identify as a patient more often seem to wind up in courts. The fact that there was no opportunity to establish the physician-patient rapport that discourages suits may contribute, but it seems more likely that physicians simply are not successful in coming to the right decisions in a telephone transaction if the patient is a relative stranger.

The use of technology in medical communications has radically altered the physician-patient dialogue and, consequently, the process of medical decision making. With "long-distance" medicine, even the issue of when and where treatment begins becomes confused. Since the duty of care is the cornerstone of liability, it is important to determine exactly when such a duty is established. At what point does the physician talking on the telephone assume clinical responsibility for the patient on the other end of the wire?

When a physician offers professional services to another individual, he or she has instigated a relationship with that person as a patient and a resultant duty of care (3, 4). This relationship has commonly been understood to evolve from face-to-face communication; however, malpractice case law has established a broader arena in which the interaction may be initiated. In *O'Neill v Montefiore Hospital*, a malpractice action was brought against an emergency room doctor who offered advice to a patient over the telephone (5). The doctor, who had never met or examined the patient, was held potentially liable as a result of that telephone conversation. The court held that a duty of care had been established by the single call. This case suggests that physicians risk establishing a duty of care when they offer professional advice over the telephone to unseen patients.

The case of Ms. Adams, presented in Chapter 1, illustrates some of the complex issues underlying the use of the telephone in psychiatric practice. The story begins with Ms. Adams' call to her therapist, Dr. Olsen, and the events that unfold are framed by a series of telephone conversations. As the case clearly demonstrates, the concepts of "relationship" and "dialogue" become much more complex when the face-to-face therapeutic encounter gives way to other modes of communication.

The initial questions that arise in the Adams case center on the ambiguity of the patient's call to Dr. Olsen. What did she expect from that call? How did she react to his referral? Some authors maintain that the telephone is indispensable for the follow-up of patients recently released from the hospital and for patients, like Ms. Adams, who are in crisis (6, 7). Ambivalent patients, communicating with the therapist by telephone rather than in person, can experience a sense of simultaneous closeness and distance. Yet, as a result of the immediate availability and intrusiveness of telephone contact (versus contact during a scheduled therapy hour), the telephone may be abused, especially by impulsive, demanding, anxious, and overly dependent patients. The therapist may struggle with an increasing sense of responsibility because of the patient's expectation that care will be provided immediately at any time and at any distance. Thus, the therapist faces a loss of control over the therapy (8).

The answering machine offers a partial solution to this problem, since it can be used as a screening device to control the access afforded by the telephone. The answering machine is a "socially correct" way for the physician to limit his or her accessibility while remaining potentially available for communication. The caller can communicate by leaving a message on the machine, and the therapist can decide when (or whether) to respond to the message, that is, when to be available for more direct, reciprocal communication.

Dr. Olsen recognizes his patient's acute distress, even over the telephone, and refers her to a local psychiatric emergency service for evaluation. The factors underlying his decision to refer her are not clear. Aside from his impending departure for vacation, perhaps the telephone communication with his patient affords Dr. Olsen a measure of emotional distance that would be difficult to sustain during an office visit. This double remove—physical and emotional—may allow him to refer her elsewhere. Of course, Dr. Olsen may also feel that his patient needs an immediate evaluation, which he, at that time, simply cannot provide. Still, by talking with Ms. Adams on the telephone and referring her to the clinic rather than seeing her, can Dr. Olsen be considered potentially negligent in his care of the patient?

Dr. Olsen elects not to call the emergency service in advance to notify them of the referral. Fortunately, the patient arrives, unannounced but safe. Dr. Newell calls Dr. Olsen to clarify the referral and obtain further information. In examining the role of *this* telephone communication in the evaluation of Ms. Adams, several questions arise: what information about his patient does Dr. Olsen convey to the resident, what information does he omit, and what information does Dr. Newell actually take in? "Oral communications without the advantage of eye-to-eye contact are subject to misunderstandings at both ends of the conversation. Feedback assures that the message is being received and understood, but it is more difficult to obtain over the telephone" (9).

Initially, Dr. Newell has several thoughts in response to the referral from Dr. Olsen. He speculates that Dr. Olsen, feeling that he is abandoning his patient, may have overreacted to her distress. Of course, such speculation may simply be the reaction of an overworked resident, irritated that his rest is being interrupted by an "emergency." It is also possible that Dr. Olsen, who has not seen Ms. Adams, is relieved to hand over responsibility for this troublesome patient by means of a single, simple telephone conversation. Finally, perhaps Dr. Olsen believes that an independent evaluation, available in an emergency setting, is more appropriate for his patient, since she seems to be in crisis. Nevertheless, Dr. Olsen describes his patient as a moderate suicide risk, adding that she is manipulative and has used threats of suicide to control the behavior of others. This telephone referral, without benefit of face-to-face communication, leaves the ambiguity and uncertainty of the current crisis in the hands of the resident.

In the third phone call mentioned in the case, the first call to Dr. Gottlieb, the resident expresses his concern that Ms. Adams may be suicidal. Dr. Newell presents the facts of the case, his evaluation, and the decision points; Dr. Gottlieb listens and inquires about the resident's confidence in the information he has gathered and in his assessment. Notably absent from the telephone call is a discussion of the abundant subjective data available. The patient is described in the case as "pale and drawn . . . in some disarray . . . manifestly depressed, tearful." Consideration of appearance and behavior, both initially and in subsequent assessments, is essential in evaluating a patient's ability to recompensate in the course of a crisis intervention. Visual cues also form a vital part of any dialogue between therapist and patient. Yet such subjective, impressionistic information is not included in the telephone consultation between Drs. Newell and Gottlieb. Of course, similar sensory data are missing from Dr. Gottlieb's experience of Dr. Newell. In the course of face-to-face supervisory meetings, supervisees commonly transmit a wealth of data, of direct clinical relevance to the patient, by their manner "in the room."

Can subjective information be conveyed as clearly over the telephone as it is experienced in the room with the patient (or with the supervisee)? Perhaps it can, but only if the two parties to the discussion adjust their habits of reporting, listening, and responding. Both must "learn to compensate for the loss of these stimuli by increasing their sensitivity to minor auditory cues, much as the blind man does when he learns to 'see with his ears' " (7). They must be alert to silences, pauses, rhythms, and intonations—the verbal and nonverbal representations of visual cues. In the psychiatric setting, critical information is conveyed not only by what is said and not said but also by the nuances—the feel—of the spoken or unspoken message. One must find new ways to communicate such impressions, visual and otherwise, when using the telephone for consultation.

The heuristics of decision making change as the selective perceptions of observer and consultant are further filtered by the telephone, making them more vulnerable to the biases of recency, availability, and locus of control (see the discussion in Chapter 3). By consulting at a technological distance, Dr. Gottlieb assumes the risks inherent in evaluating not only an unseen patient but an unwitnessed transaction between the patient and the therapist. The patient seen by Dr. Newell is not exactly the same as the patient imagined by Dr. Gottlieb, no matter how conscientious the resident is in presenting the case over the telephone. Moreover, since the consultation involves two calls, two "versions" of the patient are described and imagined, respectively. In the interval between those two calls the image of the patient may become blurred in the supervisor's mind, so that the second call conjures up a second image, which may replace rather than augment the first. Of course, these problems are inherent in face-to-face consultations as well, but the telephone adds another complex dimension.

In the fourth telephone call described in the case, Dr. Newell attempts to draw Mr. Adams into the orbit of his wife's crisis; however, this communication has the opposite effect: inviting the husband's rejection of his wife. Like Drs. Olsen and Gottlieb, Mr. Adams is physically removed from the scene of his wife's distress, and the telephone helps him maintain an emotional distance as well. His detachment from the experience may even play a role in the guilt and projective blaming that ultimately result in a lawsuit.

Some authors have found the telephone to be very helpful in the emergency setting, especially when the patient is able, by making a telephone call, to contact someone important to the immediate crisis (6, 10). Even they, however, caution that the telephone reinforces dyadic forms of communication. In the Adams case, for example, interventions and interpretations occur in the context of a series of two-person telephone calls: Ms. Adams-Dr. Olsen, Dr. Olsen-Dr. Newell, Dr. Newell-Dr. Gottlieb, Dr. Newell-Mr. Adams, and so forth. Such paired interactions make it difficult for the therapist to assess the roles and relative significance of various individuals within a complex interactional system.

As a result of the call to Mr. Adams, the patient appears "crestfallen . . . more tearful . . . and perceptibly angry." This description provides information that is vital to the ongoing evaluation. The patient's response, conveyed in visual and behavioral changes, could, of course, be consistent with a failed manipulation. Yet whatever those changes might signify, they are lost to Dr. Gottlieb and Mr. Adams, since neither is on the scene.

Technological mediation tends to minimize the perceived risks in any evaluation and decision-making process (1). The telephone, much like a mechanical translator, may have filtered out important subjective and affective information about Ms. Adams, even while conveying objective data relatively intact (11). In fact, the muted affect that is common in depression has been shown to be the most difficult to evaluate effectively over the telephone, and anxiety the easiest (6). In addition, "a spontaneous neutralization of affect is an effect of reporting, from the patient to the therapist to the supervisor. Thus, a supervisor's evaluation of the patient's affect is likely to be a diluted version of what was actually expressed in the interview" (12). Hence, the consultant must be particularly alert to the possibility that a sense of clinical urgency has been lost over the telephone line.

Dr. Gottlieb concludes that the case presented by the resident is "clear and free of ambiguity." Has she reminded herself that even a "good observer and a candid reporter" (her expressed view of the resident) is subject to his own conscious and unconscious mediation, which is further complicated by the filtering effect of the telephone? The selectivity of the resident's presentation is not necessarily negative and, in fact, is an important element in the process of supervision (13). "The model of supervision which uses reports given by the interviewer assumes that while therapists exhibit varied reactions to the material of the interview, observation by the supervisor of both the interviewer's reporting style and manner and the patient's material will yield the essence of the patient's difficulties" (12). However, the subjective cues by which the supervisor indirectly "observes" the patient within and through the supervisee are difficult to elicit over the telephone. The loss of the "ordinary counterplay of messages in which a person reinforces what he is saying verbally through his body language, or perhaps contradicts his verbal statement, thus giving a mixed message . . ." increases the risk that faulty heuristics will guide the decision-making process (6). Subjective data simply do not stand up well to technological translation.

Direct, face-to-face communication between supervisor and trainee is also vital to the process of learning in psychiatry and medicine in general. Such an opportunity for growth is regularly afforded the resident and the supervisor in traditional supervisory settings and in early-morning rounds following a night on call:

> . . . the therapist, in presenting the material, unconsciously shift[s] his role from reporting the data of his experience with the patient to "experiencing" the experience of the patient. That is to say, during the supervisory session, one [can] see evidence of a transient identification of the student with his patient. . . . In therapy the patient oscillates between experiencing and reporting while the therapist oscillates between identifying with the patient and observing him. During supervision the therapist recapitulates this oscillation of role. (13)

Such a vivid representation of the patient within the therapist fades over the telephone. Since consultation at a distance affords no direct interaction between the consultant and either the patient or the therapist, the telephone transforms an otherwise dynamic system of continuous monitoring of affects, effects, modifications, adjustments, realignments, feedback, and spontaneous corrections involved in the patient-therapist dialogue (6). The patient, the therapist, and the consultant are poorer for this transformation.

A further complication of telephone consultation is the therapist's own potential for minimizing dangerousness, as a result of a countertransference reaction to an emergency or to a particular patient (15, 16). A novice clinician—harried, frightened, tired, or even determined to achieve a rescue—may approach a patient in crisis with an agenda that has little to do with the patient. Such preconceptions may or may not be conscious and accessible for examination during the decision-making process.

Dr. Newell's initial assessment of Ms. Adams reveals his uncertainty about the risk of suicide and the need for hospitalization; the subsequent telephone consultation with Dr. Gottlieb seems to dispel that uncertainty. One can speculate that the resident's wish to avoid "not knowing" may magnify the certainty and omniscience that he attributes to the senior staff member (17). The desire to escape uncertainty—and associated feelings of inadequacy—can result in a premature closure of the consultation process (13, 17). Consultation by telephone aids this escape. Since the supervisor is not present, the resident has little opportunity to exchange his idealization of her for identification. Over the telephone, the supervisor remains the expert who is certain how to proceed rather than a therapist who can tolerate uncertainty and with whom the resident can identify (17, 18). In fact, the "phantom" nature of the consultation increases the illusion of omniscience and omnipotence by casting the supervisor as someone who can know and make decisions about a patient without having to be present.

During the suicide "autopsy," technological mediation is notably absent. The resident and supervisor now meet face to face to engage in dialogue. Dr. Gottlieb, while retaining the authority of her position, persistently transfers back to the resident all introspective responsibility for the suicide. She does not discuss her part in the decision making, nor does she acknowledge her own uncertainty or her feelings about the outcome of their decisions. Just as technology may have allowed the consultant to distance herself emotionally from both the patient and the supervisee, it may have shielded her from recognizing her own vulnerability to uncertainty.

Perhaps in an effort to be supportive, Dr. Gottlieb dissects the suicide note, placing a disproportionate emphasis on modality and hidden meanings. She tries to second-guess the nature of the suicide and argues that "the woman who overdosed may not have been the same woman you saw." However, in her attempt to reassure the resident, she unwittingly states precisely the difficulty with telephone consultation. Just as the patient who eventually killed herself may not have been the same patient Dr. Newell released from the emergency room, the patient Dr. Gottlieb imagined that night may not have been the same patient Dr. Newell saw or thought he presented to Dr. Gottlieb.

The resident uses the "autopsy" to question whether there was anything that he might have done differently. Among other issues, he must decide whether he conveyed to Dr. Gottlieb the important subjective nuances of the interview with Ms. Adams, as well as the important objective data. A woman with whom he believed he had made a mutually formed treatment decision has died, perhaps as a result of that decision—at least, so the plaintiff's attorney would argue. The resident agonizes over what went wrong.

No one was clearly in error in this case, perhaps not even the patient. Both Dr. Newell and Dr. Gottlieb appeared to act purposefully in making careful decisions, all the while weighing the risks and benefits of various choices. Yet the error, if there is any, may lie in their failure to acknowledge the importance of direct dialogue between patient and physician, and the value of subjective data thus obtained. Mutuality, dialogue and a full consideration of subjective data are compromised by the use of the telephone. Dr. Newell expresses vividly the dilemma of technological medicine and the process of consultation at a distance. Asked how it felt to be in the room with the patient, he answers, "I guess I liked the way she seemed so real in the office, you know, really present, right on the scene." That is, of course, precisely the problem: Dr. Gottlieb did not and could not know the patient in this way.

The growing dependence on all types of technology in medicine has created a buffer between patient and physician. Each patient has a personal experience of his or her illness, which can best be elucidated by a direct personal interaction. A therapeutic alliance and treatment collaboration can be achieved only in the context of shared experience. While the beeper, the telephone, the computer and all the other technological tools in the medical armamentarium often enhance our ability to diagnose and even treat patients more efficiently, they also may deprive us of the personal experience of simply talking, face to face, with patients and allowing them to talk to us. Technology, while radically changing our understanding of the therapeutic relationship, has also dramatically increased the potential for misplacing the person within a maze of data, wires, and microchips. Unfortunately, if we lose touch with the patient in the therapeutic relationship, we exponentially increase the risk of discovering that patient in the courtroom.

REFERENCES
1. Reiser SJ, Anbar M, eds. The machine at the bedside: strategies for using technology in patient care. Cambridge: Cambridge Univ. Press, 1984.
2. Willet DE. Medicine by telephone, continued: a legal opinion. Mod Med 1977;May 15:73–78.
3. Goldstein RL. The doctor-patient relationship in psychiatry: a threshold issue. J Forensic Sci 1986;31:11–14.
4. Goldstein RL. Legal liabilities of long-distance intervention. Am J Psychiatry 1986;143:1202–1203.
5. *O'Neill v Montefiore Hospital,* 202 NYS2d 436 (1960).
6. Miller WB. The telephone in outpatient psychotherapy. Am J Psychother 1973;27:15–26.
7. Cantanzaro RJ. Telephone therapy. Curr Psychiatr Ther 1971;11:56–61.
8. Rosenblum L. Telephone therapy. Presented at a meeting of the American Psychological Association, San Francisco, September, 1968.
9. St. Paul's Insurance Co. Telephone tips: a physician's most abused instrument. Malpractice Digest Sept/Oct 1979;3.
10. Beebe JE. Allowing the patient to call home: a therapy of acute schizophrenia. Psychother Theory Res Practice 1968;5:18–20.
11. Sabin JE. Translating despair. Am J Psychiatry 1975;132:197–199.
12. Muslin HL, Burstein AG, Gedo JE, et al. Research on the supervisory process. Arch Gen Psychiatry 1967;16:427–431.
13. Arlow JA. The supervisory situation. J Am Psychoanal Assn 1963;11:576–594.
14. Bursztajn H, Gutheil TG, Brodsky A. Subjective data and suicide assessment in the light of recent legal developments. Part II. Clinical uses of legal standards in the interpretation of subjective data. Int J Psychiatry Law 1983;6:331–350.
15. Winnicott DW. Countertransference. Br J Med Psychol 1960;33:17–21.
16. Kernberg OF. Countertransference. J Am Psychoanal Assn 1965;13:38–56.
17. de la Torre J, Appelbaum A. Use and misuse of cliches in clinical supervision. Arch Gen Psychiatry 1974;31:302–306.
18. Gutheil TG, Bursztajn H, Brodsky A. Malpractice prevention through the sharing of uncertainty: informed consent and the therapeutic alliance. N Engl J Med 1984;311:49–51.

SECTION V. DECISION MAKING THROUGH ETHICAL ANALYSES

chapter 13.
ETHICS AND DECISIONS ABOUT SUICIDE

Clinical decisions occur in an ethical context, whether or not the decision makers recognize the ethical nature of their decisions (1). In fact, ethical decision making about serious medical issues, such as those surrounding patient suicide, is one of the most complex challenges facing health care professionals. Formal training in medical school has traditionally focused on technical-medical skills, leaving physicians ill-prepared to tackle the ethical issues in their medical practice. Yet, perhaps paradoxically, malpractice suits often result from a breakdown in the ethical domain, rather than from a lack of medical skill.

This chapter uses the theories of developmental psychology (mainly derived from the pioneering work of Lawrence Kohlberg) to elucidate ethical decision making in the medical domain. These theories provide a systematic foundation for thinking about ethical decision making. They are empirical or "descriptive," rather than "prescriptive." This means that they are theories about actual human ethical reasoning and its development and not a code of ethics that instructs people on how to behave.

We begin with an abbreviated historical introduction into stage theory, and then we sketch out the General Stage Model defining the abstract properties of developmental stage theories and show how concrete developmental theories in five dimensions can be applied to medical decision making. Finally, the principles of developmental stage theory are used to discuss the case example presented in Chapter 1.

BACKGROUND

Current developmental stage theory has been greatly influenced by Kohlberg's (2, 3) moral developmental theory which transformed and extended Piaget's moral developmental theory, tracing the ontogeny of moral reasoning. Kohlberg's theory posits that an individual's moral development follows a series of stages. Interestingly, Habermas outlined a parallel developmental sequence for societies. Cross-cultural data from over 30 societies indeed show that moral development follows an invariable sequence—only the endpoint of development varies (4). These data also indicate that people move developmentally up through the stages only, never down, unless affected by mental illness or loss of mental capacity.

Kohlberg and his colleague Selman (5), while driving on Memorial Drive in Cambridge in 1981, had the insight that they could use Piaget's theory of the development of perspective taking—the ability to see the others' view—to create a social perspective-taking basis for Kohlberg's moral developmental theory.

Commons and Richards (6, 7) suggested that developmental theory addresses two conceptually different issues: 1) the hierarchical complexity of the task to be solved; and 2) the psychology, sociology, and anthropology of how such task performance develops. They used the hierarchical complexity of tasks as the basis for construing the notion of stage in the General Stage Model that is thus grounded in mathematical models (8) and information science (9). Commons and Grotzer (10) recently demonstrated that Kohlberg's moral developmental theory could be adequately accounted for by the General Stage Model above; Armon (11) had used both Kohlberg's moral developmental theory and the General Stage Model (see below) to create a general theory of the development of ethical reasoning. At this point, therefore, we will review developmental theory, a set of concepts that has influenced much of the thinking in this book.

General Stage Model

The successful completion of a task requires an action of a given hierarchical order of complexity. A logical analysis of those tasks shows the following (10, 12).

Actions, including reasoning, at a given order of hierarchical complexity are defined in terms of the actions at the *next lower* order of hierarchical complexity. Actions at a higher order of hierarchical complexity usually transform and organize lower order actions. We say the higher order complexity action *coordinates* the next lower order actions. This organization of lower order actions is new and unique, and cannot be accomplished by those lower order actions alone.

For example, multiplying 3 × (4 + 1) requires a distributive action. That action coordinates (organizes) adding and multiplying by uniquely organizing the order of those actions. The distributive action is therefore one order more complex than the acts of adding and multiplying alone. Although someone who simply adds can arrive at the same answer, being able to do both addition and multiplication in a coordinated manner indicates a greater freedom of mental functioning. Through such task analysis, the hierarchical complexity of a task may be determined.[a]

Dimensions of Development

This introduction will inform our discussion of the ethical decision making involved in the suicide case. In the following, we introduce stage models of individual development in five relevant domains: perspective taking, epistemology (truth), beneficence (compassion), justice (fairness), and evaluation (goodness). Underlying all other developmental dimensions are the stages of perspective taking and epistemology (12). *Perspective taking* describes the hierarchical complexity of a person's perspective on interactions among people (12, 15–17). *Epistemology* describes a person's concept of truth and reality, e.g., the concept that there exists an absolute true/false dichotomy as opposed to a state of relativism or perspectivism (18–20). *Beneficence* expresses the complexity of attachment to and caring for others (21, 22). *Justice* depicts the complexity of moral reasoning (4). *Evaluation* reflects the complexity of a person's conceptions of the good life (14, 21, 23–25). The good life includes good persons, institutions and places, good relationships, and good work.

We will then consider the institutional stage, because ethical decision making is influenced not only by the individuals involved but also by the institutional framework in which they act. Ethical decision making is influenced as much by the ethical atmosphere as by the highest stage at which people perform as individuals within an institution (26). Ethical atmosphere is gauged by the complexity of justification of processes by which institutional decisions are reached on conflictual issues.

Domain of Social Perspective Taking

The hierarchical complexity of a person's perspective on interactions among people is described in the social perspective-taking dimension of development (12, 15–17). Proficiency in understanding another person's perspective is one of the basic building blocks upon which development in the other domains depends.

---

[a]*The notion of stages:* In the General Stage Model (GSM) of Commons and Richards (7), when a person successfully performs a task at a given order of hierarchical complexity, the *stage* of the performance is of the equivalent order. Throughout the text, the GSM stage numbers appear in parentheses. The General Stage Model (7) as well as Skill Theory (13) has demonstrated that Kohlberg's (3), Armon's (11,14), and Selman's (15) half stages are actually full stages and will be referred to as such here.

In the medical context, perspective taking is necessary both for assessing the competence of the patient to make autonomous decisions and for understanding the patient's preferences. Only if physicians understand how the patient views the symptoms, illness, treatment, and life situation can they respond most appropriately; that is, physicians have to understand the patient's wants and needs by looking at the doctor-patient interaction from the patient's side as well as their own. The theory of social perspective taking can be helpful in identifying the stages in the development of physicians' perspective taking. At high stages, for example, physicians are proficient in understanding their patients and therefore relate to them successfully. In contrast, lower stage perspective taking may seriously hamper social decision making through inattention to the patient's perspective. As the physician's stage of perspective taking increases, the patient's role in the decision process also increases.

To grasp that patients form opinions of physicians based on how the physicians relate to the patients requires abstract perspective taking (stage 3, GSM stage 4a). Physicians at this stage thus understand that they have a reputation among patients, staff, and other physicians about how caring, understanding, and competent they are.

Taking another's perspective in a logical fashion requires logical perspective taking (stage 3/4, GSM stage 4b). Physicians operating at this stage may see the patients as rational or irrational, logical or illogical, but can only attend logically to either the rational aspects or the affective aspects of patients' situations at one time: On the one hand, communications that are logically organized may not address patients' affective reactions or idiosyncratic choices; on the other hand, affectively appropriate communications may not address patients' needs for empirical data about their situations. Thus, people performing at this stage cannot integrate the two variables, emotions and interests.

Stage 4 (GSM stage 5a) systems perspective taking requires the integration of two or more variables into a system. At that stage the doctor-patient interaction is seen as a network of interactive causes, for example, emotional or rational self-interests. Physicians reasoning at this stage understand that society regulates their relationships with patients; these physicians may see that the quality of their relationships with patients may even affect the likelihood that they will be sued for malpractice.

At stage 4 (GSM stage 5a), although doctors may *know* the other's perspective in an interaction, they may still prefer to view interactions from their own perspective. They may see themselves as an individual system in conflict with the hospital system. In the social context, the preferred perspective of physicians at this stage often depends on their own position in the social hierarchy. New residents, for example, may prefer the perspective of the patient over the perspective of the chief of medicine at the hospital. They may defend the patients' behavior and not hold them accountable. The assistant chief might, in turn, prefer the perspective of the chief of medicine. In sum, doctors' and institutions' perspectives of patients' concerns and problems are more complex and informed than at stage 3/4 (GSM stage 4b).

A person's reasoning may move into stage 5 (GSM stage 5b) by assuming multiple vantage points; for example, physicians report that they see their relationships to their patients in a new light after they have been patients themselves, suffering from a serious illness. People at stage 5 (GSM stage 5b) are proficient at taking and integrating multiple perspectives. This often leads to the insight that everyone—from the most difficult patient to the easiest, from the lowliest to the most influential patient—needs and benefits from respect, care, and concern. The hierarchical arrangement of the validity of perspectives, characteristic of stage 4 (GSM 5a), is replaced by the view that *all* perspectives have equal validity; thus the views from any person's vantage point are potentially valid. The person at stage 5 constructs a new perspective that integrates all the perspectives. Here, physicians may separate themselves from their patients fully, while at the same time they understand their interdependence and remain empathic. This is because doctors understand that the patients' wishes may be quite different from their own; patients' decisions to live or die, moreover, are not reflections on their competence as doctors. The ability to take multiple perspectives and to integrate these perspectives is, then, a developmental achievement.

At stage 5, physicians strive to fit the patients' points of view with their own, as well as with the wider societal perspective in which doctor-patient interactions are embedded. By coordinating the patients' perspectives with their own, doctors construct a new "supersystem." In this context, then, a treatment plan should be most effective when it integrates both the patient's and the doctor's perspectives: patients will understand their role in the treatment; doctors will understand the patients' problems and their proficiency in dealing with those problems.

Domain of Epistemology

Epistemological stage theory describes the development of the concepts of truth and reality. In the medical area relevant to our case example, a question with epistemological implications might be, for example: What are the effects of hospitalization on suicide and suicide prevention? The question would be dealt with differently at different epistemological stages. At stage 3 (GSM stage 4a), the culturally normative view (usually the view held by the local leadership) "validates" the truth. If there is a division among leadership, the modal or stereotypical view of the local community is accepted (as when the jury, faced with disagreeing experts, votes according to its own instincts). As social standards about suicide change, the truth may change.

At stage 3/4 (GSM stage 4b), logical and organized experimental methods are used to establish truth; unfortunately, only one variable at a time may be considered. For example, usually only the possible *benefit* of hospitalization on reducing suicide is tested statistically. The *cost* of hospitalization to the patient (in terms of jobs, relationship, self-esteem, stigma, and money) may be excluded from such an analysis.

At stage 4 (GSM stage 5a) the interaction of variables is taken into account. The costs as well as the benefits to the individual, doctor, and institution are logically and empirically weighed. Such weighing is inevitably biased by the position of the person or institution affected by the decision. Consider this example: statistical tests as well as summaries of percentages tend to be applied to assessing benefits of treatment, whereas only summaries of percentages usually suffice to describe the costs. Critics of hospitalization, on the other hand, reverse these approaches: the benefits of treatment are downplayed and the costs carefully documented and statistically tested. The subsystems of the cost-benefit analysis, moreover, may not be seen as mirror images of one another; critics do not consider that for every benefit there is a corresponding cost, and vice versa. During a discussion of informed consent, for example, the staff may discuss the system of benefits first. The staff may then overemphasize the possible bad outcomes of a treatment.

At stage 5 (GSM stage 5b), the benefits and the costs of hospitalization are weighed simultaneously, each system coordinated with the other; truth emerges independently of who finds it or espouses it in the institutional hierarchy. In our case, the effects of treatment and nontreatment on everyone and on every affected institution are considered.

Domains of Beneficence, Justice, and Evaluation

Apart from social perspective taking and epistemological stages, three more developmental dimensions are hypothesized to influence social decision making.

Beneficence. This stage directly describes the hierarchical complexity with which physicians reason about what they care about. What they care about may include children, parents, colleagues, groups, and possibly territories or inanimate objects. In addition, people care about friends and abstract objects including companies, town, countries, ideologies, principles, etc. (21).

Given that transference and countertransference issues are examined, doctors improve rapport with their patients if they value them. This, in turn, may improve treatment because physicians may make an extra effort to help patients with whom they have good rapport. Alternately, patients who have good rapport with their doctors may attend to their doctor's advice more closely and be more cooperative during treatment.

For all too many physicians, good rapport is limited to patients who seem like themselves. Stereotyping of patients (stage 3, GSM stage 4a) leads to differential rapport. At stage 3/4 (GSM stage 4b), valuing patients in a linear-logical manner also leads to differential attempts to establish rapport; patients who are logical and rational are valued over those who appear to be less rational. Depending on how they view the social system, some doctors reasoning at stage 4 (GSM stage 5a) think that society and its institutions benefit if *all* patients receive caring, sensitive, and thus efficient treatment. Other stage 4 doctors in contrast see benefits to the health care system, and to the institution with which they are affiliated, if patients are differentially treated on the basis of their social status.

Reasoning at stage 5 (GSM stage 5b), doctors unconditionally value their patients, irrespective of whether they like them or whether they consider them socially important. If physicians see all patients as valued persons, and therefore worthy of concern, caring, and efficient treatment, good rapport will be more likely to be achieved with all of them (stage 5, GSM stage 5b). Stage 5 (GSM stage 5b) perspective-taking skills make it possible to see the world from the patient's perspective. Hence at that stage, physicians maintain empathy, even while the patient is threatening suicide and blaming the doctor for being unable to solve the patient's problems and to eliminate his or her suffering.

Justice (or Moral Reasoning). This stage (4) is a measure of the complexity of reasoning about fairness. Physicians and patients functioning at each stage are faced with competing moral claims in making their decisions. Social decision-making process changes as the reasoning about fairness increases in complexity and becomes more inclusive.

At stage 3 (GSM stage 4a, the *group* stage), action is justified in terms of the reputation and characterization of the individuals or groups that are involved. People and groups, for instance, can be good or bad, nice or nasty, authoritative or untried. Action is often judged on the basis of individuals' or groups' underlying sentiments or motives. For example, a person at this stage may reason that a doctor is a good and well-intentioned person and thereby justified in his actions; in this way role and person may be confused. A person is viewed as a good leader because he or she has the office of the leader and fulfills the rules and regulations connected with this office. Comparably, then, people are good doctors because they do what doctors are expected to do. Physicians make decisions because they are the trusted authorities: patients are in need of help and must listen to the authority.

At stage 3/4 (GSM stage 4b), the *bureaucratic* stage, the reasons given for labeling an action as being fair and good are logical and abstract. Bureaucratic norms, laws, rules, and regulations guide behavior and are seen as "given"; they are not seen as responsive to individuals or particular situations. Role and person are no longer confused as they were at the previous stage; instead, the physician's rights and duties are seen to have a *logical* basis. Quite often physicians who reason at this stage use notions of the competence of each party to make informed decisions. Although physicians see themselves as authorities, they may share the logic of the treatment plan with the patient and reason together with the patient about appropriate treatment.

At stage 4 (GSM stage 5a), the *societal or institutional* stage, the yardstick by which to evaluate the morality of an action is the preservation (or destruction) of a system—or a society. Norms, laws, rules, and regulations form a logically coherent system. People at this stage reason in terms of how an action would impact on one's individual role and status within the system as well as on the system's capability to function. The authority of societal law, individual and group rights, and duties are all meaningful. "What would happen to society if everyone . . . ?" is a question characteristic of this stage. At this stage, justifications may be parentalistic when they refer to the authority of the expert within the system; in this case the expert is the doctor within the medical system (1). Also at this stage, doctors' justifications may be anti-parentalistic when they automatically grant independence to their patients. The rights of the patient may be seen as ascendent over the responsibilities of doctors to inform patients and to assess their competence.

At stage 5 (GSM stage 5b), the *societal universal* stage, people justify actions on the basis of universal abstract principles. These universal principles are coordinated systems (GSM stage 5a) of logical proposi-tions (GSM stage 4b). They have been articulated in all major ancient societies, in religious and philosophical works, down to the present.

Society itself is seen first as a creature of individuals and second as the context in which people develop. The principles coordinate the notions of duties and dependence with the notions of rights and independence from the previous stage; the result is true joint decision making and autonomy. Individuals at this stage of moral development recognize that the rights and duties of both physicians and patients have to be logically coordinated.

Roughly speaking, discourse among equals, who still differ in their interests and expertise, is the "due process" method of decision making. Unconventional decisions (even, for example, suicide) may be sanctioned as long as the process of arriving at those decisions is reasonable in the light of higher principles. The patient's moral claims, the physician's moral claims, and society's moral claims are coordinated and may be reconciled; in addition, the rights of the doctor, patient, and family members may be taken into consideration. Most often, the patient's right to life or to dignity supersedes the physician's right to determine treatment or duty to provide treatment; for instance, the moral duty to help a patient live is coordinated with the principled right of a patient to die.

Evaluation. This stage (14) describes how physicians identify "the good" in themselves, others, their life enterprises, and their work. The notion of what constitutes good work is critical to the physician's treatment of patients. At stage 3 (GSM stage 4a), stereotypical reasoning concerning a good patient, a good doctor, and a good doctor-patient relationship dominates the social decision-making process: typically, physicians see themselves as good, dedicated, competent helpers; their status is above that of patients. In decision making, they as the doctors *know* what is best. Note that doctors at this stage have particular difficulty with the fact that the discussion of *uncertainty* is a major activity in building the doctor-patient alliance.

At stage 3/4 (GSM stage 4b), both physicians and patients view the good physician as being the more logical and scientific one (27). Being logical and scientific, they view a good relationship as based on logical, linearly ordered communication. Indeed, science itself is defined in a narrow, simple, linear-causal mechanistic manner (28). The decision process is seen more as proceeding from the "top" down, rather than as being interactive.

At stage 4 (GSM stage 5a), the relative status of doctors is based upon their role of "saving" people within the society. Patients, because they are patients and not doctors, may be seen as lower in status; because of the law and the rules, lower status persons are to participate in decision making, but the patient must not control the process. Such control would rob physicians of their own independence and their authority; patients would make "the wrong decisions," hurting the reputation of the doctor, the hospital, and the whole health care system. In contrast with the dominant pattern, some of the doctors, reasoning at this stage and being anti-establishment, would give the patient total control. Physicians reasoning at this stage see themselves both as part of the system and as independent of it. The doctor-patient relationship is seen as one of independent parties, with the physician's role seen as more powerful; thus, a suicidal patient may be hospitalized at the request of the doctor because the doctor is in a superior position (1). In a variation the anti-establishment doctor may follow a form of mechanistic respect for the independence of the patient (see p. 9). In the former example, concerns about the patient's loss of independence are subordinate to the need to protect the health care system from excessive numbers of suicides and to prevent malpractice suits in a legalistic way.

At stage 5 (GSM stage 5b), the goals that are good for the patient, the doctor, and the society are coordinated. Physicians and patients do not define themselves in terms of status; rather they see each other as human beings who have expertise and problems and who also have rights and duties that transcend their roles in the doctor-patient relationship—rights and duties that derive from universalistic principles. At stage 5 (GSM stage 5b), doctors rely not only on their professional roles, but on their values and principles as people (in self-definition and in definition of a good person). The autonomy of the patient and doctor is recognized and supported.

THE CASE EXAMPLE: A DEVELOPMENTAL ETHICAL ANALYSIS

A number of the discussions that take place in the case in Chapter 1 bear analysis from a developmental ethical perspective. The pertinent ethical decisions and their justifications include: how the doctor should develop a treatment plan together with the patient; how the patient should treat her husband; whether the doctor should commit the patient to the hospital after the patient refuses voluntary admission; whether to interfere with the patient's possible attempts to commit suicide; how the doctors should respond to the suicide; how the husband should deal with the suicide; how he and the doctors should deal with the respective attorneys. Furthermore, a developmental ethical perspective covers the actions of the attorneys with respect to taking and trying the case, their methods of advocacy, the decision making by judge and jury, and the question of how the society should consider not only the rights of the patient and of the family involved but also the rights of doctors not to be sued frivolously.

The events of the case proceed as follows: the patient is sent to the emergency room by her regular psychiatrist, who is about to go on vacation. Here the right of the patient's doctor to take a vacation and the duty to provide coverage for the patient present a relatively complex problem. Do doctors have an unlimited duty to attend to their patients, regardless of the effects such a duty would have on doctors' lives? A number of developmental issues emerge around this question, namely autonomy, responsibility, and reciprocal role taking.

From one ethical perspective, physicians have an obligation to keep everyone alive as long as possible, irrespective of the means necessary to do so. Since the 1970s, however, the right to die has become a well-argued notion, drawing multiple and various legitimizations. One prominent argument for this right is based on the notion that persons are autonomous; hence they have the right to terminate their own lives when human dignity and function are no longer present (e.g., 3, 29, 30). Libertarians argue even further that persons are allowed to kill themselves *regardless* of loss of dignity and/or function.

Courts have repeatedly held in various contexts that competent, physically ill persons or "brain dead" persons have the right to terminate life support. But people who are suffering without identified medical causes or who are suffering from "mental illnesses" present a much more complicated problem. Although society may accept that mentally ill people may suffer, society may not grant them the competence that the decision to die requires. Yet it is the job of mental health practitioners to help their patients by increasing the patients' freedom to live their lives according to their own personal ideals (31), and part of that ideal might include dying in order not to suffer endlessly.

From both a psychoanalytic view and a developmental psychological view, the central conflict for caretakers confronting the suicidal patient seems located between these two notions: the duty to support autonomy and the duty to support life (Ref. 1, Chapter 3). In this or any context the decision to hospitalize is a serious one, because involuntary hospitalization decreases patient autonomy and is an act of parentalism, but in some cases may extend life. Likewise, the decision made in the case example to release a patient supports autonomy, at the expense of increasing the risk of suicide. Assuming that both life and autonomy are considered goods, the tension lies, as in many ethical conflicts, not between goods and harms, but between competing goods.

With the foregoing as background, we now turn to analysis of the case from a developmental viewpoint. In our case example, the patient is clearly depressed. The doctor seems to address her in a respectful manner. The patient is asked a number of questions to ascertain her status. The first problem is that the doctor does not sufficiently bring out doubts about the patient's statement that she is not suicidal (epistemological and perspective-taking stage 3/4 (GSM stage 4b). For example, the discussion of the patient's drinking implies that the patient *does* paper over the truth. If the doctor were to put himself in the patient's shoes, in the patient's disadvantaged state, would the doctor claim that she wanted to be treated like a child, as suggested later by the stereotyping of the patient by the expert witness for the plaintiff (stage 3, GSM stage 4a)? (Stereotyping here assigns the patient the "child" value for the child-adult variable.) Or would she prefer to be treated as a perfectly rational adult, as the treating doctor suggests (stage 3/4, GSM stage 4b of logical reasoning)? Doctors taking the patient's perspective might have asked how the patient plans to deal with the husband's leaving, how to deal with her anger over the desertion, and, finally, how to deal with manipulative but still potentially dangerous suicide impulses.

The doctor in large part discussed the issues from the perspective of the doctor, i.e., should the patient be hospitalized or not. Hence, the perspective of the patient is not satisfactorily considered. Such perspective taking is typical of stage 4 (GSM stage 5a) and below. With a stage 4 (GSM stage 5a)-derived notion of responsibility, the doctor has no legal obligation to hospitalize the patient. The patient can ostensibly assess the risk probabilities and benefit probabilities along with the doctor, showing at least stage 3/4 (GSM stage 4b) epistemological reasoning. Part of being depressed is that patients grossly underestimate the value of a course of remedial action, as the plaintiff's expert witness tries but fails to explain. A patient reasoning at stage 3/4 (GSM stage 4b) also cannot consider the effect of the suicide on all systems including her family, her friends, etc., when she takes her own life.

The decision to commit a patient to the hospital includes an assessment of the competence of the patient to participate in treatment planning. In the case presented here, the patient discussed her case with the doctor in what seemed to be a straightforward manner. The ready acceptance of the plan the doctor developed with the patient's participation, however, illustrates a major problem. The patient may be highly informed about a treatment but still assent rather than consent to it. Assenting to the doctor's wishes may rise out of ignorance, misunderstanding, or lack of awareness of the right to choose between treatment options. Patients may fear rejection by the doctor. *Truly* consenting (rather than simply assenting to the doctor's wishes) means involving the patient in each step of the decision process. The right to choose among treatment options should include the patient's choosing "no treatment for now," without the doctor's rejecting the patient. In this case the plan was jointly formed, but the patient, although discussing the plan, showed no emotion or particular involvement with respect to it. After finding out that her husband would not help her, the patient may well have been "just going along" with the plan (assenting) in order to get out of the hospital and carry out her real plan, suicide.

Doctors' actions that show care for the patient can be assessed as to the beneficence stage in the General Stage Model. The developmental consideration in this case is: what do the doctors in question care about and how is that caring coordinated with caring for and treating the patient? In this case, the quality of the patient's life is of concern both during treatment and afterward.

A possible focus of conflict is doctors' attachment to the institutions for which they work. At beneficence stage 4 (GSM stage 5a) the institution is the representative of the therapeutic system; at that stage, therapeutic relationships are conditional on the role defined by the institution, so that when the patient is discharged from the hospital, the institution's responsibility is seen to decrease. The boundaries of the institution may seem immovable, even when the law extends the institutional responsibility.

In such a context doctors make few follow-up calls to patients, and few "training sessions" are offered for the patient's support system. The doctor's institutional role and concern for the institution by its practitioners and administration make outreach difficult unless outreach becomes an institutional rule. Although we insist on the highest level of individual training and care within institutions, explicit training and supervision of patient support systems is often lacking. The support network is not viewed as part of the treatment team. This suggests that beneficence for these individuals never surpassed stage 4 (GSM stage 5a) because the doctor strictly applied the medical and legal system's rules rather than transcending the institutional role.

At the beneficence stage 5 (GSM stage 5b), the institution and its role would be seen to exist in service of the abstract principle of patient care and treatment, whether in or outside the institutional walls. Role boundaries between doctors, nurses, social workers, and the patient support network outside would not be as important as the total quality of the health care provider-patient treatment conditions (32).

From an evaluative stage perspective, i.e., regarding what constitutes good work for the physician, ethically responsible doctors and patients would collaboratively determine whether the patient were competent to participate in treatment planning and implementation. From an ethical perspective, competence does not mean "general" competence but rather the patient's proclivity for making choices for obtaining suitable assistance if necessary. Thus, criteria determining a patient's competence are most narrowly drawn to preserve the autonomy of the patient at stage 5 (GSM stage 5b) and the independence of the patient at stage 4 (GSM stage 5a). According to the principle of preserving patient autonomy or independence, patients should do for themselves what they can and delegate the rest: knowing when to delegate responsibility shows competence. That a patient has limitations in some area of life is not indicative of a lack of competence. Patients' logical abilities fail, however, when they cannot discern whether they are competent in seeking their own care and hence when to delegate that care when they are not. If the patient is not competent, then the doctor may take the perspective of what the patient would decide if the patient were competent. The doctor also may seek to have a guardian appointed, not for legal purposes per se but to ensure that both the rights of the patient and the wishes of the patient are independently represented within the system.

THE ETHICAL ATMOSPHERE OF INSTITUTIONS AND CARE

Meaney, Commons, and Weaver (33–35), along with Power, Higgins and Kohlberg (26) suggest that the stage of individual reasoning and the stage of what we term "atmosphere" co-determine each other. The stage of institutional atmosphere is the stage of the rationale of institutional actions—the written and unwritten policies. The stage of the institutional atmosphere can limit the stage of reasoning about action of individuals by failing to support higher stage actions or by punishing them. Likewise it can enhance them through a dialogue and alliance whereby higher stage actions and reasoning are valued, even when they challenge institutional norms. Let us consider this interaction.

Institutions are composed of individuals and individuals belong to institutions. The character of the institutions defines the individual, and individual actions define the action of the institutions. Because of the multiplicity of the stages of reasoning of people within an institution, the concerted institutional actions could exceed or fall lower than the stage of reasoning of the members (36).

In our case example, atmosphere appears in one of the major questions facing the health care system: the responsibilities of institutions once their patients obtain (or, here, retain) outpatient status. With the present organizational structure and payment methods, patient contact and follow-up are not seen to be as pressing as acute care. One high-risk period in depressed patients who threaten suicide is the period right after leaving the hospital (37); is this why absence of an offer of follow-up makes the patients' being sent home seem so tenuous?

The ethical atmosphere of a stage 5 (GSM stage 5b) institution permits an alliance not only between the doctor and the patient but between the institution and the patient. At stage 5 (GSM stage 5b), the hospital institution is also allied with community support of patients. That alliance is maintained by practicing mutual respect for all parties on a day-to-day basis. Respect for the patients' autonomy while at the hospital facilitates patients' autonomous functioning outside of the hospital. While independence from the hospital increases, both the patient and the hospital are able to deal with their interdependence.

A discussion about institutional atmosphere would be remiss if it did not address the adversarial system—itself an institution for regulating doctor-patient behavior. Whereas there are a number of methods for positively affecting the quality of professional individual contracts, American society has emphasized litigation. The resulting conflict lies among three parties: in our example, the doctors and their representatives, the patient's representatives, and representatives of the legal system including judges, juries, and attorneys. In the case example, the stage of reasoning of the atmosphere never seems to reach stage 5 (GSM stage 5b). At stage 5 (GSM stage 5b) in the justice domain for example, not only would there be a right to sue a doctor, but there would exist a corresponding duty to compensate unfairly sued doctors; that is, the patients' rights and duties need to be coordinated with the doctors' rights and duties. In the beneficence domain, even the plaintiffs' winning a malpractice suit is a loss, not only to the doctor and institution, but to medical care as a whole, as Hauser, Commons et al. show (Chapter 11, this volume). This is because, as many observers note, victory in a case is not a sufficient form of compensation for medical losses; winning a case does not mean vindication. Patients' bad feelings and bad outcome are, in the end, not compensated by money. The process seems to hurt everyone.

If the health care system functioned at the evaluative stage 5 (GSM stage 5b), the alliance between society and patients would recognize healthy interdependence. Such interdependence would foster collaboration on an optimal treatment plan rather than pitting patient and care provider against each other. At stage 5 (GSM stage 5b) of beneficence, the critogenic (legally derived) effects of such litigation represent a harm themselves, weakening the alliance between health care providers, patient, and society. Such critogenic effects may result in an overall lower quality of health care for the patient.

REFERENCES

1. Reiser SJ, Bursztajn HJ, Gutheil TG, Appelbaum PS. Divided staffs, divided selves: a case approach to mental health ethics. Cambridge, UK: Cambridge University Press, 1987.

2. Kohlberg L. Essays on moral development: Vol. 1. The philosophy of moral development. San Francisco: Harper & Row, 1981.

3. Kohlberg L. Essays on moral development: Vol. 2. The psychology of moral development: moral stages, their nature and validity. San Francisco: Harper & Row, 1984.

4. Colby A, Kohlberg L, eds. The measurement of moral judgment: standard form scoring manuals. New York: Cambridge University Press, 1987.

5. Selman RL. Personal communication. February 22, 1990.

6. Commons ML, Richards FA. A general model of stage theory. In: Commons ML, Richards FA, Armon C, eds. Beyond formal operations: Vol. 1. Late adolescent and adult cognitive development. New York: Praeger, 1984:120–140.

7. Commons ML, Richards FA. Applying the general stage model. In: Commons ML, Richards FA, Armon C, eds. Beyond formal operations: Vol. 1. Late adolescent and adult cognitive development. New York: Praeger, 1984:141–157.

8. Coombs CH, Dawes RM, Tversky A. Mathematical psychology: an elementary introduction. Englewood Cliffs, NJ: Prentice-Hall, 1970.

9. Lindsay PH, Norman DA. (1977). Human information processing: an introduction to psychology. New York: Academic Press, 1977.

10. Commons ML, Grotzer TA. The relationship between Piagetian and Kohlbergian stage: an examination of the "necessary but not sufficient relationship." In: Commons ML, Armon C, Kohlberg L, Richards FA, Grotzer TA, Sinnott JD, eds. Adult development. 2. Models and methods in the study of adolescent and adult thought. New York: Praeger, 1990.

11. Armon C. Ideals of the good life: cross-sectional/longitudinal study of evaluative reasoning in children and adults. Unpublished doctoral dissertation, Harvard Graduate School of Education, Cambridge, MA, 1984.

12. Commons ML, Rodriguez JA. "Equal access" without "establishing" religion: the necessity for assessing social perspective-taking skills and institutional atmosphere. Developmental Rev 1990, in press.

13. Fischer KW, Hand HH, Russell S. The development of abstractions in adolescents and adulthood. In: Commons ML, Richards FA, Armon C, eds. Beyond formal operations: late adolescent and adult cognitive development. New York: Praeger, 1984:43–73.

14. Armon C. Ideals of the good life and moral judgment: ethical reasoning across the life span. In: Commons ML, Richards FA, Armon C, eds. Beyond formal operations: Vol. 1. Late adolescent and adult cognitive development. New York: Praeger, 1984:357–380.

15. Selman RL. The growth of interpersonal understanding. New York: Academic Press, 1980.

16. Rodriquez JA. Exploring the notion of higher stages of social perspective taking. Unpublished qualifying paper, Harvard Graduate School of Education, 1989.

17. Selman R, Byrne D. A structural developmental analysis of levels of role taking in middle childhood. Child Dev 1974;45:803–805.

18. Benack S. Postformal epistemologies and the growth of empathy. In: Commons ML, Richards FA, Armon C, eds. Beyond formal operations: Vol 1. Late adolescent and adult cognitive development. New York: Praeger, 1984:340–356.

19. Benack S, Basseches MA. Dialectical thinking and relativistic epistemology: their relation in adult development. In: Commons ML, Sinnott JD, Richards FA, Armon C,

eds. Adult Development. 1. Comparisons and applications of adolescent and adult developmental models. New York: Praeger, 1989.

20. Blanchard-Fields F. Postformal reasoning in a socio-emotional context. In: Commons ML, Sinnott JD, Richards FA, Armon C, eds. Adult Development. 1. Comparisons and applications of adolescent and adult developmental models. New York: Praeger, 1989.

21. Commons ML. A comparison and synthesis of Kohlberg's and Gewirtz's theories of attachment. In: Gewirtz JL, Kurtines WM, eds. Intersections with attachment. Hillsdale, NJ: Erlbaum, 1990.

22. Gilligan C. In a different voice: psychological theory and women's development. Cambridge: Harvard University Press, 1981.

23. Armon C. Autonomy. In: Commons ML, Sinnott JD, Richards FA, Armon C, eds. Adult Development. 1. Comparisons and applications of adolescent and adult developmental models. New York: Praeger, 1989.

24. Cook-Greuter SR. Maps for living: ego-development theory from symbiosis to conscious universal embeddedness. In: Commons ML, Sinnott, JD, Richards FA, Armon C, eds. Adult development. 2. Comparisons and applications of adolescent and adult developmental models. New York: Praeger, 1990.

25. Kegan R. The evolving self. Cambridge, MA: Harvard University Press, 1982.

26. Power FC, Higgins A, Kohlberg L. Lawrence Kohlberg's approach to moral education: a study of three democratic high schools. New York: Columbia University Press, 1989.

27. Bursztajn H, Feinbloom RI, Hamm RM, Brodsky A. Medical choices, medical chances: how patients, families, and physicians can cope with uncertainty. New York: Delacorte, 1981.

28. Koplowitz H. A projection beyond Piaget's formal-operations stage: a general system stage and a unitary stage. In: Commons ML, Richards FA, Armon C, eds. Beyond formal operations: Vol. 1. Late adolescent and adult cognitive development. New York: Praeger, 1984:272–296.

29. Bok S. Lying: moral choice in public and private life. New York: Pantheon, 1978.

30. Bursztajn HJ. The role of a training protocol in formulating patient instructions as to terminal care choices. Med Education 1977; 52:347–348.

31. Modell A. Psychoanalysis in a new context. New York: International Press, 1987.

32. Warren, M. Personal communication. February 28, 1990.

33. Meaney M, Commons ML, Weaver JH, Shakespeare M. Ethical reasoning and atmosphere in universities. Presented at the Eastern Psychological Association, Philadelphia, Apr 1, 1990.

34. Commons ML, Meaney M, Weaver JH. Reasoning about ethics within a university. Presented at the Association of Moral Education, Irvine, CA: Nov 11, 1989.

35. Commons ML, Richards FA, In: Sonnert G, Rodriguez JA, Meany M, Weaver JA, Straughn J, Lichtenbaum E, eds. Determining the power of reasoning: developmental stage in theory and practice. Manuscript in preparation.

36. Sonnert JG. A sociological approach to higher moral stages, manuscript in preparation.

37. Bursztajn HJ, Gutheil TG, Cummins B. Legal issues in inpatient psychiatry. In: Sederer LI. Inpatient psychiatry. 3rd ed. Baltimore: Williams & Wilkins, 1990, in press.

INDEX

Page numbers followed by a "t" denote tables.